0

Columbus Landing in the New World.

THE NEW WORLD'S
FOUNDATIONS IN THE OLD

BY

RUTH WEST

HEAD OF THE DEPARTMENT OF HISTORY IN THE LEWIS AND CLARK
HIGH SCHOOL IN SPOKANE

AND

WILLIS MASON WEST

SOMETIME PROFESSOR OF HISTORY IN THE UNIVERSITY
OF MINNESOTA

ALLYN AND BACON

BOSTON   NEW YORK   CHICAGO
ATLANTA   SAN FRANCISCO   DALLAS

Norwood Press
J. S. Cushing Co. — Berwick & Smith Co.
Norwood, Mass., U.S.A.

PREFACE

THIS book is an introduction to the study of elementary American history. It tells, in the simplest form, the story of the growth of our civilization from its beginnings in the great river valleys of northern Africa and western Asia. It pictures Man as the Inventor, continually devising easier ways of working and happier ways of living.

The text attempts to show how great is America's debt to those men of other times and places, who produced the civilization our forefathers brought with them to this continent. It is desirable that young Americans should have some conception of that inheritance as a foundation for the serious study of American history.

By a careful selection of "high-light" topics, the text also attempts to build up for the pupil concepts of historical continuity and of world-wide relationships. It does this without sacrificing that simplicity in the narrative which is so absolutely necessary to effective use by the pupils for whom it is written.

The profuse illustrations throughout the volume have been carefully selected to illuminate the text, and the captions beneath them form a vital part of the book. In using them, it is worth while to teach the pupil to distinguish between illustrations contemporary with past events and those which are reconstructions by artists or scholars of a later day. In developing this distinction, do not permit the pupil to depreciate these historical reconstructions. Indeed, it is of high value to instill in him an appreciation of the sound scholarship and imaginative power necessary for their production. He will readily understand why we must often depend upon them for our most vivid ideas of past scenes — why, for instance, we have no photograph of the interior of the Parthenon in the time of Pericles, and therefore have to show it in the less realistic way used in the picture facing page 63. If, under proper guidance, he has worked out *in words* a reconstruction of the atmosphere of some past period (as suggested in exercises on page 37, page 50, and elsewhere), he will be the better prepared to appreciate pictorial reconstruction.

The short word list at the end of each chapter should be used in exercises to stimulate growth of the pupil's vocabulary. From the first, also, the pupil should be led to consult the index for assistance in pronunciation of names and unusual terms. The authors have made a special point of indicating in the index the particular map upon which each new geographical name may conveniently be found. Throughout, the physical features that have conditioned history have been emphasized — the human geography of each region treated — so as to help in articulating the pupil's study of his geography, not only with history but also with his other reading.

The other teaching aids at the chapter ends may be dismissed here more briefly. The *Thought Questions* and *Things to Do* are suggestive rather than imperative. It is advisable, however, to use the *time line* and the *map exercises* with all classes. Most of the chapters are furnished with compact *summaries*, but in a few particularly suitable cases it is suggested instead that the pupil make his own. If such a summary be worked out on the blackboard by the class, as a socialized study, the exercise may become an even more helpful factor in learning how to read — which is so large a part of learning how to study. The *lists of books suggested for further reading* have been limited to material that should be available even in schools with very little money. In larger schools the teachers will find it easy to add to them.

RUTH WEST
WILLIS MASON WEST

JULY 15, 1929.

CONTENTS

CONTENTS

ILLUSTRATIONS AND MAPS

THE NEW WORLD AND
THE OLD

THE NEW WORLD'S FOUNDATIONS IN THE OLD

CHAPTER I

WHERE DOES OUR HISTORY BEGIN ?

We Americans are proud of our country and of all it stands for.   We like to read stories of its great men and to feel that they belong to us.   It is hard for us to imagine a time when there was no United States.   The coming of the Pilgrims and the founding of Jamestown seem to have happened a very, very long time ago.

These things did happen more than three hundred years ago ; and three hundred years is a long time, many times as long as a man's life.   But after all **the United States is a young nation.**   Most nations are much older.   It is almost two thousand years since England's history began, and Egypt and China are more than three times as old as that. The lines below show how young our country is, when compared with the countries of the Old World.

EGYPT _____ 7000 years _____

                         ENGLAND ___ 2000 years ___

                                    UNITED STATES 300 years

1

You might put such lines on the board in colors and on a larger scale. There you can let two inches stand for a hundred years, or a century. Then the line for the United States will be six inches long, and England's will be forty inches. The line for Egypt, if you have room for it, would have to be one hundred and forty inches.

On a sheet of paper make another set of lines, to represent the members of your family. These would be short lines. Your own should be about a quarter inch. Can you see, then, how long to make the lines for your father and grandfather?

In many ways, groups of persons and groups of nations are alike. You learn many things from your father and mother and grandparents; and **our young nation has learned much from older nations.** Just as you and your brothers and sisters get on better if you plan your games or your work *together*, so nations, too, find it helpful to work together. Sometimes they quarrel, it is true; but they need one another in all sorts of ways.

When you go home, see how many nations you can find mentioned in to-day's newspaper. Be ready to put the list on the board to-morrow and to point out the different countries on the map. Why are these countries mentioned in American papers? Be ready to talk the reasons over in class to-morrow. Why should we try to learn more about these nations? Do you know of any meetings where people of different nations come together?

There is a special reason why we Americans are interested in the Old World. Some of us were born there, and others have fathers and mothers who were. Most of the rest of us are descended from men and women who came from the

IMMIGRANTS IN 1620. — This picture shows how the painter Merrill thinks of the Landing of the Pilgrims. The first boatload from the *Mayflower* is shown just approaching " Plymouth Rock " at the shore.

IMMIGRANTS OF 1927. — Immigrants that come through New York (as most of ours do) are detained awhile in the harbor at Ellis Island, to make sure that they satisfy our laws concerning new-comers. This group had passed the examinations and were photographed while they were waiting eagerly for the ferry boat to carry them to the New York docks.

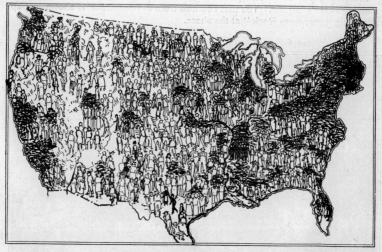

POPULATION OF OUR COUNTRY IN 1600 (above) AND IN 1900 (below).

In each picture each figure stands for about 10,000 people.

The vastly larger number of people in 1900 is one of the things due to the white man's coming.

Old World only a little farther back. **We are either immigrants or the descendants of immigrants** — whether our ancestors came to America in the 1900's or the 1600's. Except for a few families with Indian blood, no American family has lived in the New World much more than three hundred years. Before that, all America belonged to the red men.

It would be interesting for you to choose a boy or girl to take a census of the class, — as the government does every ten years for the whole country. Let your census-taker make a list of all the countries from which members of the class are descended. Some of you, he is likely to find, can trace descent back to several Old World countries.

Of course there were people living in America for hundreds of years before the first European immigrants came, but their ways of living were not at all like ours. **Have you ever tried to imagine what this country was like before white men discovered it?** There were no towns then. Instead there was only a vast wilderness thinly dotted with little clusters of Indian tepees. Great herds of elk and bison roamed over grassy plains; and bear and wolves hunted the deer through forests and swamps where to-day stand mighty cities.

All the America that we know has grown up since white men came here. Our history begins with their coming, and our ways of living have grown from theirs. *What ways did they bring with them, and where did they get them?* This book will try to answer these questions, and so show the foundations on which *our* America has been built.

Summary

Our country seems very old to us, but there are much older nations. Nearly all Americans are descended from Old World ancestors, who belonged to older nations than ours. We need to know about those other nations because they have handed down to us many of our ways of living and because to-day all nations are closely bound together. This book will tell about the life and customs of peoples of the Old World and try to show how they furnished the foundations on which America is built.

NEW WORDS

In this book you may find some words you have not used before. It is a good thing to keep a list of such words and their meanings, so that you can use them after this. Words in this chapter to put in your list would be :

census   immigrant   history   century   descendants   ancestors

You may want to add other words from this chapter. Sometimes the meaning of a word can be made plainer by a picture or poster. Can any of you who like to draw show the meaning of *census* or *immigrant* by a picture?

Ox-Carts with Solid Wheels (such as this page tells about) are still used in the Philippines. This recent photo shows several in the background, besides the one in front. Probably the use of this kind of wheel was brought to the savage Filipinos by Spanish conquerors four hundred years ago. Such wheels, indeed, are still used in backward parts of Spain and of some other European lands.

CHAPTER II

THE FIRST INVENTORS

For Thousands of Years Men have been Building Civilization, Looking for New Ways to Make Life Better and Happier

Ages ago no one could get from one place to another except on foot, as the Indians were still doing when white men first came to this country. After many centuries, men tamed wild animals — the dog, the reindeer, the horse — and trained them to carry burdens or even to carry man himself. Next they found that these animals could carry heavier loads by dragging them along the ground on sleds. Centuries later, some clever thinker invented the wheel and made a two-wheeled cart. (The first wheel, no doubt, was just a solid slice sawed from a tree trunk, with a hole punched in the center for the axle.) Men then began to build roads, over which their carts could be hauled better than over the rough ground. From that it was an easy step to four-wheeled wagons and even to fine coaches.

Then after a very long time indeed (only about a hundred years ago), a clever inventor took a great step ahead when he invented a steam locomotive which could pull a whole train of cars swiftly along two iron rails. Later still, another man discovered how to run these trains by electricity. At last, not much more than twenty-five years ago, a little gasoline engine was invented that could run a light car along a road *without* rails. And finally, with the help of improved gas-engines, we learned to fly. But we should not have our automobiles or airplanes, or even our railroads, if it had not been for the men who invented the wheel.

So it is with all our tools and even with our ways of thinking. Each age learns from the one that has gone before, and adds some new ways of its own. It may be new tools, or it may be lovely music, beautiful pictures, interesting books, more trade between one country and another, new ways of living together, better ideas of religion. **We give the name *civilization* to the sum of all the ways of making life better and happier.**

The civilization that white men brought to America three hundred years ago had been growing up in Europe for many centuries. Much of it had been brought to Europe long before from still older countries in Asia and Africa. And many thousands of years before that, the very first foundations had been laid by men who had not learned to live as nations or to write down what they did and thought. **But those earliest men made some very important inventions, which really started *our* civilization of to-day.**

THE OLD STONE AGE

The Invention of a Knife of Chipped Stone Lifted Man Into What is Called the *Old Stone Age*

The first men we know much about lived in caves. They did not know how to build houses of wood or stone, and they had no tools for such work. Neither did they have any weapons, except chance stones or broken pieces of trees. They found it hard, therefore, to protect a cave home against the fierce animals that also wanted it for a shelter.

The cave-man was much weaker than those beasts — cave-bears, mammoths, and terrible saber-toothed tigers — but he had some things they lacked. He had a better *hand* than any of them, with thumb meeting fingers

DRAWING OF A CAVE-BEAR, found on the wall of a cave in France where some cave-artist cut it into the rock about 100,000 years ago. (The drawing was very large — probably life-size.)

(instead of just a row of fingers), so that he could take a firm hold upon things. And he had a better *brain*, so that he was able to invent tools and weapons and new ways to live.

One of his first inventions was a stone knife. Some savage discovered that he could chip flakes off a piece of flint by striking it with other stones, so as to give it a keen edge and a good shape for his hand to grasp. From this invention it was easy to go on to making stone spear-heads and stone hatchets.

FLINT FIST-HATCHET from a cave in England, found in the lowest of many layers of deposits 25 feet below the present surface. The tool was about two and a half times as long as this picture.

Armed with these weapons, the cave-man could defend his home against even the cave-bear. He found it easier, also, to get meat for food, and he could now strip the skins from the animals he killed, so as to use them for warm clothing. With his knife, too, he was able to shape more delicate tools from the bones than he could make from stone — such as needles for his wife to use in sewing the skins together.

How do you suppose we know all this about the cave-men? Many of their old caves in Spain, France, and Germany have been examined carefully in recent years, and it is quite plain that thousands of years ago those caves were the homes of little groups of men. If we dig down in such a cave, we find human bones here and there all the way down to twenty or even forty feet below the present cave floor. This means that men lived there for a very long time.

The cave-woman, you see, never swept up. Dirt and refuse lay where it fell. The wind was always blowing in a little fine dust, too, from outside. And at times parts of the roof might fall down. So, century, by century, a new floor was deposited upon the old one.

In those deposits we find the bones of the animals that the cave-man ate and the tools that he used. Even in the lowest layers we find rudely shaped flint knives and ax-heads. As we examine layers nearer and nearer the top, there are more *kinds* of tools, and they are shaped *better and better*. Do you see how this tells us something about the cave people?

Far down in the deposits we find ashes and charred bones. So we know that **soon after he began to live in caves man learned to use fire.** All wild animals fear the flame; so this invention made man safer from them. It helped, too, to keep his home warm and dry; and, best of all, he could now roast his meat, instead of eating it raw.

Just how men came to use fire we do not know. Perhaps you have read the old Greek story about *Prometheus*, who stole fire from heaven for the service of man. The word " Prometheus " means " the thinker." Probably man feared fire at first, much as animals did. But lightning, or " fire from heaven," often sets forest trees ablaze, and it

A Wall Painting in the Milwaukee Public Museum

THE MAMMOTH OF THE STONE AGE IN EUROPE was a much larger and more terrible animal than our modern elephant. Still the large number of mammoth bones in cave-man homes show that the cave-men must sometimes have killed them for food. This painting by a modern artist shows how this may have been done. The mammoth has been trapped in a huge pitfall that the men have managed to dig (probably in one of his usual paths) and then covered over with brush and earth. To make sure of him, a stake, with a sharp point turned upward, had probably been set in the middle of the pit for him to fall upon so that the mighty beast would not be able to pull himself out of the hole. Even then it was no easy matter to finish him.

Savage tribes to-day kill the largest and fiercest animals in much this way.

EARLY WAYS OF MAKING FIRE.

A REINDEER engraved by a Stone-Age artist on the stone wall of a cave in
southern France — where no reindeer have lived for tens of thousands of years.
The cave-drawing is life-size. It is one of the oldest pictures we know anything
about.

may be that some "thinker" among the early men was curious enough and brave enough to watch a burning stump until he learned how to use fire for warmth.

After cave-men learned how useful fire was, they could not wait for lightning to strike a dry tree every time they needed to cook. They had to find how to kindle fires for themselves. The ways shown opposite this page were invented by Stone-Age men. Perhaps you have seen Boy Scouts use some of them. One other way was discovered after men learned to make steel (page 14); for steel will strike sparks out of flint. But that was the only improvement on Stone-Age ways of making fire until about a century ago. So men learned to guard their hearth fires very carefully.

Then, as now, each invention led to new ones. From the rude spinning tools found in the caves, we know *that the cave-woman had learned to spin.* We find arrow-heads, too, of bone and flint; so we know that *the cave-man had invented the bow.* (Why do you suppose we do not find the bows themselves?) This invention lengthened man's arm. He could now kill his game or foe from a distance. His power in the world was many times greater than before. Soon, *he began to tame the wild wolf-dog,* to help him in the hunt and to guard the opening to his cave.

WILD BOAR (charging a hunter), painted in red and black on a cave wall in southern France.

The cave-man liked to draw. Sometimes he made pictures of his tame animals. But more often he drew or carved on his bone dagger, or on the walls of his cave, pictures of the wild boar, the bear, the frightful mammoth, or a herd of deer browsing by a peaceful pool. He even learned to *paint* these forms. He got his colors much as the American

Indians did, by grinding up black, red, and yellow earths. These " paints " he then packed into hollow horns, or pressed into crayons. Perhaps you know Kipling's verses about the cave-man's drawings :

"Later he pictured an aurochs — later he pictured a bear —
Pictured the saber-toothed tiger dragging a man to his lair —
Pictured the mountainous mammoth, hairy, abhorrent, alone —
Out of the love that he bore them, scribing them clearly on bone."

The New Stone Age

The cave-men were always working over their weapons and thinking about them. At last some genius found that he could *grind* his flint knife on certain other stones so as to make the edge sharper and more even. Before long, all men near him were supplied with weapons of this new kind. They were handsomer than the old chipped-stone tools, and did better work. **Men had now advanced to a new age of civilization.** We call it the *New Stone Age*, or *Ground-Stone Age*.

A Clay Pitcher from a Swiss Lake Dwelling. (See cut facing page 14.) Notice how the early potter ornamented his work.

But grinding knives, instead of chipping them into shape, was only one of the many important inventions of that time. While men were thinking about weapons for hunting and fighting, **women were thinking about tools for peaceful work.** Probably it was some woman who wove the first *basket* out of reeds and grasses, so as to be able to carry home berries or seeds that she gathered. It is most likely that a woman made the first *clay pot*, and hardened it in the fire, so that she could carry water in it or cook food in it in new ways.

AMERICAN INDIAN PICTURE-WRITING shows that some Stone-Age men could draw or paint stories. This story was painted by a Nez Percé artist on buffalo skin and is now in the Spokane Public Museum. An Indian would read it about as follows: "A band of Sioux [on horseback] set out to make a night attack [notice moon and stars] upon a sleeping camp of Nez Percés. But the war party accidentally stampedes a herd of buffalo [the dots on the side of the buffalo show that there are many of the animals], and the noise of this stampede awakens and warns the Nez Percés, who then repulse the attack, killing and scalping some of the Sioux."

This sign writing, then, could say many things about what happens *outside* of us ; and, probably, even without an explanation, you could make more out of it than you could out of the Egyptian writing that faces page 28. But, on the other hand, those scholars who learn to read the Egyptian find that it could say nearly everything that our books can say — even about the hopes and feelings within us — and picture-writing cannot do that so well.

A Wall Painting in the Milwaukee Public Museum.

A CAVE-MAN ARTIST AT WORK (page 9). — (Just such a bison picture was really painted by some Stone-Age man on the wall of a cave in Spain.) Two of the cave-family, you may notice, are not watching the artist. Instead they have been hunting and are just bringing home their game.

THE SABER-TOOTHED TIGER, as our scientists think he must have looked. This picture is from a painting by Charles R. Knight, in the American Museum of Natural History.

The woman, too, *cared for the child*. She fed it and taught it. She even invented a way to make *cloth*, so that her child might have softer and lighter clothing than the skins of animals. Weaving cloth finally became a big part of her work. The word *wife* comes from an old word for *weave*.

BONE NEEDLES found in cave deposits, where some cave-woman dropped them ages ago. There were none better in Europe until two hundred years ago.

Farming Began in the New Stone Age

Through thousands of years the men with chipped-stone weapons had lived by hunting and fishing. They had not learned to farm; so it had always been a struggle for the cave-family to get food enough.

The women and children had done their part by gathering seeds and berries and nuts. Sometimes, no doubt, a child dropped part of the seeds on the ground near the cave. If the soil on which they fell was good, new plants would spring up there the next season and produce more seed. Many a woman must have rejoiced at finding food in a new place so near her home, and finally some *thoughtful* woman must have guessed how the thing had come about. Then, we may suppose, she *planted* a few of her precious seeds in a smooth piece of ground, after stirring it with a stick (the first *hoe*), and so raised a small crop near her own door. *Such a woman was the first farmer.*

Did you ever stop to think that wheat and oats and the other grains we see growing on our farms were once just wild grasses? The Stone-Age farmers carefully looked for the grasses with the largest amount of good seed. Since men have been raising them in cultivated fields, these plants have become even larger and better, with more and more seed. But it must have taken wise men and women at first to find out just what plants were most worth taming.

Stone-Age farmers raised rye, wheat, barley, oats, and rice, besides such vegetables as peas, beans, turnips, and onions. So, too, they tamed most of the animals that we have now in our barnyards — cows, sheep, goats, horses, and chickens.

WEAVING as shown in an Egyptian tomb-painting (ch. iii) of more than 5000 years ago — probably much like the weaving of Stone-Age women. The threads that run up-and-down (the "warp") have been first put in place, and are held straight by "loom-weights" while the cross-threads (or "woof") are drawn in.

Thousands of years afterwards the white man brought all these plants and animals from Europe to America; and here he found the Stone-Age Indians cultivating two other important food plants not known in Europe, — corn and potatoes. Since then we have learned to grow many new fruits and garden vegetables, but we have never found a new *grain* as important as those the Stone-Age men selected for us.

People of the New Stone Age Began to Live in Towns

Now that men had become farmers, the food supply was larger and surer. So people were able to live in large groups, or *tribes*. They came out of their lonely cave-homes, and gathered together in *villages* of huts built of wood or clay. Around the village stretched fields of grain and pastures for the flocks.

In each village some man, stronger or wiser than the others, soon made himself *chief*. He led his village in war, and ruled it in peace. A kind of *government* was beginning. Sometimes several villages were united under one mighty *chief*. Such a group of tribes, with its better tools and larger numbers, was then able to conquer the more backward hunting tribes near by, and make them into *slaves* to do the hardest work.

Fierce warriors of these conquered tribes sometimes escaped into the hills, and prowled about the villages at night to steal and plunder, and perhaps to carry off a child now and then. From such happenings came the old tales of giants, like the one in *Jack and the Beanstalk*, and others that you all know.

THE AGE OF BRONZE

The warriors of the Stone Age must always have been eager to try out any new kind of stone, to see whether it would make better tools than the flint tools they already had. Finally something much better was found, and it seems to have been discovered first in the valley of the Nile River in Africa.

In that valley, as in some other parts of the world, pieces of rock containing *copper* are sometimes found lying loose among other stones. If a Stone-Age hunter happened to build a campfire just over a piece of copper ore, the copper might melt and run out in bright drops. The shining metal may at first have been used for ornaments, but at last some thinker found that it could be hammered easily into tools.

RUDE STONE AXES AND A BRONZE AX. Savage tribes to-day fasten handles to their stone axes in the ways shown here.

Those tools, however, soon became blunt, because copper is a very soft metal. **Finally some early coppersmith learned** to melt a little *tin* with his copper. This mixture made the best tools that had ever been known. It could be *shaped easily* while hot — much more easily, of course, than flint could be — and when it had cooled, it was *much harder* than either copper or tin. A knife of the new metal kept its edge better even than flint, because it was not so brittle and did not chip. Such a mixture of copper and tin is called *bronze*.

It was **about seven thousand years ago** that **the men of the Nile valley outgrew the Stone Age by learning to make bronze.** With their new tools they could do many things never possible before; and, as they traded with other people, the Bronze Age civilization spread slowly around the Mediterranean.

The Age of Iron

Iron, we know now, **makes even better tools than bronze.** *Small amounts* of iron ore, also, are found in many parts of the world on the surface of the earth. But it takes a much hotter fire to melt iron than it does to melt copper, and it takes much more skill to make tools of it. Still, more than three thousand years ago some tribes in Asia Minor, and others in central Europe, learned how to work in that ore; and their iron swords soon gave them a great advantage over their Bronze Age neighbors.

The Iron Age has lasted down to the present time. Iron is still our most useful metal — though now we use most of it in the form of *steel*. Men have always used some iron that way; but lately we have learned to make iron ore into steel so easily, and we use so much of it, that **our age is often called the Age of Steel.**

These " ages " overlap, you will notice. Some tribes in the Philippines and in other Pacific islands are still in the Stone Age. The Indians were in that Age when

STONE ARROWHEADS are found in many parts of the world. These four were found in ancient graves in Egypt (in Africa). Many an American museum has similar ones that were made by our Indians. Just such heads, too, are found in the European cave-homes of Stone-Age men.

An Exhibit of the Milwaukee Public Museum

SWISS LAKE DWELLERS. — The men of the New Stone Age in Europe about whom we know most lived in villages built out over the water of certain lakes in Switzerland, with their farms on the shores near by. Not many years ago some of these lakes dried up enough so that many remains of the ancient villages were found on the muddy bottoms. This is the way a modern artist thinks one of those villages must have looked. The boats, you may notice, are "dugouts," such as some savage tribes use to-day.

STONEHENGE, on Salisbury Plain in England — the most famous ruin of the late Stone Age and one of the oldest temples in the world. It consisted of two circles of mighty pillars — each pillar a single rough slab about three times a man's height — with other huge stones laid across their tops. Within the inner circle, it is supposed, human sacrifices were offered up. Here, too, were the graves of famous chiefs. During the past centuries, many of the stones fell, and some were broken up and hauled away by the country people round about. In 1920 those that were left were set up once more — as they appear in the upper picture.

white men came to America. Indeed the Indians never had a Bronze Age. They leaped from the Stone Age to the Age of Iron when early European immigrants taught them to use that metal.

Summary

Men have been building our civilization for many thousands of years. In the Old Stone Age they learned to make knives of chipped stone. When they learned to *grind* stone tools, the New Stone Age began. Then men learned to farm, and began to live in villages instead of in caves. About seven thousand years ago the people of the Nile valley learned to make tools of *bronze*. Much later a few tribes learned to use *iron*, which we still use, in the form of *steel*, for most of our tools and machines.

New Words

civilization	*discovery*	*deposit*	*chief*	*smith*
invention	*genius*	*tribe*	*bronze*	*steel*

Thought Questions and Things to Do

1. We now count time from the Birth of Christ. Any date before that, we mark B.C.; any date after it, A.D. These last two letters stand for Latin words which mean " in the year of our Lord."

Each hundred years is called a *century*, and centuries are numbered just as you number the years of your life. When you had *finished* your first year, you were *one year old*. Until then, you were *in your first year*. If you were twelve at your last birthday, you are now in your thirteenth year, which you will finish on your next birthday. So the first century A.D. was finished at the end of the year 100; the thirteenth, at the close of the year 1300. 75 A.D. is a date in the first century after Christ; 1215 is a date in the *thirteenth* century; 490 B.C. is a date in the *fifth* century before Christ. In what century is each of the following dates: 550 B.C., 1492 A.D., 1607, 1928?

2. It is a good thing to keep a time line on the board, toward the top, while you are studying this book. For this line, let two inches stand for a century. Then a line 140 inches long will stand for seven thousand years. Divide that line into seven equal parts. Then each of those parts will stand for a thousand years. Mark

EARLY HOEING

the beginning of the line 5000 B.C. and call it also the Beginning of Bronze Civilization in Egypt. The last of the thousand years on that line is not quite finished, but you may put a mark to show about the year in which you are now living. Mark also the Birth of Christ; the Declaration of Independence; the Discovery of America. Then mark other important dates *as we come to them in the story.* Perhaps you ought to remember that dates of all things before men began to keep careful records are partly guesswork.

3. Can you find out about different kinds of travel from early times to now? Perhaps you can show them by pictures, — one set for travel on land, and another set for water travel. If you like to make models, you could have an exhibit to show the history of travel.

4. In one cave in Switzerland the bones of a thousand cave-bears have been found. Mingled with them are human bones, as well as tools and ashes. What reasons can you think of why we are sure it was the men that ate the bears, and not the bears that ate the men?

5. If you have a historical museum in your town, visit it and report on the stone tools

EARLY PLOWING — This picture (like that of the hoe above) comes from a very old Egyptian book, such as you will read of in the next chapter. Stone Age savages, who first used such tools, didn't look so neat. But does this picture help you to understand how the hoe grew into a plow?

and weapons there. In our country, these tools are usually the remains of Indian life, but some of our larger cities have also much older Stone-Age remains from other lands.

6. The *wheel* was a very important invention. Why do we put castors on heavy furniture that has to be moved about a room? Put a few stones in a box about the size of a boy's cart, and drag

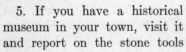

it along the ground. Now put the same load in a cart on wheels, and see how much easier it is to drag it.

7. Make a list of early inventions, putting first the ones that seem to you the most important. Can you think of any modern inventions as important? Make a list of things you have used to-day that you would not have if men had not invented ways to make fire.

8. We cannot tell exactly how the Stone-Age men came to make their inventions, but some interesting guesses have been made and good stories written about them. Kipling has some in his *Just So Stories* and in *Rewards and Fairies*. Kummer's *The First Days of Man*, Langford's *Pic, the Weapon Maker*, and Waterloo's *Story of Ab* are longer stories of the cave-man and his inventions which you would enjoy. Write a short story showing how man may have come to tame the dog, the horse, the cow, or to invent the bow, or to cook his food.

9. Other interesting books about the early days of man are Van Loon's *Story of Ancient Man*, Marshall's *Story of Human Progress*, Coffman's *Child's Story of the Human Race*, and Wells' *How the Present Came from the Past*.

Some of the Pyramids (page 23) To-day. — A photo from a distance, showing also a modern Egyptian village through the trees.

CHAPTER III

EARLY CIVILIZATIONS IN AFRICA AND ASIA

The people of great river valleys, where the climate was mild and the soil fertile, found farming so easy that they **had time to invent new ways of making life pleasanter.** In some such places they advanced very early into the Bronze Age. They cultivated wide fields of wheat, barley, and rice, and mined gold and silver, so that they became rich and powerful. With their new tools they built large towns and magnificent temples and palaces, and learned to make many useful and beautiful things. Soon the people of such countries began to trade with distant lands for things that they themselves could not make. The many towns and villages of each valley, too, united into powerful nations under strong rulers, and so were better able to keep back the tribes of hunters and herdsmen who lived in the more barren hill country about them and who were always trying to seize their fertile fields.

Four river valleys, especially, had many things most needed by men in their advance toward civilization. In those valleys, in very early times, began the great kingdoms of *India*, *China*, *Egypt*, and *Babylonia*. India and China

The Nile and the Great Pyramid

were too far away to have a great deal to do with the people of Europe until about a hundred years ago. But **much of our civilization has grown from that of Egypt and Babylonia.**

EGYPT

Egypt has been called " The Gift of the Nile "

The land of Egypt lies between the Red Sea and the Sahara Desert, with the Nile for its one river. It has a mild climate and a rich soil. Rain hardly ever falls there ; but early every summer there *are* heavy rains in the mountains farther south, where the Nile begins. Swollen by these rains, the river rushes between high cliffs till it reaches the plains of Egypt. There its banks are low, so it spreads out and floods the country for miles. When the floods dry up, the land is left covered with a fine rich mud which stays moist long enough so that in much of the valley a crop can be raised before the river floods again.

In some seasons, and in some parts of the valley, there is not enough moisture to raise a good crop. **So the Egyptians early learned to save the water in great *reservoirs*, and to let it out on the fields, when needed, by means of *irrigation ditches*,** much as we do in the western parts of the United States to-day.

There had to be some way of deciding just how this water should be given out and just how much should be allowed each person. At first each little town had its own way and its own time for irrigating the fields about it. But the men of the different towns often quarreled over the use of the water, and cut each other's dykes. **Finally the stronger towns overcame the weaker ones, till at last** (about 7000 years ago) **all Egypt was united under one powerful king.**

It was certainly a good thing for the towns of Egypt to be united. Could the union have been brought

about, at that time, do you think, in any better way
than by fighting? Are we more likely to settle such
matters peaceably to-day?

The king of Egypt was called *Pharaoh,* which meant
" House of Refuge and Justice." With his armies he was
supposed to *protect* his people against invading tribes.
With his vast numbers of officials he was supposed to see
that the ditches and reservoirs were kept in order and that
the water was let out as it was needed. In return the
people paid heavy *taxes,* either by working in the Pharaoh's
fields or by giving
him part of their
grain and cattle.

PEASANTS HARVESTING GRAIN. — A picture from
a very old Egyptian book. Can you find a reason
in this chapter why they could pile their bound
bundles in the field, instead of "shocking" them
as our farmers have to do?

The Pharaoh was
a *despot.* That is,
he could make any
laws he liked, and
could order a man
put to death. He
had many splendid palaces. When he received visits from his
subjects, he sat on a golden throne gleaming with jewels.
Before speaking to him, people had to bow to the ground
and kiss his feet. Part of the land he gave to the priests
and nobles. The rest he kept for himself, and had it looked
after by his officers.

Life was Pleasant for King and Nobles
But Hard for the Workers

All the work on the land was done by poor farmers, or
peasants, who toiled from dawn to dark. Besides the plow,
the peasant had only three tools. He stirred the ground with
a crooked *hoe,* so short that he had to bend far over to use it
(look at the picture on page 16). He cut his grain with a
short curved *sickle.* Then, after carrying the straw to a

threshing floor, he pounded it with a *flail* to beat out the grain.

Besides the grains and vegetables of the Stone-Age men, the Egyptian peasant's garden contained lettuce, radishes, cucumbers, and grapes. The last he dried into raisins or pressed into wine. He raised *clover*, too, for his master's cattle, and *flax* to be spun and woven into linen cloth. In an Egyptian barnyard there were sheep, cows, goats, scrawny pigs, ducks, geese, pigeons, storks, and antelopes.

The pigs had not been tamed long enough to be as good as the fat hogs our farmers raise. Storks and antelopes are not now kept as tame animals, except for pets. In the

Rookwood Pottery Company

This picture shows a potter of to-day finishing a vase turned upon a wheel that is driven by electric power. The Egyptian drove his wheel by his own foot — as our potters did until recently.

Bronze Age, you see, men were still learning what kinds of animals it paid best to tame. Quite late in Egyptian history, the farmers there got the horse and the chicken from Asia.

In the towns many trades grew up. *Weavers* made fine linen, almost as soft as silk. *Potters* learned to shape their jars, vases, and bowls with a wheel, instead of just by hand, and to give them a finer glaze by " burning " them in a closed brick furnace, much as we do to-day. Egyptian *glass-workers* were famous for the beautiful shapes and colors of their wares. *Jewelers* made lovely necklaces, bracelets, rings, earrings, jeweled combs. and almost every kind of

THIS LIMESTONE STATUETTE, 4700 years old, shows how Egyptian women in very early times ground grain by rolling a rounded stone upon kernels spread out on a flat stone.

ornament known to us. Egyptian monuments show pictures of *shoe-makers, cabinet makers, stone masons, carpenters, shipbuilders,* and men working at many other kinds of trades.

The workers themselves got very few of the fine things they raised in the fields or made in the shops. They dressed in coarse garments and ate plain food — mostly barley

bread and goat's milk. Their homes were crowded into little villages, just as the farmers' homes were, or into the poorest parts of the big towns. Their houses were mud hovels of one room, built along narrow, crooked alleys that were blocked with dirt. The toilers in the fields and on the canals were kept at work by the whip. "Man has a back" was a favorite proverb in Egypt. The old pictures always show the overseer of the workmen with a stick — and often show it in use.

But for the nobles and priests, and for many of their officials and servants, **life was delightful,** filled with all sorts of pleasures.

CARTOON in a book of 4000 years ago showing a lady using a "lip-stick." In her left hand she holds a mirror and a tube of paint.

The homes of the rich were roomy houses, with a wooden frame plastered over with clay which hardened in the sun.

EGYPTIAN BOATMEN FIGHTING ON A CANAL. — From an early papyrus book (page 27). Note part of the story written above and in one corner.

A MODERN EGYPTIAN PEASANT PLOWING.

"Man Has a Back."—See page 22. This shows how the Pharaohs were able to make the peasants build the pyramids.

Publisher's Photo Service

The Sphinx To-day, with pyramids in the distance—the Great Pyramid to the right. The head of the Sphinx has the enlarged face of the Pharaoh it commemorates—set upon the body of a lion, to signify power. The head rises 66 feet from the base, and the body is 187 feet long; but desert sand drifted over the feet and much of the body about 3600 years ago, and was left so until very recently.

Light and air entered at the latticed windows, across which, however, bright-colored curtains could be drawn when it was necessary to shut out a sand storm from the desert. About the house there was usually a large, high-walled garden, with fish-ponds gleaming among the palm trees.

For their Kings the Egyptians Built Great Tombs Which are still among the Wonders of the World

The Egyptians were skillful builders. Their most famous buildings were the *pyramids*. They made these for tombs for their kings. The largest was built more than five thousand years ago and is known as the Great Pyramid. It covers thirteen acres and is 481 feet high. More than two million huge blocks of stone went into it — more stone than has ever been used in any other building in the world. Some of the single blocks weigh more than fifty tons; but the edges are so polished, and so nicely fitted, that the lines where the stones come together can hardly be seen. This pyramid contained several chambers, with long passages between; and the ceilings were built so skillfully that they have never settled, in spite of the tremendous weight above them.

One hundred thousand men had to toil terribly for thirty years to build this one pyramid. The mighty stones had to be quarried in the mountains far to the southward, and floated down the Nile on huge rafts. As the pyramid was built, vast sloping heaps of earth were piled against the sides, up which the huge stones would be dragged into place. It took ten years just to make these mountains of earth; and then, as soon as the pyramid was completed, they had to be leveled away again.

There were also many *gigantic temples* for the gods and for the homes of the priests. Inside the temples, on the walls and columns, we find bands of pictures carved in the stone (as shown on page 24). This is " relief sculpture " —

a kind of carving in which the figures are only partly cut
away from the solid rock. The reliefs usually tell stories of
the life of the king who built the
temple.

**The sculptors also made
many complete statues.** The
smaller ones are often exceedingly lifelike and beautiful.
But Egyptians liked better huge
statues, like the famous *Sphinx*
(picture facing page 23). These
are less lifelike, but they have a
gloomy grandeur like that of
the vast desert stretching about
them.

**The Egyptians Traded with Each
Other and also with Far-off Nations**

Old Egypt had no true *money*.
For thousands of years all trade
was carried on by *barter*, — that
is, by giving one thing for another. In the picture facing
page 29 we see a peasant squat-
ting by a basket of vegetables
that he has brought to market.
Men who want his goods offer
him fans and vases in payment — which, however, he
does not seem to want. This
was a clumsy way of buying
vegetables for dinner.

RUINS OF A SMALL PART OF A TEMPLE.
See cut facing this page.

"Money" was invented in *Lydia,* a district of Asia
Minor (map facing page 25). Lydia had much gold
and silver, and in 650 B.C. the king of that country

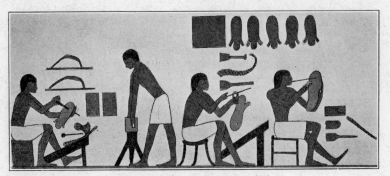

SHOEMAKERS. — An Egyptian relief.

"THE HALL OF COLUMNS" — one part of a vast, many-roomed temple at Karnak (near Thebes) built about 1500 B.C. This picture shows how modern scholars think part of the temple looked centuries ago before it fell to ruin. (For part of the ruins to-day, see the page opposite.) There were 134 of the columns. The central ones were 66 feet high, each of them spreading out at the top into a " capital " that looks like an immense bell upside down. These capitals were ornamented with carvings of the beautiful Lotus flower that blooms by the Nile, and they were large enough so that a hundred men might stand upon one of them. Compare the ruins on page 24 with Stonehenge ruins facing page 15.

DRIVING CATTLE TO PASTURE. — An Egyptian relief (pages 23-24).

AN EGYPTIAN SHIP of 2500 B.C., moving up the Nile.

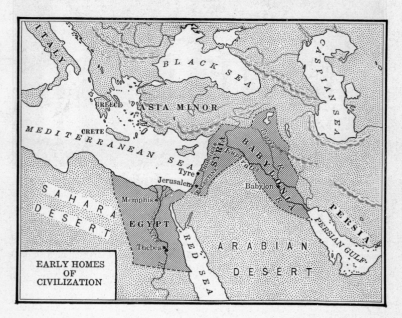

EARLY HOMES
OF
CIVILIZATION

began to mark each piece of silver with his picture and a statement of its value. Such a piece of metal is a *coin*. Ever since, *the coining of money has been one of the most important duties of governments*. Our Constitution forbids even our States to coin money. Why?

Even though they had no money, **the early Egyptians carried on a wide trade with other parts of the world.** So far as we now know, they were the first men to build sea-going ships. One ship, about 2000 B.C., brought back from Arabia "fragrant woods, heaps of myrrh, ebony and pure ivory, green gold, cinnamon, incense, apes, monkeys, dogs, and panther skins." Some of these things must have been gathered together by daring traders from distant parts of Asia.

EGYPTIAN CATTLE IN THE BARN. Notice in the right-hand picture that the masters manage the bulls by staff and rope fastened to a ring in the nose, as our farmers do. This is a picture of wooden models in the Metropolitan Museum, New York.

In return the trader could offer the beautiful and useful articles made by Egyptian workmen — pottery, tools, weapons, jewels — and also supplies of grain. Hundreds of years later, when civilization had spread all around the Mediterranean coasts, Egypt was still known as the " granary of the Mediterranean world."

We have seen how the early pharaohs made the people build huge monuments in their honor. Many of the later pharaohs, however, cared more to make Egypt prosperous by encouraging this trade that we have just described.

So they built roads instead of pyramids. One of them even opened a *canal* from the Nile to the Red Sea, so that ships might sail from the Mediterranean into the Indian Ocean, as we do now by way of the Suez Canal. That ancient Egyptian canal remained in use for hundreds of years. But when Egypt's power had passed away, the sand of the desert drifted in and choked it up.

Egyptian Priests Were often very Learned

It may seem unjust that the poor peasants had to work so hard to keep the nobles and priests in luxury. Still, by doing so, they gave time to some men to *think* about the

A DOCTOR giving a disagreeable dose. — From an old papyrus.

many strange things they saw happening in the world, and to try to find reasons for them. So **the Egyptian priests became the first *scientists*.** They studied the movements of the sun and stars across the sky, and learned that it took about $365\frac{1}{4}$ days to make a *year*. Then they made the first *calendar*. They divided the day into *twelve hours*, and invented a shadow-clock, like our sun-dial, and a water-clock which marked the passing of the hours with a silvery chime. Some of them were skillful *doctors*, even using a few remedies that are given by doctors to-day, such as castor oil.

The Egyptians were able to hand on their learning because they **had invented a better kind of writing than had ever been known before.** Many Stone-Age men had a kind of picture writing like that used by our Indians. But if you should try to write in picture writing, you would find there were a great many things you could not say. Out of the old pictures the Egyptians invented some new signs that stood for *syllables*, and they could then write many more things than before.

Indeed they even invented other signs that stood for simple sounds, as our letters do. But their "letters" were not collected into an alphabet by themselves. Instead, they were used all mixed up with the hundreds of other signs for syllables and things. Only a priest had time to learn them all; so they were called *hieroglyphs*, or "priest writing."

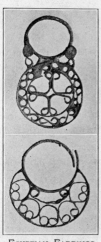

When you look at the cuts facing page 28, you will understand why one author has called this writing "a delightful assemblage of birds, snakes, men, tools, stars, and beasts."

At first these signs were carved or cut on stone. But later the Egyptians invented a kind of *paper*. They made it of the papyrus reeds which grew along the Nile. The reeds were split and soaked and then pressed together into sheets, much as wood-pulp is made into paper to-day. (Of course the Egyptians had to make their "paper" by hand, one sheet at a time, instead of putting it through

EGYPTIAN EARRINGS

heavy steam rollers as we do in our paper mills. So the papyrus sheets were scarce and costly.) On these sheets they wrote with a pointed reed, using black or red ink.

A book was a long roll of papyrus — much like the later Roman "books" that are pictured on page 48. The Egyptians wrote histories, geographies, books of science and travel, religious books, cook books, novels, and even fairy stories. The story of *Cinderella and the Glass Slipper* is an old Egyptian tale.

Quantities of these old books have been found in the ruins of Egyptian libraries and in Egyptian tombs. From them our scholars have learned much about **the religion of the Egyptians.** The poor people were ignorant and worshiped idols and animals, but the educated people had better ideas. Their religion taught that they ought to be not merely just but also merciful and kind, especially to the poor about them. One of their books gives a statement which, they thought, a good man should be able to make to the gods after his death. Here are parts of it:

"Hail unto you, ye Lords of Truth! I have not oppressed the poor. I have not caused the slave to be ill-treated. I have not starved any man. I have not made any to weep. I have not given false weight (in selling goods). I have not accused any man falsely. I have not envied other men.

"Grant that he may come unto you — he that hath not lied nor borne false witness, he that hath given bread to the hungry and drink to him that was athirst and who hath clothed the naked."

When the soul had made this last prayer (after denying forty-two different sins in all), he was put to an exciting test.

WEIGHING A SOUL BEFORE THE JUDGES OF THE DEAD. — From a papyrus five thousand years old.

His heart was taken out and placed on one side of the "scales of justice," to see whether it would balance a little image of the god of truth on the other side. If the scales did not balance, that meant the soul had lied; and then it was thrown to be devoured by a fierce dog-like monster that always waited hungrily by the scales. But if the scales balanced, it joined the souls of other good men in far-off "Isles of the Blessed" in the midst of an always-peaceful, blue, sun-lit sea. There the good souls enjoyed all the pleasures of this life without any of its pains — eating and drinking, hunting, boating, visiting, and playing games.

PART OF AN INSCRIPTION of the Pharaoh whose sculptured head is shown on page 35, beginning an account of his conquests in Asia.

EGYPTIAN NOBLES hunting ducks with a "throw-stick," or boomerang, and fishing with a two-pronged harpoon. The birds rise from a mass of papyrus reeds. Each noble has his wife with him, as well as servants. — From a tomb-painting. Notice the writing in the inscription above the picture.

EGYPTIAN MARKET SCENE before " money " was invented (page 24).

BABYLONIAN LION. — Straight north and south through Babylon ran a famous " Procession Street," or " Sacred Way," paved with huge slabs of stone. On either side of this pavement ran a high brick wall, ornamented with a border of lions in low relief, brilliantly enameled in white and yellow upon a dark blue ground.

BABYLONIA

The Babylonians, in the valley of the Euphrates, lived much as the Egyptians did in the Nile valley. They were great traders, and **invented very early a good system of weights and measures.** Our *pound* and *ounce* are old Babylonian weights. From the Babylonians, too, we get the *minutes* and *seconds* of our hours, as well as our *dozen*. They counted by twelves and sixties as well as by tens and hundreds.

There was very little stone in Babylonia ; but there was good clay for making brick, and **the Babylonians made most of their buildings of clay bricks dried in**

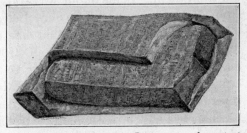

BABYLONIAN CONTRACT IN DUPLICATE. — Important agreements were sometimes written in just the same way on each of two bricks, the first one inclosed within the second. If ever necessary, the outer one could be broken open and the inside record examined.

the sun. Of course these would crumble away after many years. Then the people kept building new houses on the ruins of those that crumbled. Each new building would thus stand a little higher than the one before it, and at last the whole city would be on a high mound. To-day when travelers see a sandy hill standing up in the flat Babylonian plain they feel quite sure that an ancient city once stood there.

Even the Babylonian books were made of brick. With some sharp point a man would press the writing signs into the clay while it was soft, and then bake the book in the sun. Great libraries of these brick books have been found in the ruins of their cities — for they were not exposed to the rain and the outside weather as the buildings themselves were, and so have lasted better.

In digging into one city mound, not very long ago, an ancient Babylonian school house was found. The floor was strewn with clay *slates*, covered with writing exercises. When a boy had covered his slate, he could scrape it off with a bronze scraper and begin again. Many of these scrapers were found among the slates.

The Babylonians believed in many spirits of good and evil, and their priests had charms by which they pretended to get aid from them. Some of our ways of " counting out " come from these old charms — like our "Eeny, meeny, miny, moe."

The earliest set of laws that has ever been found was made by a Babylonian king about 2100 B.C. He had them engraved on a huge slab of stone so that they would not crumble away and be forgotten. Many of the laws are rules for carrying on business fairly, saying how debts shall be collected and interest paid. Orphans and widows were to be protected. Careless doctors and dishonest builders were to be punished :

> " If a doctor has lanced an abscess on the eye of a noble, and has caused the loss of the eye, his hands shall be cut off.
> If a builder has made a house for a man, and it has fallen and killed the owner, that builder shall be put to death."

But some of the laws seem to us very unjust, for they show that rich and poor were not treated alike. If a man put out the eye of a rich man or of a noble, his own eye must be put out ; but if he put out the eye of a poor man, he could pay for it with a small fine.

Babylonian traders traveled with their slow caravans of donkeys all through western Asia. Wherever they went with their sacks of grain and dates and their bales of leather and finely woven woolen cloth, they carried too their easier way of writing and the Babylonian rules for doing business. In this way the civilization of the Euphrates valley was later carried down to us.

SYRIA

**The Nile and the Euphrates gave Egypt and Babylonia a
start on the way toward civilization three thousand
years ahead of any people in the other lands
near them. Lying between them were two
other peoples to whom we owe much.**

Between Egypt and Babylonia stretched the Arabian
Desert, eight hundred miles wide. The only road from one
of these countries to the other curved around that desert,
through the fertile land of *Syria* (map facing 25). Mountains and rivers divide Syria into several small districts;
and in early times each of these was the home of a separate
people. Here lived Philistines, Canaanites, Hebrews, Hit-
tites, and Phoenicians, all of whom we read about in the
Old Testament. **Two of these peoples had great influence
upon our civilization.**

1. The Phoenicians lived on a small strip of coast only
ten or fifteen miles wide. It was shut off from the rest of
Syria by the Lebanon Mountains. The little district had
many good harbors for the small ships of that day, and the
people turned to the sea for their living.

At first they were fishermen and pirates. But after they
had learned some civilization from Egypt and Chaldea
(early Babylonia), they became the greatest sailors and merchants of the ancient world. The " cedar of Lebanon "
furnished them with the best of ship timber. By 1500 B.C.
their daring vessels dotted the Mediterranean.

These early ships were small open boats, driven mainly
by oars. Sometimes they used also a square sail, but only
to run before the wind. (It was many hundreds of years
before sailors learned to " tack.") They had no compass.
Their only guides, when they were out of sight of land, were
the sun and stars. Centuries later, the Greeks still called
the North Star the " Phoenicians' Star," because the

Phoenician mariners had become famous for steering by it at night. The frail Phoenician boats passed even through the straits at Gibraltar, out into the open Atlantic, and there made long voyages both north and south. One Phoenician sea captain, in the service of Egypt, took his boat around Africa, making the trip in three years.

The Phoenicians were the first colonizers. They built trading stations on the islands and shores of the Mediterranean, and left men there to mine tin and copper or to collect other wares from the wild tribes about them. Little by little these tribes learned new ways from the colonists and became civilized themselves. The colonies became powerful cities, some of which have lasted to the present day, like Tunis (Carthage) in North Africa, and Cadiz (or Gades, as they called it) on the Atlantic coast of Spain (map after page 98).

KITCHEN UTENSILS (copper), 4000 years old, found in one grave in Crete, — a large island where Egyptian and Phoenician ships would be likely to stop on the way to Europe.

Tyre and *Sidon*, the two chief ports of Phoenicia, were the richest merchant cities of the Mediterranean. To them their traders brought yellow amber from the Baltic, black slaves and ivory and gorillas from far down the west coast of Africa, and spices, gold, scented woods, and precious stones from India. The Hebrew prophet Ezekiel described Tyre in glowing words:

"O thou that dwellest at the entry of the sea, which art the merchant of the peoples. . . . Thy borders are in the heart of the seas. All the ships of the seas were in thee, to exchange merchandise. . . . With silver, iron, tin, and lead, they traded for thy wares."

From the Egyptians and Babylonians, the Phoenicians had learned to manufacture, and had become very skillful workmen. Weaver's loom, potter's wheel, metal-worker's forge and hammer, and engraver's knife were always busy in Tyre. Many of their wares have been found in the ancient tombs of Italy and Greece, in which often there is nothing else better than Stone-Age tools. This shows that those countries got their start in bronze civilization from Phoenicia. **The Phoenicians did more to** *spread* **civilization than any other ancient people.**

One gift in particular we owe to the Phoenicians. About 1000 B.C. they stopped using the old Egyptian signs for words and syllables, and instead they kept just one sign (or "letter") for each simple sound in their language. In this way, they found, they could write all their words by using only about twenty letters, instead of having to use many hundreds of signs. This kind of a collection of signs for sounds we call a true *alphabet*. The Phoenicians passed on their alphabet to the Greeks, and through them it has come down to us.

Egyptian Hieroglyph.

Egyptian Script.

Phoenician.

Ancient Greek.

Ancient Latin.

Later Latin.

OUR *A* is supposed to have grown in this way.

2. **To the Hebrews we owe even more** than to the Phoenicians. They were a tribe of shepherds and traders who had come long before from Babylonia, seeking better pastures for their flocks. They had fought their way into the land of Canaan, where they lived very simply. We need not tell their story here, for it is told very fully in the Old Testament, and you have learned it at home or at Sunday School.

The Hebrews built no great cities; they were not skilled workmen; and they had few luxuries. But they gave the world something better than any of these things. Their religion was the purest and the highest of all religions of the ancient world. **They were the first people to learn the worship of one God,** — " a spirit, not made with hands," and a loving Father who cares for all men as His children. This Hebrew religion, as you know, became later the foundation of our Christian religion.

There is another reason why we are interested in the Hebrews, or Jews, as we usually call them. None of the other peoples of whom we have been reading so far have descendants among us now. But the Jews do make several millions of our American people. More than half of all the Jews in the world are American citizens now, and one of the great Justices of our Supreme Court is a Jew.

The little Syrian countries had been a favorite trading place for their powerful neighbors on both sides of them,

HEBREW PROPHETS warning their people against the "false gods" of the tribes about them. — From the paintings by John Sargent in the Boston Public Library.

and they became also a favorite battle-ground for those neighbors. The rulers of Egypt and Babylonia were not satisfied to govern just their own lands. They wanted to conquer other nations and build up huge empires. (We give this name " empire " to any large *group* of nations with a strong one ruling the rest.) So the powerful monarchs among them in turn conquered and ruled the peoples of Syria; and sometimes, marching through Syria, one of the two great peoples conquered the other also.

A king of Babylon married a princess from a mountain country, and, to satisfy her longing for the scenery of her old home, he built, on the flat Babylonian plain, wonderful "Hanging Gardens," which became famous through all the rest of ancient times as one of "the seven wonders of the world." This picture is from a modern painting where the artist tries to show how those "gardens" must have looked. Earth was piled up in vast mounds, terrace above terrace, and planted with trees and flowering shrubs. To hold the earth in place, the mounds were "faced" with brick, and the artist thinks (you will see) that for this great work the king even brought in some stone from outside Babylonia for temples and statues.

A PHOENICIAN SHIP of about 1000 B.C., as a Babylonian sculptor pictured it on a monument. Note the shields hanging on the side at the top. This vessel stands higher than the Egyptian ship pictured opposite page 25, but it shows no other marked gain during the thousand or fifteen hundred years.

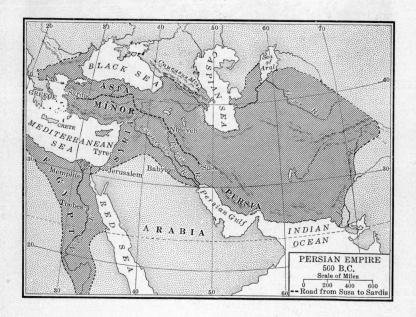

PERSIAN EMPIRE
500 B.C.
Scale of Miles

0   200   400   600

-- Road from Susa to Sardis

None of these early empires lasted very long; **but finally there came a new people, from a little farther east, to conquer and rule all the lands we have mentioned so far — and many more.**

THE PERSIAN EMPIRE

The Persians were at first a little tribe of shepherds living northeast of the Persian Gulf. They were sturdy warriors; and their boys were trained " to ride, to shoot with the bow, and to speak the truth."

About 550 B.C., one of their kings, *Cyrus,* began to conquer the great nations just west of them, and soon he **built up the largest and strongest empire the world had seen.** By 500 B.C. the Persian Empire reached from the Indus River in Asia to the shores of Greece in Europe — a distance of 3000 miles, or as far as from Washington to San Francisco.

The head of a statue of a Pharaoh who lived about 1470 B.C. and conquered as far as the Euphrates. His is the inscription facing page 28.

The Persians built roads to hold their wide-lying empire together more closely. One famous road ran fifteen hundred miles from Sardis, in Asia Minor, to their central capital at Susa. Distances were marked by white milestones; and at proper points there were good inns for the traveler. Royal messengers were always strung out along the Sardis-Susa road, on relays of swift Arab steeds, covering the distance in six days. But the ordinary trader took from six to twelve weeks for the journey, with his skins of oil and wine, or his richer wares from distant realms, laden on camels or donkeys.

The Persians did not do much to advance science or art. What they had of these things they learned from Babylonia. But they **became famous *rulers,*** with new inventions in government. Up to that time the many tribes of that region had carried on almost constant wars with one another.

Now for more than 200 years they lived peacefully together under the Persian government.

But the Persians did carry on many wars with other countries, conquering them and adding them to their empire. All the nations yielded to their mighty armies till they reached the little land of Greece. How the brave little Greek cities checked the growing power of Persia we shall see in a later chapter.

Chipped Stone Spearhead found in Egypt. There are many such proofs of a Stone Age in Egypt before the Bronze civilization there began.

Summary

The earliest civilizations arose in fertile river valleys. The *Egyptians* learned how to irrigate the Nile valley. They were the first scientists, the first sailors, the first inventors of writing by syllables, and they were great builders. The *Babylonians* made the first code of laws and invented a good system of weights and measures. Both Egyptians and Babylonians learned to make many useful and beautiful things, so that life grew more delightful; and much of their skill in handicrafts has never been lost. *Phoenician* traders planted distant colonies along the Mediterranean coast, invented a true alphabet, and carried it and the Bronze civilization of Egypt and Babylonia to the skin-clad savages of southern Europe. The *Hebrews* were the first to worship one God. The *Persians* united all the civilized world of their day (together with many neighboring savage districts) under one strong government.

New Words

kingdom	scientist	Sphinx	peasant
Pharaoh	irrigation	coin	empire
proverb	pyramid	despot	noble
excavation	calendar	alphabet	barter
hieroglyphs	tax	colony	reservoir

Thought Questions and Things to Do

1. Always keep the *map* and *the time-line* before you when you study your history. Mark important happenings on the time-line, and locate on your map the places mentioned. Print carefully on an outline map the names: *Mediterranean Sea, Nile River, Red Sea, Sahara Desert, Arabian Desert, Euphrates River, Egypt, Babylonia, Phoenicia, Syria.* Shade in lightly the kingdoms of Egypt and Babylonia. Put the pyramids where they belong. Draw in the canal of the Pharaohs, and the modern Suez Canal. Memphis and Thebes were the two greatest cities of ancient Egypt. Find them and put them on your map. Can you locate the other cities that we have mentioned?

2. Many interesting excavations are being made in Egypt and Babylonia to-day. Try to find out something about them and report to the class.

3. A class scrap-book makes the work more interesting. You will be surprised to find how many times the countries we have been reading about are mentioned in our papers and magazines. Cut out any pictures you can find, and be able to explain them to the class. Let the class choose the best ones for the scrap-book.

4. Imagine yourself taking a trip up the Nile in the days of the Pharaohs, and write an account of what you saw on the way. Or take a trip on a Phoenician trading vessel; or imagine you are a poor herdsman from the desert, and go to an Egyptian market place for food. You should be able to write an interesting account of your adventures.

5. The Nile and Euphrates valleys had no great forests. If they had had dense forests, would it have been harder or easier for civilization to start there? Could such a civilization have begun so easily in the Amazon valley?

6. Look back at page 24. What is there in the picture on that page to tell you about how high those columns are? How high do you think they are?

7. Try to write a letter in picture writing. Then try some rebus writing, in which you use part pictures and part letters. You find that much easier, do you not? That was something like the Egyptian writing. For instance, the picture of the *sun* ☉ also meant *light*. If we were in the habit of using that picture for our word "light," we could write the word "delight" in rebus writing in this way: D ☉ ; but in pure picture writing it would be impossible to make a picture of that word. One of Kipling's *Just So Stories* tells how letters *might* have grown from pictures in very early times.

8. Interesting accounts of these early peoples are found in Best's *Egypt and Her Neighbors*, Wells' *How the Present Came from the Past*, Arnold's *Stories of Ancient Peoples*, Van Loon's *Story of Mankind*. You would all enjoy the story of the Persian boy in Andrews' *Ten Boys on the Road from Long Ago to Now*.

A NOBLE LADY at the last stage in dressing. In one hand she holds a mirror, but just now she is busy with a cooling drink. A few locks of her hair have been fastened up out of the way with a hair pin, while the maid is arranging the locks below. — Part of a series of reliefs from a woman's tomb of about 2100 B.C., showing how she spent her day.

9. For some years before our Civil War there was in America an interesting "Pony Express." No railroad then reached farther west than Missouri. Mail was carried from that point to California, a distance of 2000 miles, by relays of daring riders who covered the wilderness trail in ten days. Let some member of your class look up this topic and tell the class about it, comparing the pony express riders with the royal messengers on the Persian road 2500 years ago. You will find one short account of the Pony Express in West and West, *Story of Our Country*.

BRONZE DAGGER with gold inlay work, buried in an ancient tomb in southern Greece at least 4400 years ago. There were no lions in Greece in those times. How can you explain the lions on the dagger? See pages 32, 33.

CHAPTER IV

THE GREEKS

The first *Europeans* to whom the bronze civilization of the Egyptians and Phoenicians spread were the *Greeks*. If you look at the map facing page 41, you will see reasons for this. But it was a long time before the Greeks began to keep many records, and no one knows much about them until **about 500** B.C. By that time **they had built up a better civilization than any the world had seen** — and one *more like our own* than any before it had been.

Some legends of much earlier times have come down to us. Wandering minstrels used to go from place to place, chanting long tales of the heroic deeds of brave warriors. The Greeks passed on some of these stories from father to son for hundreds of years before they were written out. The most famous of all are those about the siege of *Troy*, — a Bronze-Age city on the coast of Asia Minor which had been destroyed in very early times by a great army of Greeks. It is supposed that these songs of the Trojan War were put together about

A VASE more than 4000 years old, found in a buried city in Crete.

39

1000 B.C. by *Homer,* a blind minstrel whom the Greeks always thought the greatest of all poets. From that time to now, school boys have learned the stories he sang. (Often the Greeks called him merely "the poet.")

Geography Helped Make Greek Civilization Different from Any before It

Greece is a small country. It could be put inside almost any one of our States, and it is broken up into still smaller

divisions by steep mountain ranges and by deep arms of the sea. In early times, men could not go from one of those tiny districts to another except by rugged mountain paths or by boat. **So the different divisions did not become united under one government,** as the cities of Egypt did. Instead, each of them became the home of a separate Greek *nation.* There were about fifty of these little nations. The people in all of them, however, did speak the same language.

HOMER, the blind minstrel, and his guide, as a modern painter pictures him.

Greece is not a fertile land, like the broad valleys of the Nile or Euphrates. Still, in their narrow valleys the farmers had olive groves and small fields of grain. On the hillsides they raised grapes and figs, and, where the mountain slopes were too barren even for this, flocks of goats could find pasture.

Almost all the rivers are rushing mountain brooks, but the coast has countless good harbors. So the Greeks learned to be fishermen and sailors, until they at last became famous

This drawing from a Greek vase pictures one famous fight in the Trojan War. Achilles, a Greek hero, stands over the body of a slain friend, while the Trojans in front of him are trying to secure it in order to dishonor it. Notice the armor, especially the "greaves" on the legs.

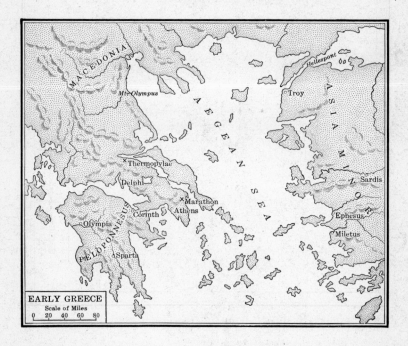

EARLY GREECE
Scale of Miles
0   20   40   60   80

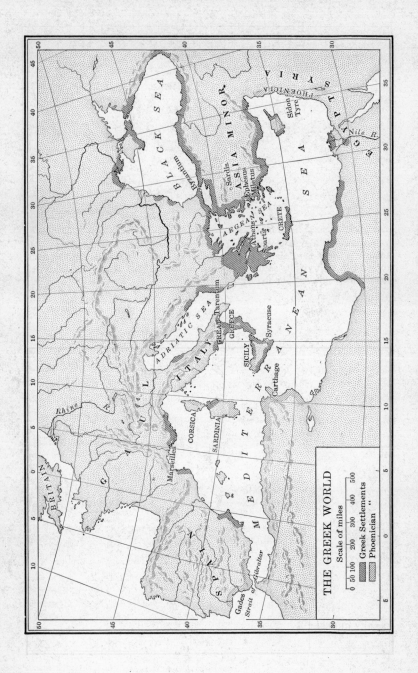

THE GREEK WORLD
Scale of miles

0 50 100 200 300 400 500

Greek Settlements
Phoenician "

BRITAIN

GAUL

Rhine R.

SPAIN

Strait of Gibraltar
Gades

MEDITERRANEAN

CORSICA

SARDINIA

Marseilles

SICILY

Carthage

Syracuse

GREECE

GREAT Tarentum

ITALY

ADRIATIC SEA

BLACK SEA

Byzantium

ASIA MINOR

Sardis
Ephesus
Miletus

AEGEAN SEA

Athens
Caria

CRETE

SEA

SYRIA

PHOENICIA

Sidon
Tyre

EGYPT

Nile R.

traders and colonizers, like the Phoenicians. Southern
Italy came to have so many Greek cities that it was called
"Great Greece." Look at the map facing this page and
notice how the Greek colonies made a fringe around the shores
of the Mediterranean and its arms. Find these important
ones: *Ephesus* and *Miletus* in Asia Minor; *Syracuse* in
Sicily; *Marseilles* in southern France; *Byzantium* (which
later became Constanti-
nople) at the opening of the
Black Sea.

WOMEN AT THEIR MUSIC — from a painting
on a Greek vase.

Greece has a mild climate, so that the people
live outdoors much of the
day. It **is also a very
beautiful country.** Everywhere is a lovely mingling
of hill and dale, with masses
of white clouds floating in
a deep blue sky. The blue sunlit sea, too, dotted with
emerald islands, is nearly always before the eye. No wonder
**the Greeks grew to love beauty more than any other people
have ever done.** They used the same word to mean *good*
and *beautiful*. The statues they made, the temples they
built, the poems they wrote, are the most perfect that
have ever been known. And since they loved the world
around them, they were always eager to learn more about
it; **so they found out more about the world than all the
peoples before them.** They learned, too, that the truest
happiness was found in *self-control* and *moderation*. Their
favorite mottoes were: "Nothing over much" and "Moderation in all things."

The Religion of the Greeks, too, Showed that They Loved Beauty

All these early peoples, except the Hebrews, believed in
many gods. Egyptians and Babylonians thought of their

gods as rather terrible creatures, often with bodies of men
and heads of beasts. But **the Greeks thought their gods
were like strong and beautiful men and women** — only far
more powerful than men could ever be. The home of their
chief gods, they believed, was the cloud-capped summit of
Mt. Olympus, the loftiest mountain of Greece. But sometimes, it was said, some of the gods came down to earth,
where any man might meet them and per-
haps get help from them.

The chief of these gods was *Zeus*,
"father of gods and men." He was god
of .the sky, and ruled the heavens and the
earth, with the far-darting lightning for
his weapon. One of his two brothers ruled
the sea, and the other the dark underworld
where dwelt the spirits of the dead.

The glorious *Apollo*, the sun-god, was
a son of Zeus. He brought light and
warmth to men. He was also god of

A MUSE with a lyre.
— A Greek cameo.

music and art and poetry. His favorite
temple was at *Delphi* on Mt. Parnassus. It was built over
a crack in the earth, from which arose thin puffs of gas.
The priestess of the temple went into a kind of swoon when
she breathed this gas, and then she would speak strange
words, which were supposed to be the words of Apollo.
No Greek liked to begin any important matter until he
had gone to this temple and asked Apollo's advice. The
oracles (as the words of the answer were called) were not
very clear, but people could usually find some meaning
in them.

Like Apollo in many ways was one of his sisters, *Athene*.
The Greeks seem to have thought more of her than of any
of their other goddesses. They said that she sprang full-
grown from the head of *Zeus*, as a wise thought does sometimes from the brain of a man. It was to Athene that they

APOLLO AND THE MUSES. — Nine goddesses helped Apollo look after different kinds of learning, — one for history, one for song-writing, one for play-writing, and so on. They were called "The Nine Muses." Sometime you will learn their separate names.

This picture is from a painting, in the Boston Museum of Fine Arts, by a famous American artist, John Sargent. Behind the head of the central figure the artist has painted a sun-disk. That symbol, together with the harp in the hand, shows whom that figure represents.

Photo by Ewing Galloway, New York

RUINS AT DELPHI TO-DAY

MODERN GREEK GIRLS (1927 A.D.) rehearsing dance and music for a revival of an ancient Greek play at Delphi. Through energy and money furnished by a Greek woman (who, however, had been born in America and had been graduated at an American college) some such play is now given there each year — in a celebration known as the Delphic Festival. In 1927 the play was the *Prometheus Bound*, written by an Athenian poet 2400 years ago. The girls in this picture represent a chorus of " Daughters of Old Ocean " who come to lament with Prometheus — who has been chained to a rock by jealous gods because he brought fire from heaven to men (page 8). This rehearsal took place, not at Delphi, but on the shore of the Aegean near Athens.

prayed for help in inventing new ways to do things. She was the goddess of wisdom.

These were only a few of a family of twelve great gods. But the Greeks believed also in many other god-like beings. Every wood and stream, every hill and dale, they thought, was the home of some spirit. All these, they believed, might sometimes take the forms of glorious youths or maidens. Many lovely stories were told about them. Sometimes the Greek writers made the gods in these stories act in silly and stupid ways, just as men often do. But the wisest Greeks had different ideas. The poet Homer exclaims, "Verily, the blessed gods love not insolent acts, but they reverence justice and righteous deeds."

The Greeks believed, too, that their gods were especially fond of seeing men use strength and skill. So one of their ways to worship was to celebrate games in honor of a god, with races and wrestling and boxing. The greatest festival of this sort was one held every four years in honor of Zeus, at the city of *Olympia*.

This drawing from a Greek vase represents a youth just crowned with an olive wreath as a victor in the Olympic Games.

These Olympic Games were for all Greeks everywhere, even in distant colonies, and no one but a Greek could take part in them. So they helped to make the Greeks feel themselves one people against all the outside world. Many men from the different nations of Greece became better acquainted with one another there.

For months before one of the celebrations, heralds traveled from city to city to announce the exact time. Then from all parts of the Greek world men journeyed toward Olympia. The only prize given there was a simple wreath of olive leaves; but every one felt that a victor in those games was a favorite of the gods and that he brought great honor to his city.   Often, on his return home, his fellow-citizens put up a statue in memory of his victory.

Above All Else the Greeks Loved Liberty

In early times each Greek tribe had its chief, who led his people in war and peace.

Early in Athenian history two youths killed a man who had made himself "tyrant" of the city. The citizens set up a statue in their honor (this picture is from a copy found now in the Museum of Naples), voted that their descendants should forever be free from all taxes, and at a yearly festival honored them by singing, —

" I'll wreath my sword in myrtle bough,
The sword that laid the tyrant low,
When patriots, burning to be free,
To Athens gave equality ! "

But **the Greeks did not let their rulers become despots,** like the kings of the eastern countries.   An early Greek king could do nothing important until he had called all the men of the tribe together and talked the matter over with them. Later on, a "tyrant" sometimes rose up and tried to rule a Greek city by force; but his rule never lasted very long.   All Greeks believed that to kill such a man was a righteous deed.

By 500 B.C. most Greek cities had become little **democracies.** That is, the people of each city ruled themselves, without any king at all.   Even in the cities that kept kings, the people came to hold most of the power.   **Of all that the Greeks taught the world, the best was this:** *to desire freedom in thought and word and act.*

The Two Leading Cities of Greece Were not at all Alike

Until about 500 B.C. Greek history is mixed up with fanciful legends, so that it is often hard to tell how much is true. But after that time there are more complete records to go by.

Sparta and *Athens* had then become the two most important cities. They were only 150 miles apart in a straight line — as near each other as New York and Albany. But they were as different from each other as French and Germans are.

1. **The Spartans** had placed their city in an inland valley, farther from the sea than Greek cities usually were, and surrounded on all sides by the peoples they had conquered. Other Greek cities had strong stone walls to protect them. Sparta was unfortified. Its people boasted, " *Our* walls are *men*." The men of Sparta **were famous warriors, but not much else.** Their one business in life was to keep down their subjects and to conquer more. **So a Spartan boy was trained only for fighting.** At the age of seven he was taken from his home to a public training house. There he lived until he grew to be a man. He was taught to run, wrestle, and

STATUETTE of a Greek boy with a thorn in his foot.

fight, and, as soon as he could handle weapons, to use spear and sword. He learned to obey orders, to bear hunger and cold and pain, like one of our young Indians, and to get along with few comforts.

When he had grown to manhood, he was moved into a military camp, or barracks, to live there with other men until he became too old to be a soldier. Even when he married, he rarely ate or slept in his own house, and he saw little of his wife and children.

Sparta had no art or learning and almost no trade. No money was allowed except cheap iron coins. The people were always opposed to new ideas. This perhaps was why Sparta never became a democracy. The kings and nobles ruled the city.   There were meetings of citizens sometimes, but they had little to say.

2. **Athens** was near the sea, and had an excellent harbor. She **became a rich trading city.**   She had also busy factories to make weapons, tools, cloths, and beautiful vases and other earthenware, not only for use at home, but also for her

traders to sell in distant lands. Her harbor was crowded with shipping from many parts of the world, and her market place and streets were thronged with foreign merchants.

Athens owed her greatness in large part to the work of *one* of her citizens. That man was *Solon.* A good while back, a small group of nobles had overthrown the king at Athens and taken his power for themselves. They had also seized most of the land.

ATTIC VASE OF about 450 B.C. now in the Metropolitan Museum in New York. The painting (in red on a black ground) shows women getting wine ready to serve.

Many of the poor farmers became slaves, and the rest tilled the land for the nobles.   But this caused bitter discontent, so that *about 600 B.C.* the Athenians were in danger of civil war — poor farmers and workmen against rich nobles.

Finally, to prevent that evil, the people all agreed to turn the government over to Solon, so that he might reform these things.   Solon had already served Athens well in war and in peace.   He was a thinker and a poet.   In his younger days he had been a trader and had visited other countries, traveling even into Egypt.   He was considered one of the wisest men of all Greece, and was so patriotic and so just that both poor and rich trusted his fairness.

Solon used his new power wisely. *He freed all Athenians who had been made slaves,* and *he gave back to the farmers the land* that had been taken away from them. But when some of the poor wanted him to divide all the land equally among all the people, he refused.

Before this time the laws of Athens had been so severe that people said they were " written in blood." *Solon made wiser laws,* less cruel and more just. He also gave Athens a *coinage,* and so helped trade to grow. He ordered, too, that *every father must teach his son some way to earn a living.* **Then he gave the people more power to rule themselves** and to manage the affairs of the city. All the citizens were to come together at regular times in an *Assembly, to make laws* and *to choose officials* to carry them out.

Solon's own rule had lasted two years, while he was busy making all these plans for his city, but now he resigned his office. This was the first time, so far as we know, that a man with great power gave it up willingly so that the people might govern themselves.

Athens had now Become a Democracy and Was Wise enough to Train its Boys To Become Good Citizens

Each Athenian citizen now had a share in managing the city, and each felt too that he had a share in its glory. Every year on a certain day all the boys who had reached the age of eighteen that year took this solemn and noble pledge :

" Never will we bring disgrace upon our city by dishonesty or cowardice. In company with comrades, or all alone, we will fight for its sacred things and for its ideals. We will revere and obey its laws. We will always try to quicken the sense of duty to the city in others. In all these ways we will strive to pass the city on to our sons more glorious and beautiful than when our fathers passed it to us."

It is for fine things such as these that we honor Athens. Her people were brave soldiers when they were needed to

defend their city; but they did not let themselves be trained into mere fighting machines. **An Athenian boy,** like the boys of Sparta, **began school at the age of seven;** but he was taken to and from school each day by a trusted servant of the family. He studied Homer and music and mathematics. Large parts of Homer's poems he learned by heart. He

This is a picture of *Roman* papyrus rolls, which were, however, almost the same in form as the earlier Greek and Egyptian books. Notice the tag, carrying a library number. As one "page" was read, it was rolled up out of sight and a new page brought to sight from the other end of the roll.

The flat book-looking thing on the cabinet is a set of wax tablets.

learned, too, to write with ink on papyrus and with a sharp instrument on wax tablets.

Every day, he gave some hours to exercising and training his body, as the boys did in most Greek cities. This training continued even after the boy became a man. In no other country have so many of the people developed such supple and beautiful bodies or prided themselves so much on their swiftness and strength.

At eighteen, when the Athenian boy left school, he had not finished the education of his mind any more than that of his body. **His wider**

GREEK RUNNERS — a relief by the American artist John Sargent, in the Boston Museum of Fine Arts.

training for citizenship was just beginning. He attended the debates of statesmen in the Assembly, watched the plays of great Athenian poets at the theater, and listened to the teachings of the wise men from all over Greece who made Athens their home. One great citizen of Athens compared the Athenian way of living with the Spartan way in these words : " *We* are lovers of the beautiful, yet simple in our tastes ; and we cultivate the mind, without loss of manliness."

Summary

Bronze civilization spread from Egypt to Greece 5000 years ago. With that start, the Greeks by 500 B.C. built up the best civilization the world had ever known. The geography of Greece (1) kept the people from uniting in one government; (2) made farming very hard but led the people to take to the sea; and (3) helped to teach them to love beauty, as their religion showed.

They also loved liberty, and many of their cities became democracies. The two leading cities, Athens and Sparta, stood for two very different kinds of life.

New Words

minstrel	oracle	tyrant	assembly
moderation	legend	democracy	citizen

Thought Questions and Things to Do

1. On the time line, mark dates for Greek history, using a different color than you used for the eastern countries. You should already have marked the place for 500 B.C. Do you remember why?

2. Locate on the map the places mentioned in this chapter. Suppose there had been a river, fit for ships, running the full length of Greece : would that have made a difference in the history of Greece? Would its history have been different if it had not been a peninsula? Give all the reasons you can think of why it is easier for us to keep our States united than it was for the Greek districts to unite under one government.

3. In what ways do you think it was bad for Greece to be divided into so many little nations? Do you see one way in which it may have been a good thing? Would new ways of living be more or

less likely to be tried out? Why was it an advantage for all to have one language? Is it more important, do you think, for people living near together to have one language or one government, if they can't have both?

4. Read the story of "Cleon" in Jane Andrews' *Ten Boys*, and also Cowles' *Our Little Athenian Cousin* and *Our Little Spartan Cousin*. Imagine yourself a Greek boy, and tell how your father took you to the Olympic Games.

5. Find all the pictures you can of Greek gods and heroes, and bring them to class to illustrate the legends. Good books in which to read these stories are: Hawthorne's *Wonder Book* and *Tanglewood Tales*, Kingsley's *Greek Heroes*, Gayley's *Classic Myths*, Baldwin's *Golden Age*, Church's *Iliad for Boys and Girls*, and Harding's *Greek Gods, Heroes, and Men*. That last book will give you a good story of Solon. Most of the other stories are legends. Do you see any reason why we should read them, since they are not real history? Can you learn anything from them about the life and ideas of the Greeks?

GREEK WOMAN SPINNING. — The distaff, in the hand, remained the best tool for spinning until the invention of the spinning wheel three hundred years ago. This is a drawing from a vase painting.

6. Think of some ways in which *our* democratic government differs from that of the Athenians.

7. In our day there are sometimes held great contests between athletes of different countries, and such contests are now called "Olympic Games." Can you see why that is a good name for them? In 1928 the modern "Olympic Games" were held at Amsterdam. Can you find out something about the contests there?

8. The index of this book tells how to pronounce new names (and many other words as well). Look there for words you do not know. The index also tells on what map to find new place names.

This is a picture of half of the inside of a Greek bowl, representing women at their toilet. The figures were painted in red upon a black ground.

CHAPTER V

THE GREEKS STOP THE PERSIANS

Before 500 B.C. the huge Persian Empire had reached the Aegean Sea (page 36). *Darius*, who was then king, even conquered the Greek colonies in Asia Minor. But those cities soon rebelled, and sent messengers to Sparta and Athens to ask for help.

The king of Sparta was not willing to try to help cities so far away. But the Athenian Assembly thought it shameful to let Greeks anywhere be made slaves. So it voted to send an army to help the Greeks of Asia win freedom. With this help, the rebels were at first successful. They even captured Sardis (page 35). But when Darius at last got his mighty hosts together, he overcame them once more.

THE FIRST PERSIAN ATTACK ON GREECE: 490 B.C.

Darius now made up his mind to conquer Greece itself, so as to punish Athens. He gave orders that one of his heralds

8422

should call out to him each day at dinner, " O King, remember the Athenians!"

Do you believe the warlike Persian Empire would have left Greece alone even if Athens had *not* helped the Greeks in Asia? If you had been an Athenian, how would you have voted about sending help?

The Persians couldn't attack Greece without ships. They were not sailors themselves; but Darius finally got together a mighty fleet from Egypt and Phoenicia, which were now parts of his empire. A Persian army of 100,000 chosen men was sent on board, and the ships moved slowly across the Aegean, stopping to seize important islands on the way. Finally the army landed at *Marathon* — the only plain of any size anywhere near Athens.

PERSIAN ARCHER of the king's guard, — from a long succession of like figures on the walls of a palace of Darius at Susa.

Sparta had promised to help defend Greece. So, when the fleet first appeared, a swift Athenian runner, *Phidippides* (who had won races at the Olympic Games), raced the hundred and fifty miles of mountain path to beg Sparta to hurry. But the Spartans said they would have to wait a week. They had a religious festival to celebrate, and their laws, they claimed, would not let them start their army out before the moon reached its full. With bitter heart, Phidippides raced back, to live or die with Athens.

There seemed little hope for the Athenians. But they marched forth, under their general *Miltiades,* to meet the huge Persian army — at least ten times as large as theirs. Even if the numbers had been equal, most men would have

The Athenian Charge at Marathon.

trembled at the idea of fighting against Persians. They were lords of the world. And yet the little Athenian army won a complete victory.

Usually the famous Persian archers scattered their foes at the very beginning of a battle by a rain of deadly arrows. But this time, while they were still getting ready to shoot, they were astonished to see the Greeks come charging toward them *on the run*. There was little time for the bowmen to get in their deadly work; and the Persians were not well armed for *close* fighting with the heavy-armed Greeks. Their large numbers were too crowded to move freely; and their chief weapons, besides the bow, were light darts and small curved swords, or scimitars. Their shields, too, were either small bronze shields or large wicker ones, and neither kind was much protection against the powerful thrust of the heavy Greek spears, with all the weight of the charging ranks behind them.

HEAVY-ARMED GREEK SOLDIER. — A drawing from a vase painting.

The Persians fought bravely; but the Athenians were fighting for their homes and for their wives and children, who would be carried off into cruel slavery if the Persians won. Their charge broke through the Persian ranks, leaving more than 6000 of the invaders dead on the field. The rest fled in disorder to their ships. The Athenians lost only 192 men.

Only old men and boys had been left to guard Athens; and Miltiades was now afraid that the Persian fleet might sail around to the harbor, and seize the city before his weary army could get back. So he hurried Phidippides across the hills to cheer Athens with news of the battle. The runner was already exhausted by the fight. But he raced the twenty-two miles of rough mountain road, shouted joyfully to the anxious crowds in the streets, " Ours the victory ! " and fell dead. (The modern " Marathon race," in which athletes of all the world compete, gets its name from this run of Phidippides.)

THE SECOND PERSIAN ATTACK : 480 B.C.

Ten years after Marathon, a new Persian king, *Xerxes*, made up his mind that he himself would lead an army to conquer Greece. Xerxes was a vain and weak son of the great Darius. First he got together the largest army the world had ever seen. Even a Persian king couldn't get ships enough to carry it, and most of it had to march by land.

On the map facing page 39 you can see that, just west of the Black Sea, Europe is separated from Asia by a narrow strait only about a mile wide. (The Greeks called that strait the *Hellespont*. What do we call it?) It was there that Xerxes planned to cross into Europe. He set thousands of slaves to building two bridges — *floating* bridges, made by joining boats together, with planks across them. Before they were finished, a storm destroyed them ; and Xerxes is said to have sent slaves with whips to lash the waves — like a silly barefoot boy who pounds a stick against which he has stubbed his toe. But at last new bridges were ready, and for seven days and nights the vast host streamed across.

The only Greek city that had been getting ready for another Persian attack was Athens. A keen-witted leader there, ***Themistocles,*** had persuaded the people that Persia was sure to try once more, and that it would be easiest to defeat her at sea. So **Athens had built warships,** until she had many more than any other Greek city.

But now, when the cities sent their leaders to a meeting to decide what to do about fighting Xerxes, **the meeting voted to put Sparta in command of all the Greeks,** for the Spartans were considered the very best soldiers. Even the fleet was to be commanded by a Spartan admiral, though Sparta had only sixteen ships out of the fleet of nearly four hundred. The Athenians had more than half of all the ships; but they showed their patriotism by giving up their claim to the command when the other cities voted for Sparta.

GREEK PEASANT. — A drawing from a vase painting.

The only road by which the Persian army could get into central Greece went through a narrow pass at *Thermopylae.* There the road between the mountains and the sea was not more than twenty feet wide. The defense of this pass was left to Sparta; and if she had sent a good-sized army there, she might have turned Xerxes back. But, though the Spartans were good soldiers, they were *not* generals. They did not like to fight far from their own city. To guard that pass they sent their king *Leonidas* with only three hundred Spartans. The rest of the Spartan force was kept at home to celebrate a festival to Apollo!

Leonidas and his three hundred did their part well. Xerxes sent a herald with orders for them to give up their arms. Said Leonidas, " Come and take them ! "   And when the herald boasted that the Persians were so many that the flight of their arrows would hide the sun, the Greek replied, — " So much the better : we shall fight in the shade."

For two days of savage fighting, the little Spartan army held the enemy back. Only a few Persians could attack at a time; and their dead were piled in heaps in front of the pass. But at the end of the second day, Xerxes found a Greek traitor who knew a narrow path *over* the mountain. The Greek army, of course, knew of this path; but Sparta had not sent men enough to guard it. During the night, Xerxes marched a part of his army over it, so as to attack the Spartans from both sides at one time.

GIRLS AT PLAY. — A painting on a Greek vase.

When Leonidas learned that the Persians had started men over this path, he knew that the end had come. He had a few soldiers with him that were not Spartans. These he now sent away to their homes. But he and his three hundred would not retreat. Indeed, the laws of Sparta forbade them to do so. At daylight, they charged out upon the Persian host and died fighting. In later times their burial place was marked by a monument with these words carved upon it:

> Go, Stranger, and to Sparta tell
> That here, obeying her command, we fell.

But after all **the Spartans had not stopped the Persians, and they would not send another army to defend Central Greece.** Instead, they began to build a stone wall across the *Isthmus of Corinth*, so as to be able to defend just the southern peninsula (the *Peloponnesus*), where lay their own city and their closest allies. Xerxes was marching at will through the rest of Greece, burning the cities that had not submitted to him at first.

The Athenians knew that when he reached them, they would be punished most cruelly of all. They sent a messenger to Delphi to consult the oracle. The priestess answered, — " Nothing can save your city ; but, when all is lost, wooden walls shall shelter the Athenians." Then Themistocles persuaded the people that " wooden walls " meant their ships. They must abandon their city at once, he urged, and fight the Persians at sea.

The Spartan admiral had ordered all the Greek fleet to move back to the Isthmus of Corinth, to help the land army defend the Peloponnesus, but at last Themistocles did get him to stop two days at Athens, to move the Athenian women and children and old men over to the *Island of Salamis.* (This island is the one nearest Athens on the map facing page 40.) These helpless people had barely reached the island before, looking back, they saw their homes and temples in flames. The Persians burned also the Athenian farming villages round about, and they expected soon to make slaves of the fugitives penned up on Salamis.

But Themistocles had planned all the time to hold the Greek fleet near Salamis a little longer — long enough, indeed, so that it would have to fight the Persians there. Over and over again, in an all-night council of the captains, he urged good reasons for this. The Persian fleet, four times as strong, had now come up ; but the Greek ships lay in the narrow strip of water between the island and the mainland, where only a small part of the Persian fleet could get at them at one time. It was just the place for the Greeks to use their smaller numbers best.

At last the admiral consented to stay and fight. Then, to make sure that he should not change his mind again, Themistocles used a strange trick. He sent a message to Xerxes, pretending to be a friend : " The Greeks are going to slip away in the night," he told the Persian king. " If you want to capture their ships, you must send part of your fleet around the island, to shut up the other end of the strait."

Xerxes did this, so that now the Greek fleet *could* not escape. Then it fought bravely. **All the next day, the battle raged,** while Xerxes looked on from a golden throne on the shore :

> " A king sat on the rocky brow
> Which looks o'er sea-born Salamis;
> And ships by thousands lay below,
> And men in nations, — all were his.
> He counted them at break of day;
> But when the sun set, where were they ! "

The huge Persian fleet was sunk, captured, or scattered in flight. The next morning, Xerxes was on his long march back to Asia by land.

This battle did not end the war; but Persia never again had any real chance to conquer Greece. **Marathon and Salamis saved Greek freedom from being crushed by Eastern despotism.** This was a good thing for all the world and for all time — not least for us to-day.

New Words

fleet   rebel   festival   traitor   herald   allies   admiral   invade

Things to Do

1. Make your own summary of this chapter.

2. You have two important dates to put on your time line. You see such dates come closer together now.

3. You will need two outline maps for this chapter: one for the Persian Empire, and one for Greece and the Aegean. List all the places mentioned, and locate them on your maps. Make the lands belonging to Persia one color and the free Greek countries another. Show important battles by crossed spears.

4. Imagine yourself the Persian herald reporting the Battle of Marathon to Darius, or a Greek prisoner at Sardis writing to his friends an account of the Persian court.

5. Write a news bulletin such as the Athenians might have posted up during the weeks between Thermopylae and Salamis.

6. List the important men named in chapters iv and v. Let each pupil describe one of those men without using his name, and let the rest of the class guess which man is meant each time.

7. Try acting out some of the scenes from this chapter, such as Themistocles in council with the other sea-captains, or Leonidas receiving the Persian herald.

THE OLIVE HARVEST IN OLD GREECE.

From a Greek vase.

CHAPTER VI

THE GLORY OF ATHENS

After Salamis the Athenians rebuilt their city on a larger scale and surrounded it with strong walls. **Then for fifty glorious years Athens was the leader of Greece.** She united many Greek cities for a time into a powerful league. With the help of this league, she drove the Persians entirely out of the Aegean and away from all its coasts, and freed all the Greek towns there.

This Period is sometimes Called "The Age of Pericles"

The government of Athens remained a democracy. Every ten days or so, all the citizens met in a great open-air Assembly. There they listened to plans put forth by the "board of generals," as they called the city council that they elected every year. Other citizens, too, might suggest plans of their own, and try to show that they were better than the plans of the generals. Then the Assembly would adopt the plan it liked best.

The man whose plans were the most popular was usually chosen president of the board of generals for the next year. But if at any time the people did not like what a general was doing, the Assembly might dismiss him from office. Often such leaders were banished from the city, or even put to death.

A great modern scholar made this picture, to show how (as he thought) the Acropolis must have looked in the days of Athenian glory. Such a picture (made from a study of remains and of old descriptions) is called a "reconstruction."

HORSEMEN FROM THE PARTHENON FRIEZE — not from the gable sculpture ("pediment" sculpture) that is shown in the picture above, but from a band of reliefs on the walls behind the columns. These marbles are now in the British Museum at London.

THE ACROPOLIS OF ATHENS TO-DAY. This view fronts differently from the front shown in the reconstruction facing page 60. The entrance (shown in front in that picture) may be seen in this photo at the rear corner of the left-hand side.

Ewing Galloway

THE PORT OF ATHENS TO-DAY is always crowded with shipping. The city at this harbor has always been known by its separate name of *The Piraeus*, and in ancient times it was joined to Athens proper by "Long Walls" that ran the four miles from city to city.

But now for a while the same man was elected president of the board year after year. This man was **Pericles.** He was a great statesman and had many wise plans for Athens. He did not try particularly to make the people like him. Indeed he was never afraid to oppose the crowd in the Assembly when he thought it was wrong. He was reserved and dignified. But the people trusted him, because they believed in his good sense and patriotism. And even when at first they seemed ready to oppose him, his splendid oratory nearly always persuaded them to adopt his far-sighted plans.

With Pericles for their leader the Athenians now made their city not only the most powerful but also the most beautiful in all the world. Greece, our scholars say, taught the world ; and Athens was called " the school of Greece." In the fifth century B.C. that one city was the home of the most brilliant company of famous artists, builders, sculptors, poets, and thinkers that any country has ever yet seen at one time.

The center of Athens' splendor was the **Acropolis.** This was a lofty, flat-topped rock, rising above the streets of the city. The top would have covered five or six of our city blocks. In older days it had been a fort, but now it was crowned with noble temples and glorious statues.

If you had been an Athenian boy, your father would sometime have taken you up the stately flight of wide, winding, stone steps that led up one side of that hill. At the top you would come to an entrance-porch whose roof was supported by tall columns of white marble. Through this porch you would pass out upon a wide level space. Below, spreading out on all sides, you would see the roofs of the city, and far off to the south you might catch the gleam of the blue Aegean. But you would turn your eyes from even those sights to the famous buildings and works of art about you. Two of these in particular you would always remember.

1. Just in front of you, towering high above even the roofs of the temples, stood a colossal **bronze statue of Athene,** the guardian goddess of the city and especially of that " Holy Hill." The broad head of the spear that the goddess

RUINS OF PART OF AN ANCIENT THEATER in a small Greek city in the Peloponnesus. Nowhere else is the circular stage so well preserved. Near it are remains of the rooms where the actors waited and dressed.

held, glittering in the sun, was the first sign of the city to the sailor far out at sea. This statue would make you think of Athens' great victory at Marathon, for the sculptor *Phidias* had formed it out of the Persian swords and shields captured there.

2. Facing you, near the center of the open space, was the most famous of all the temples. This was the **Parthenon,** a temple of Athene. You would gaze spellbound at its

THE PARTHENON in the day of its glory. — A "reconstruction." (See explanation of that term facing page 60.)

THE PARTHENON TO-DAY (more a front view than the one above).

A photograph of a "model" reconstruction of the interior of the Parthenon and of its Athene statue. This "reconstruction" is in the Metropolitan Museum of Art in New York City. (The term "reconstruction" has been explained under one of the pictures facing page 60.)

perfect marble columns and the long bands of lovely carvings on its walls. These carvings, which were also the work of Phidias, showed scenes in the story of Athene and in the celebration of a great festival in her honor. Inside the temple itself you would find Phidias' masterpiece — another statue of Athene. This glorious figure was carved out of ivory and pure gold ; and, though it was not so large as the bronze statue outside, it was nearly forty feet tall, rising from the floor of the temple nearly to the roof. To-day the Parthenon has been in ruins for centuries, but it is still considered the loveliest building in the world, and Phidias ranks as the greatest of all sculptors.

SOPHOCLES — a portrait statue. The rolls of papyrus in the vessel at his feet, you are to suppose, contain some of his plays.

Next to sculpture and architecture, the chief art of Athens was the *drama*, or the writing of plays. Every Greek city of that time had its theater. The one at Athens was like most of the rest, only larger because no other Greek city then had so many people as Athens. This theater was merely one slope of the Acropolis, with stone seats cut into the hillside, rising tier above tier in great half-circles. There was no roof, and the small stage, at the bottom of the hill, had almost no scenery.

There was no charge for admission to this theater. The city wished all its men and boys to hear the great plays that were acted there. That was part of their training as citizens. Several of the greatest Athenian poets wrote plays, but perhaps the greatest of them all was **Sophocles,** a close friend of Pericles. At some festivals thirty thousand men sat from morning till night listening in delight to his noble poetry. The few Greek plays that have not been lost are still among the world's most precious treasures.

One of the Greatest Thinkers of the World,
Socrates,
Was an Athenian of the Time of Pericles

Greece had many wise men and great thinkers, who were called *philosophers*, or " lovers of wisdom." Most of them had tried to find answers to the question, " How did the world come to be? " **Toward the end of the Age of Pericles came *Socrates*, seeking to know more about man himself.** He tried to find out what was *man's duty* in the world, and how a man could make himself wise and just and good. For his motto he took the words " Know thyself."

GREEK WOMEN GOT WATER for the household at street fountains.

While Socrates was still a young man, one of his friends asked the oracle at Delphi whether any man was wiser than Socrates. The oracle replied that there was no one wiser. When Socrates heard this, he was astonished. He had wondered about many things, and had tried to think what the truth about them could be; but he was sure he did not *know* the things worth knowing.

So he went about from one to another of the leading men of Athens, seeking some one wiser than himself. He went first to one of the " generals " of the city, who was considered a wise ruler, and asked him many questions: " What is just? What is good? What is bravery? " He found that the ruler *pretended* at first to know, but that his answers were not wise at all. So Socrates left him, saying, " Well, the oracle is right so far. That man thinks that he is wise, though he really knows nothing; but *I* know that I know nothing. So I know at least one thing more than he does."

Socrates was a kind of sculptor. He carved little images of the gods for his living. His scolding wife, *Xantippe*, was vexed because he neglected this trade so much in order to spend time talking in the market place. But Socrates didn't care about making money. He felt it was more important to train the young men of Athens to think clearly on great subjects. Crowds of young Athenians followed him through the streets, to learn from him and to enjoy his talk with other people. These youths sometimes made merry over the vain and silly men who pretended to be wiser than they really were and who were often trapped by Socrates' shrewd questions into contradicting themselves.

But the people whose ignorance Socrates showed up in this way became his bitter enemies, and were anxious to get rid of the philosopher. At last, when he was seventy years old, these foes brought a charge against him in the law courts. " Socrates," they said, " offends against the laws of Athens. He does not respect our gods, but brings in new ones; and he leads young men into bad habits."

When an Athenian was accused of a crime, he was tried, not before a jury of twelve men, such as our courts use, but before a large jury of more than five hundred citizens. Socrates felt that any such body of Athenian citizens — among whom he had lived all his life — ought to know him too well to believe the charge against him; so he would not consent to defend himself to them. The jury, by a close vote, declared him guilty. He might still have escaped with a small fine, if he had been willing to confess that he had been wrong. But when the jury asked him what punishment he would propose for himself, in place of the death penalty that his accusers asked, he answered: "O Athenians, I have tried only to do you good; and so I deserve no punishment at all, but a reward. And if you ask my opinion about *that*, I suggest that I ought to be supported by the state as long as I live, as you support those who have served the city well or those who have won honor for it at the Olympic Games."

This answer made the judges more angry than before; and they voted that Socrates should be put to death by drinking hemlock. Then he bade his judges farewell in noble and gentle words, closing: "Wherefore, O Judges, be of good cheer about death, and be sure of this, — that no evil can happen to a good man either in life or after death. He and his are not neglected by the gods. The hour of departure has come; and we go our ways; I to die, you to live. Which way is the better, God alone knows."

The trial had taken place just before a religious festival; and so, by Athenian law, a month had to pass before the execution. During this time, Socrates was kept in prison; but he was visited each day by his friends, and he had long talks with them, such as he had always most enjoyed. Two of his pupils, **Plato** and **Xenophon** (themselves afterward among the most famous of men), have each given us full accounts of these talks.

One day his friends told him they had made arrangements for him to escape to another city, where he would be safe. Socrates thanked them for their trouble, but refused to go. They entreated; but he answered gently: "Death is no evil; but for me to play truant and injure the laws of Athens would be an evil. The laws of the city condemn me to death; and, as a good citizen, I obey them in that as in other things."

On the last day for him to live, Socrates talked mainly about the life to come after death. He comforted his weeping friends by speaking of the delight he expected in the abodes of the blessed, where he could ask his questions of the wise sages there who would be able to answer him and to give him the truths for which he had sought in vain on earth. Then, when the fatal hour was at hand, he drank off the hemlock as if it had been a refreshing cup; and, bidding his friends once more farewell, he placed himself on his couch, drawing his robe about him, and lay quietly while life ebbed away.

Greek Life Was the Highest the World had Seen, but not All of It Was Good

1. *Women had little share in the better part of Greek life.* There were no schools for Greek girls. Women were not allowed to go to the theater or to other public meetings. Nor did they even meet their husbands' friends in their own homes.

Greek statuette of clay, showing a woman cooking, with a child looking on.

They were only a kind of household servant.

2. Wise as they were, *the Greeks had not gained any such power over things as we have now.* Very little machinery had been invented. The Athenian sailor had no compass. The farmer had only the same three tools that the Egyptian farmer had used. If you want to imagine how the Greeks of Pericles' time lived, you must think of traveling without railways or automobiles or even horse carriages; of sending messages without telegraph or telephone or wireless or even postal service; of cities without electric lights or gas lights,

and without pavements. You must think of even the best houses without plumbing or refrigerators, or any kind of heating except perhaps a small "brazier" (a little open stove, holding a few coals, that could be carried from room to room), or any lighting except a few small lamps that looked like bowls of oil with swimming wicks. You must

GREEK BARBER—a clay statuette.

think of sleeping in beds without sheets and of wearing clothes without buttons or even hooks-and-eyes, and of using only sandals for shoes, and wearing them without stockings. (Socrates went barefoot at all times, and all Greeks took off their sandals when entering a house. Notice the feet of the men and women in our pictures.)

3. Possibly we think too much of mere comforts. But certainly this lack of machinery to help out human labor was one cause of another real evil in Greek life. *All this fine civilization that we have described rested on slavery.* Even in Athens, for every free citizen there were several slaves. If it had not been so, the male citizens could never have spent so many days in the Assembly, listening to the oratory of Pericles, or in the theater, watching the plays of Sophocles. Without machinery, men were not able to raise food enough, or to make other necessary things fast enough, so that *many* of them could take time for anything but getting a living.

4. *The Greek cities never worked well together for long.* We have seen that they did not do so even when they were attacked by Persia. Nearly all the time some of them were

fighting with one another; and finally Sparta and Athens began a long and bitter conflict. Almost all Greece took sides with one or the other. In the end, Greece was so weakened by years of slaughter and destruction that all its cities fell, one after another, before a foreign conqueror.

SUMMARY

Soon after Salamis, Athens formed a league of Greek cities, which drove the Persians out of the Aegean. The next fifty years are called the Age of Pericles. Pericles was a political leader and orator, who, with the aid of Phidias, Sophocles, Socrates, and many other thinkers and artists, made

GREEK WOMEN POUNDING GRAIN INTO FLOUR. (The huge bowl and the mallets for pounding are stone. Cf. page 22.)

Athens the most powerful and the most beautiful city in the world. But, in spite of its greatness in so many ways, Greek civilization kept some dark blots, especially slavery and the low position of women. And the Greek cities were finally so worn out by the many wars they fought with one another that they were all conquered by an outside power.

NEW WORDS

league	*colossal*	*column*	*philosopher*
statesman	*oratory*	*drama*	*jury*

THOUGHT QUESTIONS AND THINGS TO DO

1. Do you know any buildings in your city that have columns like those you see pictured as part of a Greek temple? If not, have you at least seen pictures of such buildings in other cities in the United States? Bring some such pictures to class, if you can. This is a good way to add to the class scrap-book.

2. If a building were to be put up in your town with a sculptured frieze (a band of sculpture around the outside wall), do you think it would be well for that frieze to be a copy of the Parthenon frieze? Would it have been a good thing for Phidias to have copied the most beautiful Egyptian frieze? Have you ever seen carvings or wall-paintings on American buildings representing American scenes? Name scenes that would be suitable. You may find some toward the end of this book.

Is the mother (in this drawing from a Greek vase-painting) using a slipper or a hairbrush?

3. Which of the Greeks that you have read about so far in this book is called to your mind by each of the following phrases: a patriotic lawgiver; a wise and eloquent statesman; a shrewd leader?

4. Greek plays usually had characters from Greek history for their heroes. Can you make a Greek play of your own, and act it?

5. Hold a meeting of the Athenian Assembly, which is to decide whether it is wise to spend so much money on the buildings of the Acropolis, or whether to undertake a new expedition against Persia, or how to organize a league against Sparta.

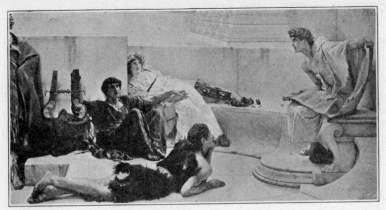

A READING FROM HOMER, as imagined by a famous modern painter. For hundreds of years after the time of Alexander, such sights could be seen, not only in Greece itself, but also over all western Asia.

CHAPTER VII

ALEXANDER SPREADS GREEK CIVILIZATION OVER THE EAST

In the Fourth Century B.C. both Greece and Persia Were Conquered by the Macedonians

Just north of Greece lived the *Macedonians.* They were a good deal like the Greeks, but became civilized more slowly. About 350 B.C. they were made into a united nation of conquerors by their ruler *Philip.*

Philip had lived in Greece when a boy, and now he taught his people to admire Greek ways and to imitate them. He built up a splendid army (not exceedingly large, but well armed and well trained), and used it first to conquer many half-civilized tribes about him. Then he turned to the cities of Greece and conquered them one by one because they proved unable to unite against him. Afterward he treated them kindly, and most of them grew to like him.

While the Greek cities had been busy with the long wars between Sparta and Athens, Persia had started to threaten them again. So now Philip planned to invade Asia and to conquer the Persians in their own home. But he died, just as he was ready to start out, and his plan was carried on by his son *Alexander*, then only twenty years old.

Alexander had been a fearless, headstrong boy, with an excellent mind. He was fond of Homer, and he knew the Iliad by heart. One of his tutors was *Aristotle*, a Greek philosopher and a pupil of Plato (p. 66). From this teacher, Alexander learned to admire Greek art and science.

In 334 B.C., at the head of the army Philip had made, **Alexander crossed the Hellespont into Asia.** Most of the rest of his short life he spent in wars of conquest. He never avoided a battle, and never lost one. He won many striking victories over huge Asiatic armies, marched across pathless, burning deserts and over lofty snow-capped mountain ranges, **and became master of Asia as far as the Persian Empire had ever reached.** He even led his army over the passes of the mighty Hindukush mountains down into the fertile plains of northern India. Then, crossing the Indus River, he won new realms *beyond* the limits of the old Persian world — until at last his faithful soldiers refused to follow farther.

Alexander then turned back as far as Babylon. That city he made the capital of his vast empire. But when he died there only two years later, at the age of thirty-two, **the empire at once fell to pieces.** For the next two hundred years its many kingdoms were ruled by descendants of Alexander's generals. But these rulers fought constant selfish wars with one another, and finally they were all conquered by a new state that was rising in the West — *Rome* — of which we shall soon read.

Alexander Mixed the Best Parts
Of Greek and Persian Life
Into a New Civilization

Alexander was one of the finest soldiers the world has ever seen. But he is best worth remembering because he was more than a mere fighter.   Like his father, he admired Greek life, and he wished all the people of his vast empire to adopt Greek ways.   So he started Greek colonies in every part of his conquests, all along the line of his marches.

Of course the people in these new cities were not all Greeks. Most of them were Asiatics, or *Orientals*, from the country around.   But each new city did have a *core* of Greek citizens — either worn-out soldiers left behind by Alexander, or new immigrants from Greece in search of fortune in the rich Orient. For a long time these Greeks were the leaders.   Each city built its temples on the plan of Greek buildings. Each had its theater, where the inhabitants listened to the plays of old Greek dramatists and of new ones. For centuries Greek was the everyday speech in the streets.   And though no

ALEXANDER THE GREAT. — A sculptured head now in the Copenhagen Museum.

city had anything now to say about the government of the kingdom in which it lay, still nearly every one of them did have an Assembly, to manage *its own* affairs.

Of all the new Greek colonies in the East the most famous was *Alexandria,* built by the conqueror himself at the very mouth of the Nile.   Here, for some centuries back, there had been only haunts of pirates among marshy sands and swamps.   Now in a few months there appeared the strong walls, beautiful buildings, and busy streets of a mighty metropolis.   This city soon led the world in wealth and trade and learning.

The Greek colonists in Egypt and Asia were wise enough to learn many good things from their Oriental fellow-citizens. Greeks and Orientals intermarried, indeed, so that a new race grew up, with a new civilization, partly Greek, partly Oriental.

The New Wider Greek World Gained Much New Knowledge Largely through the Work of Scholars at Alexandria

Alexander had been an eager explorer as well as a soldier and a colonizer. While in India he built a great fleet of many hundred ships and sailed down the Indus River until

A GREEK CARPENTER. — From the statements under other pictures can you guess how this picture was made?

he reached an ocean that the Greeks had not known anything about. Then he sent the fleet on, under his friend *Nearchus*, to explore this newly-found " Indian Ocean " and to seek a way from the mouth of the Indus to the mouth of the Euphrates. (Follow his route on the map facing this page.) The maps that Nearchus made, and the collections of new plants and animals that he brought back to Babylon with him, added much to the Greeks' knowledge about the world. Many of those collections Alexander sent to his old teacher, Aristotle, to help him in his studies.

When Alexander's empire broke up, one of his Greek generals named *Ptolemy* seized upon Egypt. He and his successors (all known as *Ptolemies*) were lovers of learning. **One of them built a great university at Alexandria.** One part of this was a large library of half a million books. Many men were employed there to write out careful copies

GREEK GIRLS AT PLAY. — A modern painting of ancient Greece by Leighton.

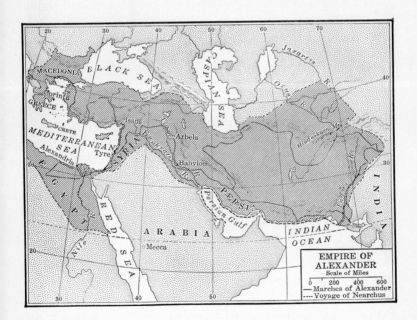

EMPIRE OF
ALEXANDER
Scale of Miles
0   200   400   600
—— Marches of Alexander
---- Voyage of Nearchus

ALEXANDRIAN LIGHTHOUSE, as a modern scholar pictures it from ancient descriptions. This tower stood until 1326 A.D. — more than sixteen hundred years — and was one of the "Seven Wonders" of the ancient world.

DEATH OF SOCRATES, — as a modern painter represents it. His friends, and even the prison officer who holds the poison, are deeply moved; but the philosopher, reaching carelessly for the fatal cup, is absorbed in his unfinished conversation. At the stairway in the background are his weeping wife and children, to whom he has just said farewell. (Reread the account of Socrates on pages 65–67.)

of the most valuable books to send to scholars in other cities. The university had also vast botanical and zoölogical gardens, with collections from distant parts of the world. All the teachers and great scholars who worked in the university were paid from the treasury of the Ptolemies.

Aristarchus, one of the scholars at this university, was the first man to teach that the earth and planets revolve around the sun. Another scholar there, *Eratosthenes*, invented the way we still use to measure the circumference of the earth; and he found out very closely indeed just what the distance is. He figured that it was a trifle *more* than 25,000 miles. (How much is it?) All scholars of that day knew that the earth was round, and they used globes in teaching geography.

Men now began to use their new knowledge to improve everyday life. The new cities had wide, paved streets, and were well lighted at night. They had also good water systems, with fountains and public baths. In all these matters, they were far ahead of the Athens of Pericles — and indeed of much later cities of the time of Columbus, or even of George Washington.

The first Ptolemy built a *famous lighthouse* in the harbor of Alexandria, on the little island of *Pharos*, to protect the growing commerce of the city. The tower, with many stories, rose 325 feet into the air; and from the top, at night, a group of reflecting mirrors threw light far out to sea. "All night," said a Greek poet, "will the sailor, driving before the storm, see the fire gleam from its top." The first lighthouses built by the United States, more than two thousand years later, had little improvement, if any, upon this Greek-Egyptian work.

The man of that day who did most to use knowledge in these practical ways was **Archimedes** of Syracuse. He was the Edison of his time. He found out just how the *lever* works; and, in explaining it, he said: "Give me a place outside the world to stand and to rest my lever, and I will move the world with it." When a Roman fleet attacked his city, Archimedes set fire to the ships by huge *burning-glasses*. (You have seen boys use small ones, probably, to make some one jump.) And he also invented *hurling-engines* that threw huge rocks from the walls upon the besiegers.

In Egypt there had always been some low ground that was never fit to plant because it remained wet too long after

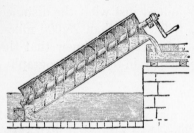

THE FIRST PUMP (ARCHIMEDES' SCREW).

the yearly flood. Archimedes invented a queer spiral pump to drain such lands. He wound a hollow tube of metal around a cylinder, spiral fashion. Then, when the lower end was placed under water, and the cylinder was made to turn rapidly (by a crank), the water rose through the tube and could be carried off at the top. This device, known as " Archimedes' screw," is still used in the low lands of Holland to drain off the sea water that sometimes gets in through the dykes there. (In Holland the crank of the " Screw " is turned by a windmill, but windmills were not invented until long after Archimedes' time.)

Once Archimedes had spent a long time in trying to find some way to solve a difficult problem of this sort. The right way flashed into his mind while he was bathing in one of the great public baths; and he leaped from the bath and ran home through the streets without his clothing, shouting happily, " Eureka! Eureka! " (*Eureka* is a Greek word meaning, " I have found it.")

This sort of absent-mindedness was finally the cause of his death. After a three-year siege, the Romans did at last capture Syracuse and began to plunder the city. Busied with a new invention, Archimedes did not know what had happened. He had set out with his new delicate machine in a box, to carry it to the palace of the king of Syracuse, who was always much interested in his work. An ignorant Roman soldier, running upon him in the street, supposed the box contained gold, and killed Archimedes for it, and then, disappointed in his hopes, smashed the invention.

In the second century B.C. all the lands of Alexander's Empire were conquered by Rome, whose story we are now going to read. But the new Roman world soon learned to admire the civilization of those lands. So most of it became Roman, and some of it was finally passed on to us.

SUMMARY

In the fourth century B.C. both Greece and Persia were conquered by the Macedonian rulers, Philip and Alexander. Alexander started Greek colonies wherever he went, and so spread Greek civilization. His empire broke up at his death; but Greek learning continued to advance for 150 years more, and it was then passed on to the Roman conquerors of the Greek world.

NEW WORDS

capital   *lever*   *spiral*   *science*   *Oriental*

THOUGHT QUESTIONS AND THINGS TO DO

1. Alexander is sometimes called " the Great." List the reasons why you might call him so.

2. Show the boundaries of Alexander's empire on the map, and trace the route of his march.

3. Make a model of a Greek city such as Alexander might have founded. What are some of the buildings you would have in it? What other things would you put in to make it look like a Greek city? *Dress* figures for Greeks and Orientals, and put them in the streets of your model.

4. Can you explain Archimedes' lever, or show how it works?

5. List all the things you can find in the chapters on Greece which make the Greek ways of living seem more like ours than the ways of earlier peoples did.

6. Arrange the following names in the right time order: Pericles, Solon, Alexander, Themistocles, Archimedes, Phidippides. Then write an important fact connected with each one.

VERY OLD OLIVE TREES BY A ROAD NEAR ATHENS TO-DAY. — A donkey, as shown in the photo, is a favorite means of travel in the rough parts of modern Greece.

The most famous Roman weapon was a short sword for close fighting. Each soldier in this group carries one.   Can you make them out?

CHAPTER VIII

EARLY ROME

" Westward the Star of Empire Takes Its Way "

If you look at the map facing page 41, you will see many reasons why civilization did not reach Italy as early as it did Greece.   In the first place, Italy was farther away from the Eastern countries where civilization began.   Besides, there were no chains of islands leading to it from Asia, as there were to Greece.   Do you see how important that was in the days when sailors had no compass to guide them in a new sea and so liked to creep along cautiously from coast to coast?

To be sure, Italy was not far from Greece; but all its harbors were on the side *away* from Greece.   Its eastern coast was very rocky.   Still, quite early, a few Phoenician traders did sail on from Greece to the shores of Italy; and by 800 B.C. the Greeks themselves had begun to plant colonies on its southern coasts (page 41).   From these, civilization spread slowly to other parts.

The Italians Could be United into One Nation More Easily than the Greeks Could

Italy is a long, boot-shaped peninsula, with its toe almost touching Sicily. On the north it is shut off from the rest of Europe by the Alps, a curving range of high and rugged mountains. These mountains keep off the cold winds, so that Italy is mild and sunny. Oranges grow there in the latitude of New York. (How much farther south than New York do we have to go in America to grow oranges?)

Rivers and small mountain ranges divide all Italy into districts about the size of our counties. They are larger than the districts in Greece, however, and it is much easier to get from one to another than it is in Greece. These districts were then the homes of different peoples. The Greek peoples, you remember, were never able to unite until a foreign ruler conquered them. But, in time, the Italian peoples were all to be joined together into one nation by a city in Italy itself. That city was Rome.

Early Rome was both a Fort and a Trading Post

The first Italians we know about **lived in little farming villages.** In early times each village had its own king, as in early Greece. Usually a village was built near a hill, just as in Greece, and the hill was made into a fort by building a wall around it, part way up the slope. The temples of the tribe were inside the walls, and the whole tribe could take refuge there if a strong enemy attacked them.

Near the middle of the long peninsula was the *Tiber*. South from that river, there spread out a fertile plain, dotted with many little hills just fit for village forts. This plain was the home of an Italian people called *Latins*. On the other side of the river lived the powerful *Etruscans*, who often tried to conquer the Latins.

In very early times, one Latin tribe built a strong square fort on a hill close to the Tiber. This was **the Roman tribe,**

and their fort was called **Rome.** From the beginning, it
was the special job of the Romans to keep back the Etruscans. They were the champions of all the Latins against
that foe, and so they became more skilled in war than the
other Latins.

Sometimes, when **Latins and Etruscans** were not fighting,
they **traded with each other.**   The Latins were plain farmers,
but the Etruscans were skilled in many other ways also,
especially in working in metals.   So if a Latin needed a new
plowshare or a knife, he would drive an ox across the plain
to the bank of the Tiber, to trade it to some Etruscan for

the tool. (Later, when the Romans began to use money, their first coin was a piece of copper with the figure of an

EARLY ROMAN COIN.

ox stamped upon it.)

Just below the Roman hill-fort, the Tiber was so shallow that a man could wade across. Such shallow places were called *fords* and were very useful in the days before there were many bridges. The Romans had built their fort near the ford to keep Etruscan armies from crossing by it to invade Latium. But they were glad to have peaceful Etruscan traders use it to bring over manufactures of metal and wool and linen, to exchange for Latin oxen or hides or grain.

Sometimes, too, a Phoenician or Greek ship sailed up the river from the sea, to trade at this place where Romans and Etruscans met. After a while, regular market days came to be held each month in a level space at the foot of the Roman hill, and so Rome grew richer than other Latin cities, as well as more powerful. When Rome had become a great city, one of the most famous places in it, with

SO-CALLED WALL OF SERVIUS — thirteen feet thick and fifty feet high. It consisted of a huge pile of earth in the middle, faced on each side with immense stones fitted together without mortar. See page 84.

the most splendid buildings, was the *Roman Forum*. That was the place where these early markets were held. (The first meaning of the word *forum* was *market*.)

Rome Becomes " the City of the Seven Hills "

You can see now two ways in which geography helped early Rome. There was still a third way. **The hill on which the Roman fort stood was one of a *group* of *seven***

"THE GREAT DRAIN" (see page 84). The Romans learned how to arch their drains from the Etruscans. (The Greeks had never used the arch.)

hills. In some war between Etruscans and Latins, an Etruscan tribe managed to get across the river and fortify itself on one of those hills, close to Rome. This made it hard for the Romans for a time. Then before long a band of invaders from a mountain tribe to the west seized another of the seven hills. The three forts must have fought one another for a long time, but no one of them was able to capture the others. They were so near together that they couldn't very well go on fighting all the time. They had to make peace in order to raise food. **So finally the three hills**

joined together in one city — an exceedingly large and power-ful city for those days.

Now the Romans learned to be great builders. Before long, they built *one mighty stone wall around all seven hills.* Old Roman legends say this wall was built by a certain king

AN ETRUSCAN CHARIOT, now in the Metropolitan Museum in New York. Made, probably, about 700 B.C.; found in 1901 in an ancient Etruscan cemetery. The body of the chariot is of bronze, the surface of which is worked into beautiful figures. Even the wooden parts of the chariot had been covered with bronze.

The Etruscans seem to have brought the use of the wheel into Italy.

Servius. If we visit Rome to-day, we can still see parts of that wall, and also parts of the immense stone *drains* the early Romans built to carry off the water from the swampy ground between the hills. About this same time, too, according to the legends, the Romans built *a narrow wooden bridge* across the Tiber, where the old ford had been.

The remains of the old stone walls and of the drains are the most trustworthy records we have of those early days. Romans did not learn how to write until much later. The early history of Rome is mostly made up of fanciful legends

Seven kings are told about in these legends. **The last one was *Tarquin the Proud*.** He was so wicked and cruel that (about 500 B.C.) the people drove him and his family from the city. Then they took a solemn oath that there should never again be a king in Rome.

Tarquin fled to Etruria, and *Lars Porsena*, king of one of the cities there, promised to help him and " swore that the

great house of Tarquin should suffer wrong no more."
Porsena gathered a mighty army, and marched on Rome to
restore Tarquin to his throne.

The bridge across the Tiber, so useful in peace, now became a peril. The Romans had tried to make it safe by
building a fort at the farther end; but
Porsena's army quickly captured this fort
and advanced to the bridge itself. The only
way now to save Rome was to destroy the
bridge before Porsena could cross. It would
take some little time to do this with such
tools as the Romans had. (What quick way
would we use?) So the Roman general
called for volunteers to give their lives for
their city by holding that farther end of the
narrow passage while his army was tearing
down the bridge behind them. Then a
young Roman noble, Horatius, with two
brave companions, hurried across, in front
of the advancing Etruscan army, and kept
the bridge with sword and spear.

PART OF AN ETRUSCAN
VASE PAINTING.

Three by three the noblest of the Etruscans attacked the
Roman three, but were overthrown and cast into the rushing stream beneath. Then, as the bridge began to totter
under ax and crowbar, friends called to the three champions
to save themselves. Horatius' two companions did race
back in safety to the Roman side. But Horatius himself
waited, to make sure, until the bridge crashed down in ruin
into the yellow flood. Then, refusing still to surrender
(though the generous Porsena offered to spare his life), he
threw himself, clothed in armor as he was, into the turbulent
waters and *swam* sturdily across to safety. When the later
Romans told this story to their sons they would say,

" And our Father Tiber
　Bare bravely up his chin,"

Summary

Civilization moved westward from Greece to Italy. Italy could be united more easily than Greece could. Rome had three advantages in uniting it: (1) it was in the center of Italy ; (2) it was built beside a large river, fit for commerce ; and (3) it was built where there was a group of seven hills — so that several different cities there finally united into one large one. The early history of Rome is mixed up with legends, of which some are partly true.

New Words

champion   *ford*   *forum*   *frontier*   *invader*

Things to Do

1. Show on a map how civilization was moving westward. Shade the earliest homes of civilization a deep blue; make the first European lands to become civilized a lighter blue; then make Italy and Sicily a still lighter shade. Keep this map; later on, you can show on it what countries Rome civilized, marking them with *bars* of the Roman shade.

2. Mark on your time line the date when Rome drove out the kings. What were Greeks and Persians doing at that time?

3. You ought to read some of the Roman legends. Each of you might report on one of them to the class. There are good stories in Harding's *City of the Seven Hills*, MacGregor's *Story of Rome*, Lovell's *Stories in Stone from the Roman Forum*, Tappan's *Story of the Roman People*. You should also read the story of Horatius in Macaulay's *Lays of Ancient Rome*, and you may like some of the other poem-stories in that volume.

A School. — From a Roman relief. The outer roll of the "books" that the boys are studying has been broken off from the sculpture. Compare with the cut on page 48. The standing boy holds a case of writing tablets.

CHAPTER IX

THE ROMAN REPUBLIC

After the Romans drove out their king, they decided to elect every year *two* officers in his place. These two they called *Consuls*. A still more important part of the new government was the *Senate*, made up of three hundred men, who were elected from the oldest and noblest families *and held office for life*. From time to time, too, the Consuls called together an *Assembly* of all the fighting men; but this had less to say about the government than the Senate had.

We call this kind of government a *republic*, because it had no king. But it was not democratic, like the Greek cities. The common people did not have much say in it. *Our* government is both a republic and a democracy.

The Romans Quarreled among Themselves
For Two Hundred Years

The common people had to fight in the Roman army, but they had very few rights in the Assembly. The nobles had everything their own way for a long time, not only in the Senate, but in the Assembly also.

These nobles were not rich. Many of them, in fact, were only poor farmers with a few acres of ground. But they were very proud of the fact that they were descended from old families who were supposed to have lived in Rome since its beginning. They would not allow their sons and daughters to marry outside these old families; and so, gradually, **two distinct classes grew up:** *patricians,* or nobles; and *plebeians,* or common people, who could not trace back their ancestors to the first families of Rome.

The patricians made all the laws. So they **found it easy to keep the plebeians from holding any office and from using any part of the public land** — land that Rome took from cities she had conquered. Such land was used only for the good of the patricians. Therefore, as Rome conquered more and more of her neighbors, the patricians grew richer; but the plebeians, who made up the rank and file of the army, sometimes had not enough time left for farming. Thus they grew poorer and poorer and gradually drifted into debt. Then if the debtor could not pay at the proper time, he and his land became the property of the man from whom he had borrowed. Many debtors were thrown into dungeons and torn with stripes.

The plebeians became more and more dissatisfied with all this. Not long after 500 B.C., a war broke out with a neighboring tribe, and the plebeians refused to fight. At last one of the Consuls won them over by promising to set free all debtors. The plebeians then helped to win the war. But when it was over, the other Consul refused to let the debtors go free. (You see, when one Consul started to do anything, the other could stop him by saying " Veto," which meant " I forbid.")

Soon afterward the war broke out again, and again the

plebeians were persuaded by new promises to help save Rome. But this time, instead of coming back to their homes after the war, they wisely waited *in arms* outside the city, to see whether the just laws they had asked for would really be given them. The Senate refused to permit such new laws. **Then the plebeians marched away to the Sacred Mount,** three miles from Rome, and started to make a new town of their own.

This " strike " frightened the patricians. To get the plebeians to come back, **the Senate now consented that each year they might choose officers of their own, called Tribunes.** A Tribune had almost as much power as a Consul, except that he could not lead the army in war. He could say " Veto " to any act of a Consul or of the Senate. It was his special duty to protect plebeians against patrician officers, and the door of his house always stood open so that a plebeian might reach him easily at any hour.

Still the plebeians had gained only a small part of what they needed; so **the contest went on,** much as before. In Greek cities such struggles between rich and poor often caused bloody civil wars, but in Rome the two classes never took up arms against each other. The plebeians gained their rights, slowly, one at a time, by getting new laws passed whenever they could. It took more than a hundred years; but this was much better for all Rome than a sudden change, brought about by violence. **By 300 B.C. the plebeians had become the equals of the patricians.**

All Romans, both patricians and plebeians, had great respect for law. They were the first people to teach the world that it is perfectly right for men to try to *change* a law *by any lawful means*, but that it is necessary to obey the old law (unfair though it may seem) until it has been so changed. The United States is one of the countries that have learned this lesson best.

In Every Time of Great Peril
Some Patriot Arose to Save Rome

While Rome was still weakened by the long class strife that we have just been reading about, **the neighboring peoples several times almost conquered her.** Once, in particular, the *Aequians,* from the northeast, marched into Roman territory, plundering the outlying farms and threatening the city itself. A Roman army was sent out against them under a Consul, but the Aequians trapped it in a narrow valley where soon they could starve it into surrender.

In this moment of peril **the Roman Senate voted to put all power into the hands of one man,** until the danger was past. This was called appointing a *Dictator.* For this office the Senate chose *Cincinnatus,* an old patrician soldier who had served Rome well in fomer wars.

Cincinnatus was living on his four-acre farm some miles from the city. The messenger of the Senate found him plowing. But at the call he left oxen and plow in the furrow and hurried to Rome. Before dark that day he had enrolled in a new army every man able to bear arms, and at night he marched forth against the Aequian army. Each of his men carried five days' food and a number of wooden stakes. Reaching the Aequian camp before daylight, he had his men silently surround it and then drive the stakes into the ground in front of them, for a wall.

As soon as the Aequians found out what was going on, they hurried to attack these besiegers. At once the first Roman army, which they themselves had surrounded, began to attack them in the rear, and soon they had to give up. Cincinnatus did not put the Aequians to death or make them slaves. He let them go home ; but first he made them admit that Rome was their master. He drove two spears into the earth, with a third fastened across the tops ; and then he compelled the Aequians to pass under this " yoke," bending low beneath it and carrying no arms, to show that they were as much the servants of the Romans as the oxen that plowed Roman fields with the yoke on their necks.

On his return to Rome, the Senate gave Cincinnatus a great "triumph." A splendid procession followed him as he rode on a chariot through all the principal streets, and the people everywhere greeted him with cheers as the savior of his country. But Cincinnatus was not made vain by all this. On the sixteenth day after he had been appointed Dictator, his work all done, he resigned his office and went back to his plowing.

For this simple and noble conduct, Cincinnatus became more famous than for his generalship. It was remembered many centuries later, at the end of our Revolutionary War, when George Washington and his fellow officers gave up their high offices and went quietly back to their farms and workshops. That was why they formed themselves into a society called " the Cincinnati." And when some of those officers afterward made a new home in what was then our frontier, they called their city Cincinnati.

Now Rome Swiftly Became Mistress of All Italy And Learned to Rule it Wisely

After plebeians and patricians became *united*, so that for a long time there was no more strife at home, Rome began to conquer the other towns of Italy. By 275 B.C., or about fifty years after the death of Alexander, she had become mistress of all Italy south of the Po valley.

Rome won because her people understood team work and knew how to obey orders. And she kept what she had won because she was wise enough to treat the conquered Italians generously. She let most of the towns keep their own consuls and senates and assemblies, and go on managing their own affairs in their own way. Many of their people, indeed, she made full Roman citizens, with all the rights that the people of Rome had.

Rome herself managed those matters that concerned Italy *as one whole*, such as making peace and war. But she protected the other cities so well, and treated them so justly, that they were glad to be under her rule. No other conqueror had ever ruled its subjects as well as Rome did. Never before had so many people in so large a territory had a share in the government. (Our kind of government, in which *all* the people are citizens and choose a congress to make the laws, is much better, but it was not invented until many centuries later.)

Ewing Galloway

The Appian Way To-day. — Compare the ruins at the side with the monuments in the picture facing page 117.

Rome Built Roads to Help Hold Italy Together

The first "Roman Road" was begun in 312 B.C. It ran south from Rome three hundred miles to Tarentum, one of the Greek cities in the south of Italy. Travelers still drive over this *Appian Way*, as it is named from the great Roman, Appius Claudius, who planned it (page 96). By 200 B.C. several such roads — all leading to Rome — stretched across Italy in different directions. Later, when Rome had conquered a vast empire outside of Italy, that, too, was covered with a network of these roads (map facing page 98). They were the best means of travel the world was to see until railroads were invented about a hundred years ago.

These roads were built so that the Roman army could march quickly from place to place. Therefore they were always made as straight as possible. Hills were graded down to easy slopes. High mountains were tunneled. Across mighty rivers great bridges were built, resting on rows of stone arches, which sometimes rose a hundred feet from the river bed. Marshy lands were spanned by stone viaducts for miles at a stretch.

Such a road was costly. First the workmen removed all loose soil, down to a firm layer of earth. This they packed hard. On it they placed a layer, several inches thick, of large stones; then one of smaller stones; then one of still smaller ones, or of gravel. As these three layers were put in place they were cemented together into one solid mass about two feet thick. The top was then leveled smooth; and upon it was laid a surface of huge smooth blocks of stone, with the edges joined so nicely that the surface seemed one vast stone. The remains of these roads, sometimes in good condition, " still mark the lands where Rome has ruled."

The roads were used, of course, for travel and trade, as well as for marching armies. Inns grew up along them at proper distances from one another, with relays of horses for government messengers and for travelers. Travel was either by horseback or in carriages (chariots) or in litters swung along comfortably on the shoulders of slaves. Along the sides stood regular milestones, each one showing its distance from the gates of Rome. The Roman general Julius Caesar once journeyed from the Rhine to Rome — a full eight hundred miles — in eight days, even though part of his way was across the Alps. This was more than twice as fast as our President John Adams was able to travel in the year 1801 from Washington to his home in Massachusetts.

The Third Century B.C. was the Best Period of Roman Life

Even after the Romans became rulers over all Italy, they continued for nearly a hundred years to live plain and simple lives. They liked to hold up *Manius Curio,* a famous

conqueror of the Greek part of Italy, as an example of the
best kind of Roman citizen. Curio had been given three
magnificent "triumphs" for victories over the foes of Rome.
But, like Cincinnatus, long before, he was a farmer and
owned only a few poor acres. Ambassadors from another

country came to him once
at his home with a gift of
gold, to win his favor.
They found him in his small
hut, peeling turnips in the
chimney corner. There was
nothing else in the house to
eat; but Curio refused the
gift. Said he: " The man
who is content with this
dinner hath no need of gold.
I count it glory, not to
possess wealth, but to rule
those who do."

CONFERRING THE TOGA. — When a Roman
boy reached the age of fifteen, the father
clothed him for the first time in a man's
toga, to show that he had become a man.
This was the occasion for a joyous family
gathering. In this picture the abandoned
hoop means that the young man has put
aside his boyhood toys.

The most common food
was a porridge of ground
meal or pease, boiled in
water. (This remained the
chief food of the poor for
hundreds of years in
Europe: " Pease porridge
in the pot, nine days old.") When the Roman farmer had
meat, it was usually pork sausage. Barley flour, without
yeast, was baked into flat round cakes of bread. The usual
drink was water or goats' milk, but a few people were beginning to use wine, after the fashion of the Greeks.

Dress was as simple as the food. Each man wore a
simple " loin cloth " of linen, such as you saw on the Egyptian workmen in the pictures in the first part of this book.
Over this there was worn a short-sleeved woolen shirt (the

Roman *tunic*). This came down to the knees. At public gatherings and for ceremonies, the man wore over this clothing a white woolen blanket, gathered about him in graceful folds. This was the Roman *toga*.

Men went barefoot or wore sandals, as the Greeks did. There were no stockings. Hats were unknown, except for the helmet in war. A man who belonged to a family from which senators were chosen always wore a broad gold ring, to mark his rank. Women wore a short tunic, with a longer one over it, and, for the street, a blanket-wrap somewhat like the man's toga. They were fond also of rings, bracelets, and pins, made of copper, silver, or gold.

Education was very simple. Poor boys had no schools. At seven, the boy of a well-to-do Roman was sent to a school taught by some Greek slave. He learned only to read and write, and to figure a little with Roman numerals. (You can easily satisfy yourself that to do this last was no easy matter. Try to multiply ccxliv by

A ROMAN MATRON as sculptured on her tomb.

lxix without thinking in our figures.) Much attention was given to athletic games — running, wrestling, and using spear, sword, and javelin.

Rome had a special officer to look after the conduct of the people. Every five years the Assembly chose two *Censors*. A Censor could even turn a Senator out of office, or take away a man's citizenship, to punish him for bad conduct in his private life.

The Censors also had charge of public works for the good of Rome. Appius Claudius (page 92) was Censor when he built the Appian Way. He built also the first Roman aqueduct at that time, to bring pure water to Rome from the Apennines many miles away.

The Roman religion was something like that of the Greeks. Their chief god was the god of the sky, and he was called

Jupiter. They had a goddess of wisdom and industry, called *Minerva*. Do you remember the Greek names of these two? The Romans even copied the Greek stories about these gods and about many others.

ROMAN GRIST MILL. — The man holds a bag of grain to pour into the mill to be ground into flour by the turning mill-stones. The first such mills were turned by man-power, but even that was an improvement over the ways shown on pages 22 and 69.

SUMMARY

Rome was a republic, but not a democracy. The plebeians struggled for two hundred years to gain more rights in the government, until (about 300 B.C.) they became equals of the patricians. While the class struggle was going on, Rome was often attacked from outside by neighboring tribes, but she was saved by heroic leaders, such as Cincinnatus.

All Romans had great respect for law and were able to do good team-work. When class strife *within* had ceased, Rome soon conquered all Italy. Then she ruled it generously and justly, and bound it together by fine roads. The third century B.C. was the best period of Roman life, which remained plain and simple.

NEW WORDS

consul	*patrician*	*tribune*	*toga*	*nobles*	*litter*
senate	*plebeian*	*dictator*	*aqueduct*	*chariot*	*tunic*
republic	*veto*	*triumph*	*censor*	*yoke*	*helmet*

Thought Questions and Things to Do

1. Put on an outline map of Italy the places and the names of tribes mentioned in this chapter and in the last one before it.

2. On the time line mark the few dates given in this chapter. What were the *Greeks* doing during the long struggle between classes at Rome?

3. Dress some models of Roman citizens.

4. Can some member of the class report on how we make our good automobile roads to-day, so that you may compare it with the Roman way? Do you know how long we have had such roads? When you read about the Roman roads, did you remember about any earlier people who built good roads? In what other way was that earlier people like the Romans?

5. Characters in Roman legend and history have been made the heroes of plays by modern writers. Could your class write and stage a play with Cincinnatus as a hero?

6. Read the story of the Roman boy in Jane Andrews' *Ten Boys*.

A ROMAN SHOEMAKER

CHARIOT RACE, — one of the favorite sports in the Roman amphitheater (see page 101). This is the way a modern painter pictures one.

CHAPTER X

ROME WINS THE WORLD

After Uniting Italy under Her Rule
Rome Conquered All the Mediterranean Lands

A conquering nation never likes to stop fighting. It always wants new conquests. The Romans soon began to reach out across the sea — to Sicily, North Africa, and Spain. By 200 B.C. Rome had become mistress of all the *western* shores of the Mediterranean. Then she turned *east*, and in the next half-century (by 146 B.C.) she had brought under her rule the old empire of Alexander *as far as the Euphrates in Asia*. The Mediterranean was to be " a Roman lake " for six hundred years — almost twice as long a time as separates us from the Pilgrim Fathers.

There were two good things about this Roman conquest: (1) The kingdoms of the East had been spending much of their time in fighting one another (page 72); and *to this part of the world*, on the whole, *Rome brought order and peace.* (2) The peoples west of Italy, on the other hand, had remained half savage until *Rome conquered and civilized them.*

98

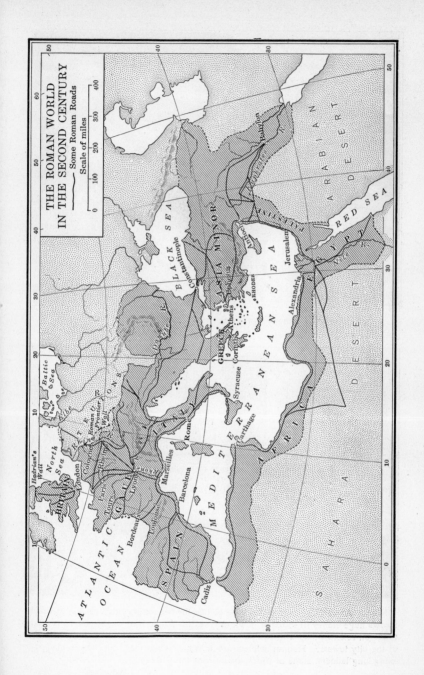

THE ROMAN WORLD
IN THE SECOND CENTURY

—— Some Roman Roads

Scale of miles

0   100   200   300   400

ATLANTIC
OCEAN

Hadrian's
Wall

North
Sea

BRITAIN

London

Colonna

Paris

Tours

Bordeaux

Toulouse

Baltic
Sea

Elbe

R. RHINE

Roman Frontier Wall

GAUL

Lyons

Rhone

Marseilles

Barcelona

SPAIN

Cadiz

MEDITERRANEAN SEA

Rome

ITALY

Carthage

Syracuse

AFRICA

SAHARA

DESERT

BLACK SEA

Constantinople

GREECE

Corinth Athens

RHODES

ASIA MINOR

Antioch

PALESTINE

Jerusalem

Alexandria

EGYPT

R.

Babylon

R.

ARABIAN DESERT

RED SEA

DESERT

IMAGINARY ROMAN STREET SCENE in front of a barber shop.

ROMAN ARMY STORMING A TOWN. — Notice the two hurling engines, one of which throws huge stones fit to batter down city walls. At the back of the picture is a tall tower on rollers (filled with Roman soldiers) which has been pushed up against one of the city towers. Roman soldiers are trying to scale the walls in one place by using long ladders, some of which the citizens throw down.

The *story* of the conquests, however, is not pleasant.
Roman soldiers were proud of their discipline, and they
fought bravely for their country, many times against over-
whelming odds.   But often the wars had been brought about
by greed for riches, and sometimes they were waged with
great cruelty.

After the Greeks in southern Italy had been conquered,
Rome became more and more a trading city, and a new class
of wealthy merchants grew up.
These men were jealous of richer
trading cities on the shores of
the Mediterranean, like Syracuse,
Corinth, and Carthage. So they
tried to find excuses for fighting
these cities, to destroy them and
get all the trade for themselves.
The merchants became very
powerful at Rome, and could usually persuade the Senate and Assembly to see things their way and
to vote for war.

Roman Catapult — a war engine like a huge cross-bow, to
hurl stones and darts.

For a time, too, **the Romans
forgot their old wise ways of
treating conquered cities,** especially outside Italy.   They
called each conquered country a *province*, and sent some
Roman general to govern it.   Many such a governor used
his power mainly to gain plunder for himself and his friends,
even carrying away whole shiploads of treasure from the
beautiful cities of the East.   Sometimes, too, he started new
wars needlessly with free peoples near his province, because
by such a war he might win new territory for Rome and so
get the honor of a " triumph " for himself.

A Roman " triumph " was a splendid sight.   The Greek
historian, *Plutarch*, has described for us the triumph of the

Roman general who conquered Macedonia in 168 B.C. It took three days for the long parade to march from the gates of Rome through the principal streets and on through the Forum up to the temple of Jupiter, while all the time throngs of shouting and cheering citizens, clad in their white togas, crowded the window spaces and the platforms that had been built for spectators along the way.

On the first day passed two hundred and fifty wagons loaded with paintings and marble statues that had been robbed from Greek cities. The next day was given to a long procession of wagons filled with rich armor that had been captured, followed by three thousand men each carrying a basin filled with *silver* coins, or some silver goblet or vase or other such dish.

But the proudest sight of all was kept for the third day. On that day came first long lines of men carrying basins of *gold* coins, or dishes of gold. Then followed the chariot of the Macedonian king, with his golden armor piled on the floor and his crown resting on the seat. Behind the chariot walked the captured children of the king — two little crying princes and a little girl. Then followed, some distance behind and all alone, the captive king himself, on foot and clothed in black. And finally came the victorious army, with song and music, greeted by the loudest cheers of all, with the triumphant general at its head, riding in a splendid chariot and robed in a purple toga embroidered with gold.

The proud Romans gloried in these signs of their power. But they gave no thought to the terrible sufferings of the people they conquered. This same Roman general had paid his soldiers by letting them plunder at will seventy rich but helpless cities. This meant more misery than can be told for hundreds of thousands of people, whose homes and families were broken up and whose lives were ruined.

Rome's Conquests Gave Her a Rich Empire
But Made Her Poor in More Important Ways

The army was no longer made up of citizen-farmers, who left their plows for a few weeks or months to defend their country at need.   Instead, it **was a trained body of soldiers** who made fighting a life business.   From the age of twenty to forty-five they lived always in camp, hoping for war and more plunder.

In fact not many citizen-farmers were left.   A few had become wealthy land-owners with large country estates. These they now cultivated by the toil of large gangs of slaves, who had been captured in war.   They raised huge crops which they could sell cheap, since they paid no wages. Farmers with only a few acres could no longer make a living because they could not afford to sell their crops for such low prices.   Neither could they get work to do from the big landlords, because there was so much slave labor.

So the small free farmers of Italy drifted to the cities — especially to Rome.   There they huddled together in poor tenements with little to do.   Once they had been the most important part of the Roman people; but now **they became a mob of landless men,** ignorant and brutal, fed from the public treasury, and amused by great public shows. Never again could Rome have a Cincinnatus or a Curio.

The entertainments that the city mobs liked best were the *gladiatorial games.*   These usually took place in some vast circular space surrounded by rising tiers of seats, much like one of our foot-ball stadiums.   Such a space was called an *amphi*theater, because it resembled *two* theaters placed back to back.   The level space in front of the seats was the *arena.*   One amphitheater (the Roman Coliseum) could seat nearly fifty thousand spectators.

When the crowd had taken their seats, a procession of gladiators (" swordsmen ") marched around the border of the arena, so that the spectators might have a good chance to pick their favorites. These gladiators were usually captives or slaves who had been trained to fight, perhaps with a promise of freedom if they should win a number of contests. When the spectators had had time to bet on their favorites (for Romans bet wildly on these contests, as some people still do on prize fights), the gladiators began a long series of deadly combats, either by twos or in larger groups. When one was seriously wounded or disarmed, his victor paused for the spectators to give a signal for mercy or for death. If the crowd held their thumbs *up*, the vanquished man was allowed to live; but " thumbs down " was the order for the conqueror to slay his helpless rival.

Usually the gladiators fought with swords, armed, like Roman soldiers, with helmet and shield. But the mob liked excitement and change; so sometimes a man fought with wild beasts, or beasts with each other. Sometimes a bear fought a lion, or an elephant a tiger. One of these shows lasted 123 days, and cost the lives of more than ten thousand gladiators.

As the Roman citizens changed for the worse, the *government* changed too. The *Senate* was now made up mainly of men who had enriched themselves while governing some province. It was no longer fit to rule. If any province, like Sicily or Greece, was being robbed by a cruel and greedy governor, the people there might ask the Roman Senate to punish him. But that kind of Senate was not likely to do so.

The new Roman *mob*, too, was quite unfit to govern the world, or Italy, or even themselves. It sold its votes to the candidate who offered the largest gifts of free grain or the most gorgeous free shows. Men went armed to the elections; and when rival candidates for office bid against each other for the mob's favor, riots broke out, and sometimes thousands of men were killed in the streets. Indeed, some of the civil

"Thumbs Down!" See page 102. The defeated gladiator appeals for mercy, in vain, to the Vestal Virgins (priestesses of the Roman goddess Vesta) in the front row of spectators. — From a modern painting.

The Coliseum at Rome To-day. — During the Middle Ages a great many of its fallen stones were used by Roman nobles to build their castles and palaces.

ROMAN STREET, in front of a food shop. — A "reconstruction" by a famous German scholar. If you have forgotten the meaning of "reconstruction," see the explanation facing page 60.

wars between selfish and ambitious rivals disturbed the whole Roman world.

There were still many good Romans who mourned deeply all these evil changes. Most of them could not see how to do anything about it, but a few great-hearted leaders did try to bring about reforms. Some of them seemed to succeed for a while; but in the end they all failed — either killed in civil war or murdered by the daggers of assassins.

But this kind of misgovernment could not last forever. **Finally the Roman** *Republic* **gave way to the Roman** *Empire,* ruled by one master. Then there was peace once more throughout the Roman world — but *peace without freedom.* We cannot have liberty unless we are willing to keep ourselves fit for the duties of free men.

Summary

By 146 B.C. Rome had conquered the Mediterranean lands, bringing order to the quarreling East and civilization to the barbarous West. But often her wars were unjust and cruel, and she had begun to lose some of her best qualities: (1) Most of the work in Italy came to be done by slaves; (2) the small farmers, no longer able to earn a living, drifted to the cities, where they became ignorant mobs, fed and entertained at public expense; (3) the government became bad, since both Senate and Assembly-mob had become unfit to rule. So at last the Roman Republic changed to the Roman Empire, ruled by one man.

New Words

province	Roman	mob	plunder	riot
gladiator	amphitheater	arena	assassin	candidate

Thought Questions and Things to Do

1. On the map show Rome's conquests to 146 B.C. Does the map show any advantage that Rome had for conquering and ruling

the Mediterranean lands? Locate all the cities mentioned in this chapter. Why were the Romans slower than the Greeks in beginning trade by sea?

2. Read the stories of Tiberius Gracchus and Caius Gracchus and of their mother Cornelia in Harding's *City of the Seven Hills,* Tappan's *Story of the Roman People,* or O'Neill's *World's Story.*

CAESAR CROSSING THE RUBICON (pages 109–110). — A modern painting.

DEATH OF CAESAR (page 112). — A modern painting. The assassins are just leaving
the Senate House, brandishing bloody swords.

CHAPTER XI

JULIUS CAESAR ESTABLISHES THE EMPIRE

How Caesar *Prepared* to Make Himself Master

The man who finally overthrew the outworn Republic and
established the Empire was *Julius Caesar.* Caesar had been
trained both as an orator and as a soldier. He came from
an old patrician family, but he took the side of the common
people. Like other reformers, he wanted to put the poor
people of Rome back upon farms of their own. But in
order to get himself elected to office so that he could carry
out his plans, he was willing to *buy* the favor of the mob in
any way he could get it.

The first office to which Caesar was elected put him in
charge of the public shows. Then he gave the most magnificent games that had ever been seen at Rome, spending upon
them not only all his own fortune but also all he could borrow
from the money-lenders, besides the public money that was
always allowed. After that, the Assembly mob was ready

to elect him to any office he wanted.   He quickly became one of the two or three leading men at Rome.

But Caesar knew very well that he could not count long on the favor of the mob.   He knew, too, that the Senate both feared him and disliked him, because he really was on the side of the people.   The favorite of the Senate was **Pompey the Great,** who had just brought back to Rome rich booty from wars in the East.   The Senate gave Pompey a splendid triumph, so as to win the mob to his side.

Caesar then decided that he too must win victories.   But he did not ask the Senate to send him to a wealthy Eastern province where there were rich cities to plunder.   At that time a savage people called *Gauls* lived in the Po valley in northern Italy and in the region we now call France, on the other side of the Alps.   Rome had already conquered the Po valley and a narrow strip of southern France.   Caesar asked for these districts for his province, so that he might bring under Roman rule the unconquered tribes in the rest of the great country of Gaul, or France.

During the next nine years he fought war after war, and proved that he was by far the best Roman general.   The jealous Senate had given him only a little army.   But his soldiers soon became so devoted to him that they would follow him anywhere, and, with his small force, he won surprising victories.   His first war, however, was not to *conquer* Gauls but to *defend* them from stronger and fiercer barbarians than they themselves were.

These were the *Teutons* who lived across the Rhine. Just when Caesar reached his province, **one of these Teuton peoples,** with their women and children, **had crossed into eastern Gaul and begun to conquer it.**   They had huge bodies, with fair skins and yellow hair and fiercely blazing blue eyes.   In battle they seemed to have no fear of death, but rushed upon their foes with terrifying shouts.   To the smaller Italians, and even to the mighty-limbed Gauls, they appeared unconquerable.

If these Teutons became masters of part of Gaul, they would be dangerous neighbors to Caesar's province and even to Italy. **So Caesar decided to attack them.** His soldiers had not yet come to know and trust him, and at this news they almost mutinied. But Caesar knew how to manage them. "Stay safely in your tents, then," said he, "if you are such cowards. My Tenth Legion, at least, is made up of brave men and will not desert their general. If necessary, I will attack those clumsy savages with that regiment alone." The shamed army begged their commander to forgive them — though some still wept, and many made their wills. Then Caesar overcame the Teutons in a great battle and followed their flight to the wide, swift Rhine. A few of

SLINGERS were an important branch of the Roman army.

them escaped to the other side in boats; but most of the invaders (even the women and children) were massacred.

Then Caesar carried the war into Germany itself. In twelve days, with surprising speed and skill, he built a wooden bridge across the broad Rhine. With swift marches, he attacked and destroyed village after village among the German forests and swamps, and, after eighteen days, recrossed the bridge and broke it down behind him. It was four hundred years before the Teutons again broke into Gaul or Italy.

When he had driven back the Teutons, Caesar soon found excuse for attacking the free Gauls. Sometimes he was terribly cruel to tribes that resisted him, but he dealt kindly with all who yielded to him. **During his nine years in Gaul, he conquered it all and began to Romanize it.** The Gauls learned to speak Latin, to build cities, and to live as the Romans did. Caesar even made many of them full Roman citizens. Later, when he had become master of Rome, he made some Gauls members of the Senate.

Within two centuries after Caesar's conquest, Gaul was one of the most highly civilized parts of all the Roman world. The law and language and customs of France to-day are in large part Roman. At a later time, France was for centuries " the teacher of Europe." She never could have been so, if Caesar's conquest had not brought Roman civilization to her.

Caesar also carried the Roman standards into Britain. The people there were kinsmen of the Gauls, and had sometimes given them aid against Caesar. So **in 55 B.C.**, and again the next year, he crossed the Channel with a great fleet. He defeated the Britons in a few small battles, but he did not try to make their country a Roman province, as he had done with Gaul.

A hundred years later, however, other Roman rulers did conquer and Romanize all of Britain up to the highlands of Scotland. One of the things that we remember Caesar for is that he paved the way for bringing civilization to Britain.

How Caesar Became Master at Rome

Caesar was now becoming the most famous man in the world. His enemies in the Senate did not want him to win any more victories, so they would not let him have another term as governor of his province. They also refused to let him celebrate a triumph, in spite of all that he had done for Rome, because that would have allowed him to bring his victorious soldiers back with him. Instead, they ordered him to disband his army at once and to return to Rome as a private citizen — on pain of death if he did not obey.

Caesar and his friends were sure the Senate meant to have him assassinated as soon as he should lose the protection of his army. It would not be the first time such a thing had happened, and some of his enemies were boasting openly that now it would happen to him. Indeed two Tribunes who had taken his side at home had already been set upon with daggers and had barely escaped with their lives to Caesar's camp.

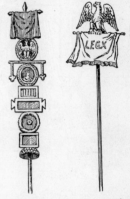

Caesar was in the Po valley when he received word of the Senate's decree against him. During his long wars in Gaul, he had built up a splendidly trained army of fifty thousand men; but these were now far beyond the Alps on the distant borders of Gaul. With him he had only his favorite Tenth Legion — about five thousand men. If he obeyed the Senate and went to Rome alone, he would be giving himself up to the daggers of his enemies. If he stayed quietly in his province, or if he entered Italy with even the Tenth Legion, he would be giving the signal for civil war between himself and Pompey.

Such standards were the Roman "flags." The standard of one legion differed a little from that of another, but nearly always they had somewhere the eagle emblem, — so that the standards of the army were sometimes called "the Roman eagles."

Caesar made his choice quickly. At once he set out for Rome, at the head of his faithful legion. At the last moment, when he reached the banks of the little Rubicon River, which separated his province from Italy, he did hesitate for a few precious minutes. But soon he spurred forward again, crying out, " The die is cast."   (Did you ever hear the words " He has crossed the Rubicon " used of some one who had just made an important decision?)

Pompey the Great had been slowly gathering large armies in Italy for the Senate, but everywhere the people favored Caesar, and his rapid march surprised and terrified his foes. Within two months, almost without a battle, Pompey and the Senators had fled from Italy and were trying to raise new armies in other parts of the Roman dominions—Greece, Asia Minor, Egypt, Spain, North Africa.

This kind of hurling engine is seen also in the large picture facing page 99, but here you can see better how the " cord," or rope, was drawn back into place by working a crank. It was loaded with iron balls, much like a small cannon ball.

But Caesar gave them little time.   During the next year and a half he followed his fleeing enemies to all those parts of the world, defeating and scattering the forces they had raised against him and putting down other rebellions against Rome.   After one of his victories he sent back to Rome the famous message, " I came, I saw, I conquered."

Some of Caesar's friends now wanted to make him king.   Caesar refused that *title*, because he saw that the people of Rome still hated the name.   **But he did take the** *power* **of a king.**   He had himself appointed to all the important old offices.   He became Dictator *for life*, and Censor for life, and was given the power of Tribune for life. But the title that he liked best was *Imperator*, the name by which the Roman army in the field of battle saluted a victorious general.   This became the usual name for the head of the new monarchy, and from it comes our word *Emperor*.

How Caesar *Used* His Power

It was in *January of 49 B.C.* that Caesar had " crossed the Rubicon." **He lived only five years more; but** in that short time, besides all his wars, **he worked out many great reforms** and began even greater ones. Carthage and Corinth, and other noble cities that had been destroyed by the jealousy of Roman business men, were rebuilt. *The provinces were made equal to Italy itself,* and *received the same laws.* The governors were no longer allowed to rule as they pleased and to fill their own pockets by plundering the provinces. They were now the servants of a stern but just master, who cared equally for the welfare of all parts of the vast empire.

FREE DISTRIBUTION OF BREAD by the government. Free grain soon took the form of free loaves, and well-to-do citizens came to prize their right to a share.

In Rome itself Caesar found a helpless mob of 320,000 idle men who had to be fed by the government with free grain. Half of these he succeeded in placing in new homes where they could support themselves once more and lead a better kind of life — some of them in the cities that he rebuilt, and some on small farms in Italy. (If he had lived longer, he would probably have done more to cure this evil.)   He also improved the coinage of Rome, built many splendid buildings there and in other leading cities, carried out the first complete census of Italy, and corrected the calendar.

The old Egyptian " year " (page 26) was now almost three months out of the way, because it had counted only the 365 *whole* days, dropping the quarter day of each year. So now winter came in what had once been a late spring month. Caesar adopted the leap-year plan that we still have ; and he put the seasons in the right months again by adding eighty days to the year 46 B.C. He also rearranged the months, and one of them was named for him. (Can you tell which one of our months that was?)

When Caesar had put down all resistance, he generously pardoned the old nobles and allowed them to come back to Rome. He was warned that they were plotting to murder him ; but he refused the bodyguard that his friends wanted to give him. " It is better to die at any moment," said he, " than to live ever in the fear of dying." On the Ides of March (March 15), 44 B.C., as he entered the Senate House, a band of plotters struck him down. They had gathered about him in a body, pretending that they had a favor to ask. When their swords flashed out, Caesar at first stood stoutly on his defense and wounded one of the assassins. But when he saw his friend Brutus among them, — a noble whom he had especially favored, — he resisted no longer. Exclaiming sadly, " What! Thou, too, Brutus! " he drew his toga calmly about him, and fell, pierced with more than twenty wounds. (See picture on page 105.)

Caesar was a tireless worker, but he always had time for gracious courtesy in dealing with all classes of people. The world has seen few men with so great mental power. He was a *many-sided man*. Says a modern historian, " He was great as a captain, statesman, lawgiver, orator, poet, historian, grammarian, mathematician, architect." If you study Latin in the high school, you will read the histories that he wrote in his tent at the end of weary days during hard campaigns.

Caesar and Alexander are the two great military captains whose conquests have done the most for civilization.   Both were snatched from their work by an early death; but, as a man, Caesar is far the greater.   His calm self-control saved him from the stormy fits of passion that sometimes seized Alexander; and, though he was a master in war, he had none of Alexander's boyish liking for mere fighting.   He preferred to build up, rather than to tear down.   It was fitting that the name *Caesar* should become the title (as it did) of all succeeding rulers of the Roman Empire for many centuries to come — though only the first five of those rulers belonged to Caesar's family.   It is interesting, too, to remember

A MARBLE HEAD (now in the British Museum) said to be the work of an old Roman sculptor, to portray Julius Caesar.

that the titles *Tsar* and *Kaiser* were just different ways of writing Caesar.   But in all the two thousand years in which proud rulers bore that title, no Caesar of them all was the equal of the first one.

SUMMARY

Caesar took the side of the common people against the selfish nobles.   He drove back invading Germans across the Rhine, conquered and Romanized all Gaul, and even invaded Germany and Britain.   When the Senate ordered him to return to Rome without his army (so that his enemies might slay him), he " crossed the Rubicon " and began civil war with Pompey and the Senate.

When he had put down his foes, he returned to Rome and carried out many reforms.   Jealous nobles assassinated him when he had ruled only five years, but his work was to go on after him.   He had made the outworn Republic into a new Roman Empire, and he had begun to give equal and just laws to all parts of that empire, without favoring any one part (not even Rome itself) more than others.

New Words

reformer   Romanize   Roman legion   Imperator

Thought Questions and Things to Do

1. Mark on the map the lands civilized by Cæsar.   Compare Caesar's empire with Alexander's.   Alexander united older lands : Caesar added new ones.

2. Compare the Romanizing of Gaul with the way Alexander spread Greek ways in the East.   Do you know of any parts of the world to which *we* have carried our civilization?

3. Read Shakespeare's story of Julius Caesar in Lamb's *Tales from Shakespeare*.   Read also Harding's *City of the Seven Hills*, Tappan's *Story of the Roman People*, and O'Neill's *The World's Story*.

4. Imagine yourself a Roman citizen in the time when Caesar was crossing the Rubicon, and write your ideas about it.   Were the ideas of all Romans of that time the same?

5. Your class would find it interesting to dramatize scenes from the life of Caesar.

TEUTONIC BODYGUARD OF THE ROMAN EMPEROR MARCUS AURELIUS (180 A.D.). — From the reliefs on a triumphal column. (See also page 129 and facing page 118.)

CHAPTER XII

THE ROMAN WORLD

Julius Caesar's Work was Carried on by Augustus

The assassins had struck down Caesar, but not his work. The kind of government he had set up was to last for many centuries. Sometimes there were disputes as to who should be the emperor; but always nearly every one agreed that there must be *some* emperor over all the Roman world.

The first ruler after Caesar was his nephew *Augustus*. He quickly crushed the rebellious nobles, and then ruled forty-five peaceful and prosperous years. He carried forward many of Caesar's plans. He also rebuilt splendidly most of the public buildings of Rome, so that he could say before his death, " I found Rome brick and leave it marble." The other chief cities, too, he adorned with noble buildings — temples, theaters, and public baths.

But the most important thing that happened in this long reign had nothing to do with emperors and courts, and probably was never heard of by Augustus: it was the birth of the child Jesus, in a manger, in a distant corner of the Empire.

" Rome was the whole world, and all the world was Rome."
For More than Two Centuries, Life was Peaceful and Prosperous

The Roman Empire, compared with Alexander's, did not
extend so far to the east, but it included much more of
the west (maps facing pages 74 and 98). It stretched from
the Euphrates to the Atlantic, and bordered the Mediterranean with narrow bands of land both north and south.
Indeed, that inland sea was now the main *highway* of
the Roman world, — more important for trade and travel
than even the famous Roman roads on land. The Empire
contained about as much territory as does the United States,
and had about eighty million people. (How many has the
United States?)

The Empire was defended largely by *natural* boundaries.
On the south there stretched away the Arabian and Sahara
deserts — an impassable belt of desolate sands. On the
west rolled the stormy waves of the Atlantic. On the
remaining sides, north and east, lay the wild North Sea,
the broad Rhine and Danube rivers, the Black Sea, and the
Euphrates. And along the rivers, stood the mighty Roman
legions to watch and guard.

Outside the rich and peaceful Empire there wandered
vast hordes of barbarians, eager for plunder and always beat-
ing against the boundaries for a chance to break through. So
at the weak spots strong walls were built to help out the
natural defenses. In Britain, one emperor built a stone
wall across the island from sea to sea, to protect the Romanized part from the wild *Picts* of the Scottish highlands.
(The Romans called these highlanders " Picts," or
" painted," because they daubed their bodies with war
paint, much as our Indians used to do. When Caesar invaded Britain, two hundred years before, all Britons used
war paint, but those in *Roman* Britain had given up that
custom.)

THE APPIAN WAY.

The army which guarded this Roman world was not large.
It numbered only some 400,000 men, even counting the
sailors in the large navy that kept the seas safe from pirates.
Our own country, with few foes to fear, keeps half that
many men under arms, and modern Europe has ten times
that many soldiers. That small Roman army, too, was
nearly all kept on the exposed frontiers.

Within the Empire the people rested for more than two
hundred years in " the good Roman peace." Everywhere
was a busy and happy prosperity, so that the din of arms on
distant frontiers hardly made itself heard. **Never before
or since has so large a part of the world known so long a rest
from the horrors of war.** A famous English historian has
said that a wise man would rather have lived during that age
than at any other time in the world's history.

Nearly all the people lived in *cities.* There were a few
large places, like Rome, Alexandria, Carthage, Ephesus,
Corinth, and Antioch ; but only a few cities had as many as
twenty thousand people. Yet even the smaller towns had
fine baths, aqueducts, temples, and schools. In Gaul,
Caesar had found not one real city, — only villages of huts,
surrounded by stockades. But two hundred years later,
Roman Gaul had 116 flourishing cities, some of them with
famous schools that drew students even from Italy.

Many of the people living in the city and its suburbs were
farmers, whose fields stretched away from the town in all
directions. Each town, too, had large numbers of *shop-
keepers* and of *skilled workmen* of many kinds. These
workmen were organized in " gilds," or unions (all weavers in
a weavers' gild, and so on) ; and a baker or a mason would
usually have two or three *slaves* to do the heavy unskilled
part of the work.

There were also *engineers, architects, bankers, teachers,
physicians,* and *dentists,* as well as wealthy *merchants* who
traded on a large scale instead of just keeping little shops.

Usually, also, there were a few *nobles*.   Some of these became lawyers; some wrote books; some made the higher officers of the army; and nearly all of them, besides their town homes, had also fine country houses, or *villas*, with large estates, which were worked by slaves.

AQUEDUCT IN SOUTHERN FRANCE, built about 150 A.D. by a Roman emperor to supply a city with water from springs 25 miles distant.   Water pipes were carried through hills by tunnels and across streams and valleys on arches like these. This aqueduct has vanished (its stones used for other buildings) except for the part on this bridge across the Gard river; but here it is still possible to walk through the pipes on the top row of arches.   Some of these Roman aqueducts remained in use till very recent days.

It has been possible for us to learn a great deal about the homes and streets and work and play of the people in a Roman city because of a strange and terrible accident.   Mt. Vesuvius in Italy to-day is an active volcano.   In early Roman times it was plain that it *had been* a volcano many years before, but its fires seemed extinct.   Groves and rich vineyards covered its slopes, and cities had been built about

TRAJAN'S COLUMN in Rome — the finest example of a favorite kind of Roman monument. It is 100 feet high, and the spiral bands of relief sculpture that circle it contain 2500 figures — commemorating conquests by the Emperor Trajan. Some other emperors had similar columns. Reliefs from one of them are shown on pages 115, 129.

ROMAN GARDEN SCENE. — The master of a country house is being carried out through the garden in a *litter* (a favorite way for rich Romans to travel).

RUINS OF THE FORUM AT POMPEII, with a view of Vesuvius "the Destroyer" in the distance.

its base. Suddenly, in 79 A.D., its fires burst forth, and a fearful eruption spread thick layers of ashes and lava over the country roundabout, burying two of the cities many feet deep.

Years passed, and the buried cities were almost forgotten. But, after more than sixteen centuries, a deep well happened to be dug just above one of them. It reached down far enough to uncover some interesting remains. Since that time skilled excavators have uncovered that ancient city of Pompeii, finding the houses with their furniture and ornaments, the shops with their tools, and the public buildings, all just as they stood when the volcanic flood came rolling in upon them. In some of the larger American museums you can find many remains from Pompeii — pictures, statues, vases, furniture, and even *models* of the buildings.

It is plain that Roman city life was rather pleasant for all but the slaves and the poorest workmen. We know from the books of the time that every city had its forum, or public square, surrounded by stately public buildings. Pompeii shows that in even a small town those temples, theaters, halls, and public baths might be of beautiful marble.

The Romans were not great artists, like the Greeks, but **they were good builders.** They thought the Greek buildings very beautiful and made many of theirs much like them; but almost always their large buildings had one thing that Greek buildings did not have. In very early times they had learned to use *arches*, probably from the Etruscans. They found arches especially helpful in their bridges and aqueducts (pages 83, 118), but they used them also in nearly all public buildings. Sometimes they built a *roof* out of many arches that joined at the top, forming an immense *dome* as in the pictures facing page 118 and (from the inside) facing page 132. (Do you know of buildings in America that have domes?)

Roman cities had many more public baths than our

modern cities have. The baths were immense temple-like buildings of splendid marble. In the bathing rooms, there were silver faucets for hot or cold water, and marble tubs and basins and swimming tanks. Often, too, the buildings contained libraries, picture galleries, gymnasiums, and eating rooms. Slaves were on hand, to rub the bodies of the bathers and to anoint them with oil and perfumes. Many people spent a large part of their spare time in these buildings, some of which on most days were free of charge, like great public club houses. At Rome the public baths could take care of 60,000 people at a time. Even to-day Rome gets its water through four aqueducts that were built during the early empire (four that are still left, out of many more at that time), and few other modern cities have so good a supply of water.

Well-to-do Romans had also learned from the *Greeks* how to build convenient and lovely houses. To be sure, the houses were usually built close to the street, and the openings on the street were few and small; but within there was much space and beauty and open air and sunshine.

Just back from the main entry there was always a large hall and reception room, where the master received guests and did business with his agents and stewards. Much of the central part of this Hall (or "inside porch," or "court") was left open to the sky, unroofed, and the rain water that entered through the roof opening drained into a marble basin in the middle of the floor — where also there was usually a playing fountain.

At the rear, this first "court" opened into a second spacious court, with flowering shrubs and glorious marble statues, stolen long before, perhaps, from some Greek city. Here, too, were marble seats and benches around another fountain; for the life of the household was largely carried on in this open court.

Around both hall and rear court were rooms, large and

INTERIOR OF A ROMAN PUBLIC BATH BUILDING, as a famous German
scholar "reconstructs" it.

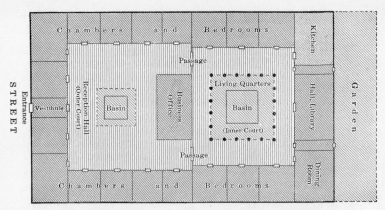

GENERAL PLAN FOR A ROMAN GENTLEMAN'S HOUSE

INNER COURT OF A ROMAN HOUSE, as represented in a modern painting. The master is coming in from the Reception Hall.

small, — libraries, baths, work rooms, sleeping rooms. At the back of the house were the kitchen and pantry. The paving of the courts and the floors of the rooms were usually of different colored marbles, the pieces arranged in patterns (*mosaics*), often in the form of plants or animals. The walls were hung with costly, brilliantly colored tapestries, and the ceilings were richly gilded. Stairways led from the courts to an upper story of narrow sleeping rooms and work rooms. Sometimes there was a third story. It took a good deal of room to supply sleeping quarters for the troops of household slaves; but many of them slept in the court or on the floors of the halls.

The villa of a nobleman had all the comforts of his city house — baths, libraries, museums, mosaic pavements, gilded ceilings, and tapestried walls. Around it spread lovely park-like grounds, with ornamental shrubbery and fishponds and playing fountains, and with beautiful marble forms gleaming through the trees.

A villa was usually the center of a large farm. Indeed the rich landlords, with the gangs of farm slaves who heaped up wealth for them, were about the only people left to live in the country. The wretched huts of the slaves huddled against the walls that surrounded the villa grounds — a dark background for all the villa's magnificence.

There was Much Trade and Travel in All Parts of the Empire

Trade flourished as never before, and as it was not to flourish again after the fall of Rome for at least a thousand years. From every frontier the splendidly built military roads ran toward Rome, and from them a network of good roads spread out over each province. The ports of the Mediterranean were crowded with ships, much like those in which Columbus, eleven or twelve hundred years later, was to cross the Atlantic, and the sea was dotted with happy sails. One merchant of Asia Minor tells us, on his gravestone, that he had sailed around Greece to Italy seventy-two times.

Indeed, Roman traders pressed on to savage tribes far beyond the boundaries of the Empire, just as Dutch and English traders of three hundred years ago journeyed into the savage interior of America. From the distant coasts of the Baltic they brought back amber, furs, and flaxen German hair with which the dark Roman ladies liked to deck their heads. Such goods the trader paid for in toys and trinkets and in wines and sometimes in Roman swords and armor — as our colonial traders got their furs from the Indians with beads and whisky and guns and knives.

Some daring traders made still longer voyages to the rich regions of the Far East, even as far as China. From India and the islands southeast of Asia came a steady stream of silk, indigo, pearls, sapphires, and rubies. That same new East sent to Europe also costly spices, like *pepper* and *cinnamon*, and two other new delicacies for the table. (1) For the very rich a delicious sweet *syrup, drawn from the Eastern sugar cane,* began to take the place of honey, which had been the only sweet known before in Europe. (2) Roman physicians sometimes ordered boiled *rice* for wealthy patients who could afford such a luxury.

There was much travel, too, for pleasure. The people of one part of the Empire wished to see and know all the other parts of the great Roman world. Travel was safe and swift and comfortable, even between places as far apart as London and Babylon. Guidebooks showed routes and distances, and inns along all the great roads furnished resting places and meals and relays of horses. It was almost as common for the gentleman of Gaul or Britain to visit the wonders of Italy or Egypt as it is to-day for an American to visit Paris. Sometimes these visitors had the bad manners to scrawl their names on monuments and buildings, much as some modern travelers do. A famous statue in Egypt still bears a scratched bit of writing, telling that it was visited by a Roman gentleman, " Gemellus," with " his dear wife Rutilla " and their children.

One thing made travel even easier than in our day. That was the fact that **all people of the Empire could understand one another.** Latin was the language of the Western part, and Greek of the Eastern ; but all educated men in each part spoke the language of the other. Young Romans from all over the Empire came together at the universities of Athens or Alexandria or in the newer schools of Gaul or Italy. And everywhere the works of the old Greek writers were studied, much as we study the works of Shakespeare — and so some of them were saved for modern times.

The Empire was a vast " melting pot." Trade and travel, good government, a common language, just laws (the same everywhere), and centuries of prosperity molded the many races of the Roman world into one people. Gaul, Briton, African, Greek, Asiatic, all called themselves Romans and felt that they belonged to one nation. In the fourth century A.D. this noble feeling was put into fit words by an Egyptian poet :

> " Rome, Rome alone, has found the spell to charm
> The tribes that bowed beneath her conquering arm ;
> Has given one name to the whole human race,
> And clasped and sheltered them in fond embrace.
>
> . . . .
>
> Though we tread Rhone's or Orontes's shore,
> Yet are we all one nation ever more."

(The Orontes was a river in Syria, and the Rhone was a river in southern Gaul.)

There was one more reason why the Empire became so united in feeling. The emperors had found a way to let all parts of the Empire know what the government was doing, along with certain other matters that concerned them all.

There were no newspapers yet; but, almost every day, the officers of the emperor posted up a written *bulletin* in the forum of the capital city. The governor of each province, too, did the same thing in *his* capital. Then scribes copied these bulletins and made a living by peddling the copies

to rich people who wanted to know what was in them without standing before the bulletin boards in the crowded forum to read them. Copies of one city's bulletins were often sent to other cities, to be posted in *their* forums.

A bulletin always contained any new laws that had been made by the emperor, with important decisions by his judges in the law courts, and news items about the emperor's family and powerful nobles and other interesting people. Accounts of frontier wars found a place — especially if there had been a glorious

Part of a wall-painting at Pompeii to show the different things going on in the forum there. The men in this part of the painting are reading a bulletin that rests on the sloping board in front of the sculptured horsemen.

victory. In each large city, the bulletin would give the program of coming gladiatorial games, with the results of those that had just been held, and other news about famous gladiators. (Quite like our newspapers, after all, only much smaller.)

Private persons were not permitted to post bulletins in the forums; but, in the lack of newspapers and of printing shops, they did find a way to publish advertisements and other notices by scratching or painting them on the walls of the houses — which, you remember, came close to the street (page 120). There were complaints that some men scraped off other people's notices from a street-wall so as to write their own there — much as our bill-posters sometimes unfairly cover up one notice with another. Wall space, you see, was very much in demand. When Pompeii was uncovered, its street-walls were found scrawled over with private advertisements and notices — some of them urging people to vote for or against certain candidates in a city election for which the time had almost come.

SUMMARY

Augustus carried on the work of Caesar, and for centuries there was always some emperor to rule the Roman world. The Empire reached from the Euphrates to the Atlantic, stretching along the shores of the Mediterranean, which was its chief highway. The people for the most part lived in fine cities, enjoyed peace and prosperity for more than two centuries, and came to feel that they were all one nation.

NEW WORDS

arch	*mosaic*	*suburb*	*volcano*	*excavator*
dome	*villa*	*gild*	*lava*	*bulletin*

THOUGHT QUESTIONS AND THINGS TO DO

1. Show the boundaries of the Roman Empire, and draw the walls where the Romans built them. Do you think such walls would help much in war now? If you had been deciding where Roman legions were most needed, where would you have put them?

2. From the map facing page 98, find the names and places of some of the most important Roman cities. Which of them are important to-day? Name the countries of to-day that are in the territory which made up the Roman Empire.

3. Imagine yourself taking a trip in Roman times, and give an account of it.

4. After studying the plans and pictures, make a model of a Roman courtyard.

5. List the advantages of living about 100 A.D.   Do you know any other country that is sometimes called " a melting pot of races "?

6. Without looking up the matter, see if you can write the following in the right order in time.   (Then check your work by your time line.)

a. The Phoenicians carry civilization to Europe.   *b.* The Greeks drive back the Persians.   *c.* Bronze civilization begins in Egypt.   *d.* Solon makes Athens a democracy.

7. In what order did these countries become powerful: Athens, Babylonia, Persia, Rome, Egypt, Macedonia?

8. Good books that tell how boys of the Empire lived are Johnston's *Little Roman Cousin* and Stuart's *Boy through the Ages.*

ROMAN FORUM, as a modern scholar thinks it must have looked in Caesar's time.

APPEAL TO A ROMAN EMPEROR FOR JUSTICE by a legionary, or common soldier. This painting on the wall of the Supreme Court room in the Wisconsin Capitol suggests the influence of Roman law in *our* history. See page 130.

CHAPTER XIII

THE ROMAN EMPIRE COMES TO AN END

On your time line draw a broad band of *white* from 31 B.C. (the beginning of Augustus' reign) to 300 A.D. For nearly all that time the Empire was happy and prosperous. During the last hundred years of it, however, there were many short wars between rival generals who wanted to rule the Empire. Then followed two centuries of disorder and suffering before the Empire finally came to an end. You might mark that last period by a band of *red*.

The People came to be Divided into Few Rich and Many Poor

More and more the wealth of the Empire fell into the hands of a few rich men. By 300 A.D. these few were very rich indeed, but the rest of the people were getting poorer and poorer. The landlords with great estates sold grain so cheap that men with small farms could no longer make a living. Look back at page 101 and see how the free farmers

127

of Italy had been driven from their farms long before this time by the rich landlords. Something like that happened now all over the vast Empire.

But now the poor farmers did not all go to the cities to become idle and hungry mobs. Some of them found another way to keep themselves and their families alive. The landlords really needed workers, if they could get them cheap enough, because the supply of slaves was giving out, now that Rome was no longer conquering new countries. So now **many men who had had to give up their own farms worked on the great estates as** *serfs*.

SERFS IN ROMAN GAUL baking bread — as pictured in an old manuscript.

This was a new kind of worker. *A serf was a sort of halfslave.* He worked for a master without getting any wages. Instead he was given a little patch of ground (sometimes from the farm that had once been his own) on which he might work in his spare time to raise food for himself. Most of the time, however, he had to work on his master's land, and he had to work there *whenever he was called on*, even though his own little crop might be ruined if he left it.

Besides this, a serf had to make his master many presents out of the little that he had — a chicken, now and then, a few eggs, a bushel of grain. *Still he was better off than a slave.* He did have a hut of his own. That and his little piece of ground could not be taken away from him. On the other hand, he could not take himself away from the land. If the landlord sold the land, the serf went with it to the new master.

As time went on, there came to be hundreds of thousands of serfs in Western Europe. Indeed, for hundreds of years after the Empire came to an end, and even after the discovery of America, much of the farm work in Europe was done by serfs.

By 400 A.D. the Empire had Grown so Weak That Tribes of Teutons began to Break in

There were not so many people in the Empire now as there had been during its good centuries. Most people were too poor to have large families, and serfs and city mobs could not give their children good food or the right care. Finally there were not enough workers left to get done all the things that were needed. So the emperors began bringing in hundreds of captive barbarians and giving them as serfs to the landlords.

TEUTONS SERVING IN THE ROMAN ARMY. — From the relief sculpture on a triumphal column of a Roman Emperor of about 180 A.D. (a column much like the one facing page 118). More commonly, however, the Germans fought on foot — as in the cut from the same source on page 115.

It was harder and harder, too, to get soldiers enough to defend the frontiers, and so the emperors began to hire free Teutons to serve in the Roman army for pay. Before long, nearly all the soldiers and many of the generals were Teutons.

And then, about 400 A.D., whole Teutonic nations began to come in _as conquerors_, bursting through the frontier barriers, with their women and children and flocks and herds. They wandered to and fro, plundering and destroying until they felt ready to settle down in a new home in some part that pleased them.

The Eastern Part of the Empire Lasted a Thousand Years Longer

By 500 A.D. Western Europe had been broken up into many different countries, each ruled by some Teutonic people (map opposite page 142). In the eastern part of the old Roman world the Empire kept alive for another thousand years, but it had lost much of its power. Its chief city was Constantinople.   The emperors there more and more came

A COIN OF JUSTINIAN. Notice the fine engraving.

to rule as despots, like the old Egyptian and Babylonian kings. We usually speak of what was left of the Empire as the *Eastern Empire* — or, sometimes, as the *Greek Empire*, since all the people there spoke Greek (page 123).

In later years this Eastern Empire had very little to do with Western Europe, and so had not much effect on our history.   But we do owe it one important thing.   **One of the emperors, *Justinian the Great*, gathered together all the laws of the Roman Empire, and had them written out in good order.**   We call this a *code* of laws.   These Roman laws were fair and just; and this putting them together in an orderly way made it easier to pass them on to other countries. The Justinian Code is a large part of the law of many European lands to-day and of our State of Louisiana—first used there when that district belonged to France.

The Roman Empire Had Lasted Long Enough in the West To Give the Christian Religion a Good Chance To Spread over All Europe

As we have seen, Jesus was born in the reign of the Emperor Augustus (page 115).   In the year 26 A.D. he began to teach his new religion of peace and love and brotherly kindness. Some of the Hebrews welcomed his teachings, but the priests feared that he was turning the people away from the old religion. They went to the Roman governor and accused Jesus of stirring up a rebellion against the Roman government. So he was put to death.

But his disciples went on with his work in all parts of the Roman world. (Can you think of three reasons why it was easier for them to carry their teachings to all parts of that world then than it would have been at any earlier time?) Everywhere they went, the poor and unhappy listened to them eagerly, and little Christian churches sprang up in nearly every city.

Soon, however, the Roman government began to perse-cute the Christians cruelly, in order to make them give up their beliefs. There were several reasons for this. (1) The little societies of Christians held their meetings *secretly*, and so the government feared they might be plotting rebellions. (2) The first Christians thought it was wrong to fight, and would not serve in the army even when the Empire needed soldiers. (3) The Christians refused to make sacrifices to the old Roman gods, as every one was expected to do at certain times.

This last fact was the chief reason why Christians were persecuted. When crops failed, or a barbarian people invaded the Empire, or a frightful plague broke out, many Romans believed that the old gods were punishing the whole Empire because they had not received all the usual sacrifices. For a long time, too, many people thought the Christians did horribly wicked things at their secret gatherings. They did not really know much about the Christians anyway, and so it was easy to believe any dreadful story that was started about them.

Even some of the best emperors thought it their duty to crush the new religion, and carried on cruel persecutions.

But the Christians were ready to suffer terrible deaths rather than give up their faith. Some were burned at the stake. Some were thrown to wild beasts in the arena. It would take volumes to tell the stories of these heroic Christian martyrs — who often were hardly more than boys and girls.

And so **persecution did not crush Christianity.** Instead, the Church grew steadily. People began to think there

This picture (from a famous modern painting) shows a group of Christian martyrs exposed in the Coliseum to be devoured by hungry lions. The cage of the beasts has just been opened. The martyrs are kneeling in prayer.

must be something true and fine about a religion when such numbers were willing to die rather than give it up. They became curious about it, and, as they learned more about Christianity, they became Christians themselves. By 300 A.D. many rich and powerful persons had joined the Christian Church.

The Church now was getting too strong to be persecuted. **Finally, in 312 A.D. one of the emperors began to show special favor to the Christians.** This was the Emperor *Constantine.* He ordered that all persecutions should be

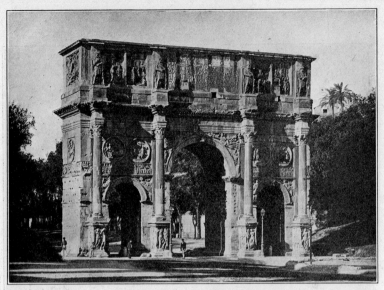

ARCH OF CONSTANTINE (page 132) commemorating a victory that made him Emperor.

CHURCH OF ST. SOPHIA, CONSTANTINOPLE, built by Justinian (page 130). The whole interior is lined with costly, many-colored marbles. This view shows only 18 of the 40 windows around the lower part of the vast dome. In 1453 the building became a Mohammedan church (ch. xx).

ARCH OF TITUS TO-DAY, with the Coliseum in the distance. (Titus was son of Trajan; see facing 118.) A triumphal arch, spanning a street, was a favorite Roman structure to celebrate victories. The relief sculpture on this arch celebrated the capture and destruction of Jerusalem by Titus in 70 A.D. after a rebellion by the Hebrews against Roman rule. Those citizens who had not been slain in the siege, or who had not perished in the flames of their city, were sold into slavery. Ever since the Hebrews have remained a scattered people, without a national home — until the recent attempt to restore them to Palestine.

stopped, and then very soon most of the people in the Empire joined the Church. Later, another emperor ordered that there should be no other religion in the whole Empire, and even began to persecute those who still tried to worship the old gods.

The Church had a government of its own, something like that of the Empire. In every town or village, and in every division of a large city, there was a *priest*, to look after the religious services for the people there. In the *chief* church of each large town there was a *bishop*, to oversee the priests of his neighborhood. Usually, too, one bishop in each Roman province was over all the rest of the province and was called an *archbishop*. And the bishop of Rome, or the *Pope*, was thought of by every one in Western Europe as head of the whole Church. All these officials of the Church were called the *clergy*.

Before the Empire came to an end, **Christian missionaries began to go outside the boundaries of the Empire,** to carry their religion to the barbarians. So when the Teutons broke over the boundaries in the fifth century, many of them had already become Christians, and if they had not, they soon did become so. Although Western Europe did split up into many nations, the people in all of them still belonged to one great Church.

Summary

After two prosperous centuries the Empire began to grow weaker. A few very rich men had come to own all the land, so that the old free farmers everywhere were becoming either city mobs or serfs. About 400 A.D. the Teutons began to break into the Western Empire.

Much of the Roman civilization was destroyed; but much of it, too, was saved, to mix with the new ideas of the Teutons and form a new civilization. Before the barbarians came, the Christian religion had spread over all the Empire.

New Words

serf	persecution	missionary	bishop	pope
code	martyr	invasion	archbishop	clergy

Thought Questions and Things to Do

1. Without looking at the time line, see if you can write the following in the right order. Then check up by looking at the time line.

a. Julius Caesar starts the Empire. *b.* Constantine adopts the Christian religion. *c.* Rome conquers all Italy. *d.* Rome drives out the kings. *e.* Rome conquers the Mediterranean world.

2. Write a letter from a Roman noble about the Christians. Perhaps you might show how he changed his ideas as he learned more about the Christians.

Hall of a public bath-building, erected in Rome by an emperor of about 300 A.D.; now the Church of St. Mary of the Angels.

EARLY TEUTONIC SMITHS WORKING IRON. — A wall painting in the Milwaukee Public Museum.

CHAPTER XIV

THE TEUTONS

The Teutons were a Savage People When They Broke into the Empire

We have told how terrifying the Teutons looked to the Romans in the time of Caesar (page 106). These fierce barbarian warriors had changed their ways very little in the four hundred years after that time. **They still lived much as some of the American Indians did when Columbus discovered America.** The land beyond the Rhine, where they had their homes, was a wilderness of forest and swamp. They had only small clearings for their little villages and for their narrow fields.

Their homes were built of roughly hewn logs, or sometimes of reeds and twigs woven together. Often their cattle and other beasts lived in the same room with the family. Their dress was still largely of skins of deer or bear that the men had killed, though the women did spin a little coarse linen and woolen cloth.

The women, too, cared for the cows and goats and tilled the small patches of grain. Sometimes the woman of the family

135

had the help of a slave or two to watch the herds of pigs that fed on acorns and roots in the forest, and to do some of the other unpleasant work.   The Teutonic warriors themselves were too proud to work.   When they were not fighting or hunting, much of the time they gorged themselves with meat and drink, and lay about the fire, gambling or sleeping.

TEUTONIC CHIEFTAIN calling his followers.

There was only one kind of workman whom they honored. That was the *smith*, who at his forge in the forest hammered out iron into weapons and armor.

Fighting was their sport as well as their business. The bravest and strongest among them was usually chosen to be the king of the tribe, to lead them in war. But they did not let their kings decide many things for them. If anything important was to be done, such as deciding on war, or moving their homes to another part of the forest, all the free men of the tribe came together.   This was called a *folk-moot*.   Here the warriors listened to the plans of their chiefs. If they wished to vote *no*, they muttered together disapprovingly. But if they wished to vote *yes*, they clashed their spears against their shields, for they thought the sound of arms the most honorable noise they could make.

Their government had no officials to protect people against violence. Each family had to protect itself. If any one were slain in a quarrel, then all the other members of his family must join in avenging the injury. They might do this by killing the murderer, or, quite as well, by killing some

THOR, as pictured by the modern painter Gehrts.

BATTLE BETWEEN NORSE GODS AND EVIL MONSTERS, as pictured by the modern painter Gehrts. You can see Thor with his hammer, Woden with his spear, some of "Woden's Daughters," and human heroes.

THE RAINBOW BRIDGE TO VALHALLA (page 138), as pictured by the modern painter Gehrts.

member of his family.   (This sort of war between two families
is called a " feud.")   But if the relatives of the murderer were
willing to pay a reasonable sum of money to the injured
family, then the feud was dropped.   Such money was called
" wergeld," or *man money.*

EARLY TEUTONIC VILLAGE — as a famous French scholar (Parmentier) thinks it
probably looked.   The three men seated in the center are gambling.

Do families in any part of our country ever have feuds
somewhat like those of the early Teutons?   Do you think the
Teutons would have been so likely to have had them if they
had had courts of justice and policemen, as we have?

The Teutons worshiped many gods.   The chief one was
Woden, god of the sky and god of war.   He was thought of
as always holding a spear.   One day of the week was named
for him, — " Woden's day," which we call Wednesday.
Next to Woden, the Teutons worshiped *Thor,* god of storms.
When it thundered, they said Thor was hurling his hammer
across the heavens at some evil one (the wonderful hammer

that always came back to his hand). * "Thor's day" is our
Thursday. *Freya* was the goddess of joy and fruitfulness.
(Which day of our week was named for her?) Two other
heathen gods gave their names to Tuesday and Saturday,
while our Sunday and Monday were the "Sun's day" and
the "Moon's day."

The Teutons did not try to build temples to their gods.
They liked better to worship under spreading oaks in their
sacred groves. There sometimes they sacrificed captives
to Woden.

In the German forests and in the Northern Scandinavian
lands, **the long, dark winter was a bad time of hunger and
cold.** It came on, said the Teutons, when for a time the
gods were overcome by wicked ice-giants of cold and darkness. Always there was war between these giants and the
gods. The home of the gods — the huge palace of Woden —
was *Valhalla*, a place of warmth and sunshine and feasting.
Every morning the warrior-daughters of Woden rode out
across the rainbow bridge from Valhalla to earth. At night
they came galloping back, carrying the warriors who had
been killed that day in battle. The souls of these heroes
remained in Valhalla to feast with the gods and to help them
in the fight against the evil ice-giants.

The Teutons believed also that, besides the great gods in
Valhalla, there were spirits that dwelt in rivers and mountains and forests. Dwarf-like gnomes, they said, lived in the
earth, guarding its precious jewels and making its metals
into wonderful tools and weapons; and not far away in the
forest, there were beautiful fairies who often worked strange
tricks upon mortals.

Indeed, the Teutons gave us not only most of the fairy
tales that delight our children, but also our beautiful Christmas customs of hanging the mistletoe and burning the Yule
log. The Yuletide was a joyous heathen festival with them

for many centuries before it became our Christian Christmas. It was the season when the days were just beginning to get longer — because, said the Teutons, the gods and heroes of Valhalla were getting the upper hand in the fight with the frost giants. (What day of the year is the shortest?)

There was much that was bad and terrible about the savage life of the Teutons; but they had also some good things that the old Roman world needed badly. That world had come to a standstill. For two or three centuries it had not advanced in any new way. Its people no longer *did* anything for themselves (because the government did everything for them), and so they had even stopped *thinking* for themselves. They had lost their spirit of independence.

The Teutons were brave and truthful and loved freedom. They **brought into the Roman world new life and a new chance to advance.** In the long run their fresh energy and their spirit of proud independence helped Europe to begin again the march of progress.

The West Goths were the First Teutons To Win a Home within the Empire

For centuries before they broke into the Empire, the savage Teutons had heard many stories of its wealth and glory. Traders had brought them tales of rich cities, of broad and fertile fields, of fruit-laden orchards, and of sunny vineyards. They wanted to leave their narrow clearings in the damp and cold northern forests to win better homes and an easier life in those Roman lands. Indeed, many of them had been serving in the Roman armies (pages 115, 129), and others had been made Roman serfs.

The first Teutons to break through as conquerors were a group of tribes known as *West Goths*. They had been living just north of the Danube. They had traded a good deal with the Romans south of the river, and had learned some Roman ways. Now, more warlike and barbarous peoples came crowding up behind them, so they begged the emperor to let them cross the Danube and settle within the Empire. The Empire needed more men (page 129), so the emperor let them come in. He promised to treat them well, but the promise was soon broken by his careless or greedy officials.

Then the angry Goths rose against the Roman armies and defeated them in a great battle near Constantinople. From that time no one was able to drive them out. They settled for a while in the lands north of Greece. After a few years their young war-leader *Alaric* led them into Greece itself, and they carried off vast amounts of plunder from many rich cities there.

But Alaric would not be satisfied till he had conquered Rome itself. So finally the whole nation of Goths — men, women, and children — marched west into Italy, plundering everywhere as they moved. At the news of their coming, the cowardly emperor fled from Rome. For eight hundred years the old capital of the Roman world had not seen an enemy within its walls. But now, *in 410 A.D.*, Alaric besieged it and forced it to surrender.

For days the victorious Goths busied themselves in sacking Rome, killing people when they chose and carrying off whatever pleased them. Things like libraries, statues, and paintings, which they did not know enough to use or enjoy, they destroyed. Only the churches were spared, by the special order of Alaric.

Wherever the barbarians conquered, indeed, they destroyed much of the old civilization "just for fun," like mischievous boys. A story of this sort is told of one warrior who was plundering a beautiful villa where the floor mosaic (page 121) pictured a lovely swimming swan. The warrior dashed the marble mosaic to pieces with his battle ax, in rude sport, — to make sure, he said, whether the swan were alive or not.

The West Goths did not stay in Rome. Alaric meant to conquer the whole empire; but on his way into southern

Italy he died suddenly of a fever. His followers did not wish the grave of their proud leader to be known to his enemies. So captives were put at work turning a swift stream from its channel. Then in the old river bed a grave was dug to receive the body of the king with his favorite horse and his rich treasure. When the river had been turned back again into its old course, the captives were killed; so no one ever learned afterward where the king of the West Goths was buried.

The Goths now gave up the idea of conquering the whole Empire, and decided to find a place to settle down. They left Italy and marched west. In southern Gaul they found the *Vandals*, another Teutonic people who had broken across the Rhine while Alaric was conquering Rome. **The Goths drove these Vandals before them, into Africa, and took south Gaul and Spain for themselves.**

The Four Centuries from 400 to 800 A.D.
Are Called the *Dark Ages*

While Alaric had been leading his West Goths through southeastern Europe, **many other Teutonic nations had begun to break into the Empire,** to seize parts of it for themselves. The *Burgundians* settled in eastern Gaul, and part of France is known by their name to-day. A little later the *Franks*, who were finally to give their name to the whole of old Gaul, began to conquer the northern and central parts. The *East Goths*, and afterwards the *Lombards*, seized new homes in Italy, part of which is still called Lombardy. Tribes of *Angles* and *Saxons* found their way by boat across the North Sea to Britain. (Map facing page 142.)

Until about 600 A.D. swarms of barbarians followed one another through Europe, killing and plundering as they pleased. Then it took two centuries more for these conquering invaders to begin to be civilized. We call the whole four hundred years *the Dark Ages*.

Show the Dark Ages on your time line. (Notice that the first century of this period was the last century of the Empire.) How does the period compare in length with the time since Columbus discovered America?

OLD ROMAN BRIDGE, at Ronda Gorge in Spain, which lasted on through the Teutonic invasions and indeed is still in use. (See page 119.)

When Europe did begin to get itself in order again, it had become a very different place from the Europe of Roman times. It was now divided into many little districts under different rulers, and those rulers were all Teutons. The old cities were in ruins. Schools had disappeared. Roads and bridges were no longer kept in repair, and so there was neither trade nor peaceful travel. Indeed there were almost no skilled workers left to make beautiful or useful articles to sell.

In southern Gaul, and in parts of Italy and Spain, it is true, a few of the old Roman cities remained, and the people there kept up some of the Roman ways. But even those cities had almost no trade, and they were much poorer and had fewer people than in the old days.

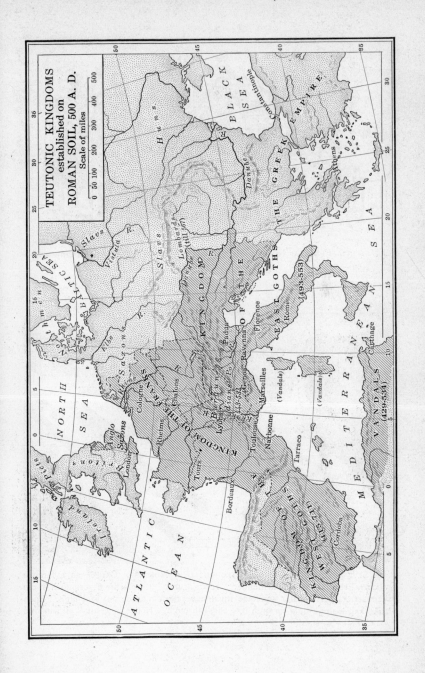

TEUTONIC KINGDOMS
established on
ROMAN SOIL, 500 A. D.
Scale of miles
0 50 100 200 300 400 500

FEAST IN A FRANKISH NOBLE'S HALL, as pictured in a tenth-century manuscript.

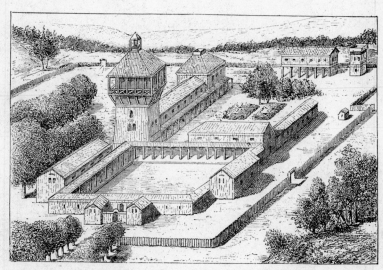

A SEVENTH-CENTURY WOODEN STRONGHOLD IN NORTHERN GAUL — as a famous modern French scholar, Parmentier, "reconstructs" it, from the descriptions in old manuscripts. The outer stockade must have been nine or ten feet high. Each stake had a small hole through it to shoot through. Notice how small all windows were. Why so small?

For a long time the Teutons would not live in the cities. Even in the country the fine marble villas of the Romans seemed like prisons to them. The only way they knew to live was in little villages, with woods and open fields around them. So they built wooden homes such as they had known in Germany. They did, however, sometimes build strong stone forts to keep off enemies, since now they could get stone quite easily, just by tearing down beautiful Roman buildings.

The only work the Teutons knew anything about was farming; and that was carried on now in a much poorer way than in the days of the Empire. Hundreds of thousands of acres which for centuries had been rich each year with crops, grew up now to brush and briars and finally to forest. Much land, too, went back to dismal swamps, since the old drains were not kept up.

Most of the work on the farms was still done by the

CHAIR made at Ravenna (Italy) in the 6th century, with beautiful and delicate wood carving, showing how the old Roman craftsmen kept on working in some cities of southern Europe.

serfs. All the centuries of strife and confusion had made little difference in the way that kind of people lived. Many of them, of course, had been killed, or had starved when Teutonic raiders had carried away the crops. Some of the bolder and stronger ones, too, had fled to the forests, to get their living as robbers and thieves. But a good many of them remained in their little farming villages; only now they tilled the land for a Teutonic master instead of for a Roman lord.

As time went on, in one way and another **the conquering Teutons and the conquered Romans found ways to live together in peace.** They began to intermarry; and in

SEVENTH-CENTURY FARM SERFS in what had been Roman Gaul. — From an old manuscript.

time all the people of each district thought of themselves as *one* people. **So, slowly, there grew up the new nations of Western Europe** — *English, French, Spanish, Italian, Dutch, Swiss, Belgian.* And these new peoples soon began to try to build a new civilization out of the ruins of the old. The Teutons had added some new ideas of their own to what was left of Roman ways; and, in the end, **this mixture was to make a better civilization in Western Europe than the Roman world had had.**

The other nations of Western Europe — *German, Danish, Norwegian, Swedish* — were built up by Teutonic peoples *who had stayed at home* and had never mixed with the Romans. Farther to the east were still other peoples who were not Teutons at all, the Slavs, Finns, Tartars, and Huns. All these were to be civilized later. For a time now, civilization was to spread north and east, instead of west (as we shall see in chapter xvi). Then, after a few hundred years, **the nations of Western Europe were to carry their new civilization westward once more,** — this time across the Atlantic. For these were the nations that were to found colonies in America.

Once All This New Europe United
To Drive Back the Huns

Once, early in the Dark Ages, the Teutonic invaders helped to keep off a more terrible peril than themselves. Countless hordes of *Huns*, wild horsemen from the vast plains of central Asia, were pressing westward into Europe, with their flocks and herds.

Milk and meat from these herds made most of their food. In war they moved from place to place swiftly, on their shaggy ponies. Indeed, they almost lived on horseback at all times; and the lasso, along with bows and lances, was a favorite weapon. They covered their horses with the scalps of their enemies. Some of their tribes painted their bodies for war, and others burned horrible scars upon their faces with hot irons, so that they might seem more terrible in battle. They were small in body, but very quick and active. To the Romans, and even to the fierce Teutons, they seemed a sort of wild beast, rather than men. Their faces were more flat than the faces of European peoples, and they had wide pug noses. The Roman writers like to say that they had no noses at all, but only horrible holes in the middle of their ugly faces.

The first Teutons who broke into the Roman world were really trying all the time to get away from these frightful Huns — who were pressing upon their rear. Then a little later **there arose among the Huns a great military chieftain named** *Attila*. This man united all the scattered tribes of Huns into one huge army, and in 451 A.D. he led them across the Rhine. They swept down upon Western Europe like a cloud of devouring locusts upon a fertile field. Attila himself liked to boast, " Where the hoof of my horse treads, grass never grows again."

Fortunately, when the Huns came into Gaul, the Roman power there had not altogether gone. **Near** *Chalons*, **Attila was met in battle by the last Roman legions** that were ever

seen in the West, under the Roman hero *Aëtius.* But
Aëtius did not have to fight alone. **Romans and Teutons
were wise enough to stop fighting each other and to unite
against this new danger.** Theodoric, king of the West Goths,
had led up his host from Spain to help turn Attila back.
And from the corners of Gaul came Frank and Burgundian
armies.

The " Battle of the Nations " was one of the really " de-
cisive " battles of the world. Huge numbers were slain.

ATTILA AND HIS HUNS. — A modern painting.

But at last the generalship of Aëtius, the discipline of his
legions, and the valor of his allies won the victory. Attila
left three hundred thousand dead on the field, it was said;
and the shattered fragments of his host rolled away again
toward Asia. Western Europe was saved for the new
nations, to be formed later by the union of Roman and
Teuton.

In his retreat, Attila passed through Italy, and some of
the people who lived near the head of the Adriatic fled from
him, seeking refuge in a group of islands there. These
people were *Veneti*, an old Italian tribe; and this settlement of theirs grew into the great city of *Venice*.

SUMMARY

The Teutons in their old homes lived much as the Indians did before white men came to America. They loved freedom and had a spirit of independence that helped Europe to make a new start. The first to break into the Empire were the West Goths, who sacked Rome, and finally settled in Spain. The four centuries from 400 to 800 A.D. are the Dark Ages. During the first two of those centuries many Teutonic peoples were swarming into the Empire, destroying and plundering as they moved. During the last two centuries the Romans and Teutons in Western Europe began to grow together into new nations, ready to build a new civilization. Once during the earlier period, Romans and Teutons united long enough to drive back the Huns (451 A.D.).

NEW WORDS

folk-moot   feud   wergeld   Valhalla   gnomes   heathen   allies

THOUGHT QUESTIONS AND THINGS TO DO

1. Study the maps facing 118 and 142. Which would be the easier to make? Which is most like the map of Europe to-day? How many of the peoples mentioned on page 144 can you find on a modern map of Europe?

2. Can you make models for an early Teutonic village?

3. Read the story of " Wulf the Saxon Boy " in Andrews' *Ten Boys*, for a good picture of early Teutonic life. You will like also to read Baldwin's *Story of Siegfried*, Mabie's *Norse Stories Retold*, and Tappan's *European Hero Stories*.

4. Imagine yourself a boy with Alaric, and tell what you saw and felt. Remember what the sight of a Roman city must have made that boy feel.

5. Imagine yourself a serf in Gaul when the Goths came there, and tell what happened to you and around you.

CHAPTER XV

THE CHURCH IN THE DARK AGES

When the Empire Fell, the Church became Stronger than Before

You may be surprised that the Christian Church was not destroyed by the violence and bloodshed of the Dark Ages. Instead, it grew stronger than it had been before. The churchmen did not flee from the barbarians, as some of the emperors did. In many a conquered town a bishop, or even a humble priest, faced the invaders fearlessly, and, with stern rebukes, commanded them to show mercy to the helpless townsmen. Such unselfish daring struck the savage conquerors with awe; and often, if they had not already become Christians, they soon did so.

These fierce warriors, it is true, may not have been very good Christians at heart, even though they had become Christians in name. But at least they did have respect for priests and bishops, and were willing to listen to their advice. So the Church became a great power for good. It protected the weak, stood for peace, and taught right living.

Before long, there was not a person in all Western Europe, Roman or Teuton, **who did not belong to the Church.** The priests, all through the centuries of disorder, united people in marriage, baptized their children, buried their dear ones, and constantly taught them the duties of a better life. They promised forgiveness of sins to those who repented of evil

148

Theodosius I ruled the Roman world a little before the year 400. He was one of the greatest Emperors; but at one time, angered because the people of a Roman town had murdered a number of his Teutonic soldiers, he had ordered a cruel massacre of thousands of the citizens. When he next appeared at church (at the Cathedral of Milan), *Bishop Ambrose* refused to let him take part in the worship until he had confessed his sin and done penance in sackcloth and ashes. Twelve centuries later the Dutch artist Rubens painted this picture to celebrate the courage of St. Ambrose. (Theodosius had always been devoted to the Church. He was the Emperor who first forbade all heathen worship, closed the old temples, and put an end to the Olympic Games because they were in honor of a pagan god.)

In his retreat after Chalons (page 146), Attila planned to sack Rome. There was no force there to resist him; but *Pope Leo the Great* met him and, by entreaties and threats, induced the barbarian to turn back. About a thousand years later the artist Raphael (page 271) celebrated Leo's peaceful victory by this painting on the wall of the papal palace, the *Vatican*, in Rome, where it may still be seen.

and who gave freely to the Church, and threatened everlasting punishment to all others. The most reckless and bloody chieftain, as death drew near, trembled before the humble priest who claimed power to close the gates of Heaven against him.

The new Teutonic kings found themselves ruling over more Romans than Teutons — sometimes ten or twenty times more. They had many hard questions to settle, quite different from any they had known in their old homes beyond the Rhine. Often there was no Teutonic law to fit these matters. But nearly always there had been a Roman law that fitted. **So the Teutonic kings turned to the Church for help,** for the churchmen were the only people left in Western Europe who knew the old Roman law.

Besides, not only the kings but all the smaller chiefs and nobles needed the help of the churchmen in other ways. These bold conquerors could handle a sword, but their fingers had never learned to manage a pen. They had now become lords of large estates, with power to rule people of many sorts living upon their lands. **They had to have clerks and secretaries who could keep records and advise them about the Roman customs.** Almost always these secretaries were churchmen, because for a long time they were about the only people left in Western Europe who could write. **Little by little, these advisers of the landlords and rulers** brought back many of the old Roman customs and so **helped save the old civilization.**

Western Europe had split into many nations; but in all of them the Church had one law, one way of doing things, one head, one religious service. A priest taught his people in their native language, of course, but he conducted the sacred service of the Church in Latin, in whatever country he lived. If priests from Britain, Spain, Italy, chanced to meet, they were able to speak together in Latin. Besides, the

Pope was above kings. His word was law throughout all Western Europe. **There were many nations, but only one Church.**

The *Monks* Did Most of All to Save Civilization

Even before the Teutons had come into the Empire, a good many Christians had become *monks*. These men thought the best way to save their souls was to go off by themselves in little groups, away from pleasures and temptations, so as to live quiet and holy lives. The home of a group of monks was a *monastery*.

POPE GREGORY THE GREAT (590–604) sending forth missionaries. — As pictured by a monk in an old book.

After the barbarian invasions began, there came to be a great many more monasteries — and also *convents* for women who wished to become *nuns*. For four hundred years a man or woman who loved a peaceful life had little chance to find one except in these places. Many a noble, and even powerful kings, grew tired of power and strife and found peace in the humble religious life of a monk.

When a man became a monk, he took three vows. He promised never to have any property of his own, never to marry, and to obey the head of the monastery in all things. He was allowed to live in a monastery for a year before taking these vows, so as to learn just what life there was like. But when he had once taken them, he could never go back to an ordinary life among men.

There were many rules for a monk to obey.   He must fast often, and spend many hours of each day in prayer.   He must also do hours of useful work each day, for the monks believed in the proverb about Satan and " idle hands."   Indeed, one of their mottoes was " To work is to pray."   Besides, they had to raise crops to support themselves.

A monk must be humble.   Even when at work in the fields he was expected to keep his head bowed and his eyes downcast.   He must be silent and waste no time in idle talk.   His dress was a long robe of coarse woolen cloth of black, gray, or brown.   It was tied about the waist with a cord, and it had a hood, or cowl, which could be pulled up over the head, so as almost to hide the face.   Monks were looked upon as more holy even than the priests.   So a man in this dress was nearly always safe, even in those days of violence — especially if he could mutter a few words of " priests' Latin," to prove that he really was learned enough to be a monk.

A group of monks usually

ABBEY OF CITEAUX. — From a monkish painting in a manuscript of the 12th century, as reproduced in Parmentier's *Album*. (A large monastery was often called an abbey.)   Notice the fields of grain culti- vated in narrow strips, as explained on page 196 and facing that page.

started their monastery in some deserted place — a swamp or deep forest or a barren wilderness — where no landlord would be likely to disturb them.   At first they put up just rude huts for shelter.   Slowly, by hard and constant toil, they drained the swamps, cut down the forest, and turned the bare places into fertile gardens. After a while, stately towers of stone took the place of the humble wooden huts.

The most important and most beautiful part of every monastery was its *church*, where the monks met for sacred worship several times each day. Usually that building formed one side of an open square, and the buildings in which the monks lived made the other three sides. One was taken up by the rows of narrow cells in which they slept. On another was the long dining hall. On the fourth were the library and writing rooms.

CLOISTERS OF SALISBURY (England) TO-DAY.
Built about 1300.

This whole square was called the *cloister*. The open space was often used for a graveyard. Around all four sides of that open space was a covered porch where the monks would come for quiet walks when their work for the day was done. Outside the cloister, but near it, were the work rooms; for the monks made everything that was used in the monastery. So here were blacksmith shops, bake-ovens, shops for spinning, weaving, and dyeing, and for tanning leather and making it into shoes, and for other kinds of work. In time the monks became so skillful in all these things that neighboring villages learned a great deal from them. The nuns, too, in their convents did fine kinds of weaving and embroidery that people of later times have been glad to copy.

Around all these buildings of the monastery ran a high and strong stone wall. But one important building sometimes had to be outside the wall. This was the monastery *mill* for grinding grain into meal. Late in Roman times, men had learned to make flour by grinding grain between two heavy millstones *turned by water power*, instead of by a horse—as in the picture on page 96. So the mill had to be built where there was a stream of running water.

Outside the wall, too, lay the monastery fields for grain and the woodlands and meadows where herds of cattle and swine were pastured. For hundreds of years the monks were the best farmers in Europe. They learned how to do many things in the old Roman ways; they raised the best crops of grain and fruit; and they bred the best kind of cattle to be found anywhere. From these monastery farms the people roundabout, after a while, learned to farm better than they had been doing.

MONK AND PUPIL—a dictation exercise; as pictured in an old book.

The only schools of the Dark Ages were kept by the monks. They taught gladly not only the bright boys who were planning to be monks or priests, but also anyone else who wished to come to them to learn. **And for hundreds of years they wrote the only books that were made in Western Europe**—sermons and hymns and records of happenings that they thought important enough to write down. Even with the help of their records, we don't know a great deal about the Dark Ages; but the little that we do know comes mostly from their books. Some of their beautiful hymns have been sung in all Christian churches ever since.

In their dimly lighted cells the monks copied *old* books with painstaking care, and often they decorated each page that they wrote with beautifully painted capital letters and with

A Bishop Crowning an Early King of the Franks (8th century) in the Cathedral of Aachen (page 159) — as a modern scholar (Parmentier) imagines the scene.

Cloister at Mont Saint-Michel (France). Older students would know at first sight that this building was not put up earlier than 1200 A.D. In the picture above it, you will notice that the arches are the round Roman arches; but in the thirteenth century, as you are told elsewhere in this book, there came in a new style of building, called Gothic, of which one trait was the *pointed* arch. (See also the cloister pictured on page 152, and the cuts on 227, 231, and facing 237, 238, 239, etc.)

Church for all Western Europe, with one language, one service, one government, and one teaching about how people ought to live. The monasteries that grew up during the Dark Ages helped to save civilization by the hard work and skill of the monks, by their love for learning, and by their holy lives.

New Words

monk   monastery   nun   convent   cowl   cloister   abbot   dole

Thought Questions and Things to Do

1. Make a model of a monastery.

2. Make a list of reasons why a man or a woman in the Dark Ages might wish to take the three vows. Do you think there were more reasons then than now?

3. This is a good place to look back for a review of the schools of the various peoples we have read about. You will find still others before we come to the schools of to-day. Which of them all do you like best? Let members of the class write school-boys' diaries for all the different periods.

4. List the important things invented by the Romans and handed on to us. What inventions of other peoples did they save for us? In what ways did the Church help to save all these things?

HEATHEN VIKINGS (page 157; some of Charlemagne's chief enemies) burning the dead body of a comrade in his ship — the most honorable funeral among them. The Viking village may be seen at the foot of one of the cliffs that border the fjord.

CHAPTER XVI

THE EMPIRE OF CHARLEMAGNE

Charlemagne Saved and Spread Civilization

During the Dark Ages **the Franks had conquered all of Gaul and part of western Germany. Then, a little before 800 A.D., a very great man became their king.** His name was *Charlemagne,* or Karl the Great. A Frankish priest, who was his secretary, wrote down a great many things about him, so that we know just how he looked and lived.

Charlemagne, says this priest, was very tall and strong, with yellow hair and large blue eyes. His face was usually cheerful and kind, but when he did become angry, his eyes blazed with flames of fire. He ate and drank little, and dressed simply; but on very important occasions he wore an embroidered cloak and a jeweled crown. He liked to ride and to hunt, and he was a very good swimmer. After he was a grown man he learned to read; but though he practiced faithfully, all he ever learned to write was his name.

Charlemagne ruled for forty-six years (768–814). He was not fond of fighting. But just at this time new swarms of barbarians were attacking Europe, and **he had to spend a large part of his life in wars** against them. The greatest danger came from the fierce *Saxons*, who lived near the North Sea from the Rhine to the Elbe (map after page 158). After years of trouble, Charlemagne decided that the only way to stop their attacks was to conquer them in their own country and make them civilized Christians. (The cut facing 167 shows *how* he had to convert some of them.)

It took nine long and cruel wars to master the Saxons. Time after time, Charlemagne was victorious, but as soon as he turned his back they rose against him again. Finally he punished them by a horrible massacre. After winning a great victory over them, he demanded that they surrender to him forty-five hundred of their chiefs and best warriors, and then he put to death all those helpless prisoners.

In the end the Saxons were subdued and baptized. And **when the fighting was over, Charlemagne ruled them wisely and kindly.** He sent colonies of Franks among them. Churches and monasteries were built in the Saxon forests, and civilization spread slowly eastward to the Elbe River, — into a region which the Roman Empire had not been able to conquer.

Charlemagne also led his armies down into Italy to help the Pope against the Lombards (page 141). The Pope had become a ruler (just like a king) over a large stretch of territory in Italy. Now the Lombards had seized all of his lands except Rome itself, and were trying to capture that. Charlemagne defeated them and sent their king to a monastery. Then he gave the Pope back his lands and made himself king of the rest of Italy.

These were only a few of Charlemagne's wars. On every frontier warlike peoples were threatening his lands. Invaders even came by sea — the savage *Vikings*, who took that name because their homes were along the *viks*, or bays, of Denmark and Norway. (Sometimes these Vikings were called *Northmen* or *Norsemen*.   Can you see why?)   Charlemagne beat them off finally by building fleets of larger ships than theirs.   Then they stopped troubling the lands of the Franks during the rest of his reign — though they plundered far and wide in other countries.

Charlemagne became " Emperor of the Romans "

If you look at the map after this page, you will see that **Charlemagne came to rule over most of Western Europe.** He did not have Britain or Spain or the Scandinavian lands. But he did have large territories east of the Rhine.   It was his earnest hope to set up a firm and good government over all the peoples of his vast dominions, so that a better civilization might grow up there.

In the year 800 he visited Rome again, to help the Pope put down rebellions in Italy.   On Christmas Day, as he knelt in prayer before the high altar in the Church of St. Peter's, **the Pope placed upon his head a gold crown and saluted him " *Emperor of the Romans.*"**

This new title brought Charlemagne more respect from the many peoples in his wide realms, and so gave him more authority over them, than he could ever have had with just his old title " king of the Franks."   No Saxon or Burgundian or Lombard or Goth liked to be reminded that his nation had been made subject to the Franks.   But all of them, as well as all the old Roman populations, were proud to think of themselves as belonging to a new " Roman Empire " of the West.

Still you must not think that the " Empire of Charlemagne " was like the old Roman Empire in much else but its name.   We have already read a little about how people lived in 800 A.D.   Western Europe was still ignorant and poor and full of misery.   All Charlemagne's power could not keep down the bands of robbers or build up trade or even make good roads.   He could get no money from his people

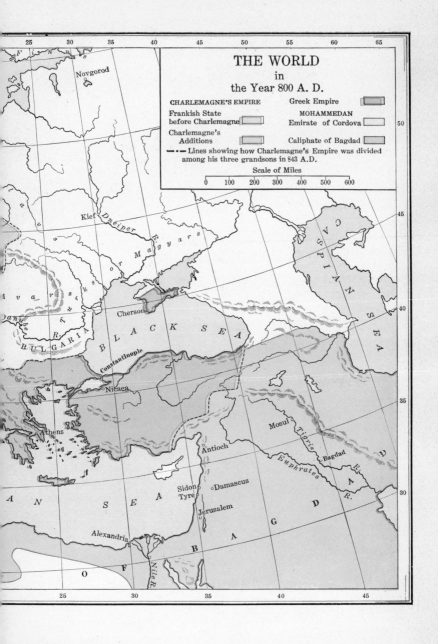

THE WORLD
in
the Year 800 A.D.

CHARLEMAGNE'S EMPIRE   Greek Empire

Frankish State
before Charlemagne   MOHAMMEDAN
Emirate of Cordova

Charlemagne's
Additions   Caliphate of Bagdad

---- Lines showing how Charlemagne's Empire was divided
among his three grandsons in 843 A.D.

Scale of Miles

0   100   200   300   400   500   600

for taxes, because there *was* almost no money. Instead of
paying taxes, his subjects served him in war as soldiers,
without pay, and his nobles served him as governors and
officials without salaries.

The Emperor's court was supported by his many farms,
scattered over the country. It would have been hard to
carry the grain and other food stuffs
from these to Charlemagne's capital,
far in the north, at Aachen. So
Charlemagne and his court moved
from one farm to another and ate the
produce on the spot where it was
raised. In this way, too, the Emperor
could see to it that each farm was well
taken care of. He himself made exact
rules for the farming and took great
care that his stewards got each chicken
and each egg that was due from his
serfs. It was an anxious day for the
steward of a royal farm when he
learned that it was his turn to receive a visit from the keen-
eyed Emperor.

Serving-man with lamp in
time of Charlemagne, pic-
tured in an old manuscript.

Charlemagne tried his best to start schools. He did all
he 'could to help the monastery schools, and he opened
some new ones, under the charge of his bishops, in towns that
had begun to grow up. At his own court he set up a " School
of the Palace " for sons of his nobles. He persuaded the
most famous scholar of all Europe, the English monk *Alcuin*,
to come there to teach, and he himself often joined the young
people at their lessons.

**Charlemagne's rule has been called " a point of light in
the Dark Ages."** In many ways he made things better
than they had been for four hundred years. He put down
some of the robbers and kept out barbarians. He took great
care to appoint good officers to look after the distant parts

of his empire, and he made many just laws. He helped to keep the old Roman Empire and civilization from being forgotten, and he spread civilization farther to the East. His Empire was a union of several different peoples of Western Europe, and it showed that they could be much better off as friends under one government than as enemies.

IMAGINARY SCENE IN THE SCHOOL OF THE PALACE. — The modern artist who painted this picture has given Charlemagne a full beard, but writers of his own time all say that he wore only a mustache. (See also the cut facing page 167.) The white-bearded man a little behind Charlemagne is Alcuin.

Sad to say, **when Charlemagne's firm hand and wise head were gone, there was no one strong enough to keep his Empire together.** The map after page 158 shows how his three grandsons divided it. The eastern part (which had never been part of the Roman Empire) was later to grow into the *German nation*. The western part, where the people were a mixture of Franks and Roman Gauls, later became *France*. In the other part, between these two, many little nations grew up. From time to time France and Germany swallowed most of these, and kept on quarreling over the rest of them until just a few years ago.

It was a long time before there was a strong and good government for any of these divisions of the Empire. This was partly because Charlemagne's descendants were weak men. But even good men and strong rulers would have found it hard to govern well during the next centuries. **The Norse pirates were plundering everywhere.** After they had ravaged the coasts, their light boats would swarm up the rivers.   Then the Vikings would take horse and ride through the country far and wide, sacking many a village and farmstead.   They even stabled their steeds in the cathedral of Aachen, the favorite capital of Charlemagne.

For these worshipers of Thor and Woden robbed even the monasteries and churches, which the early Teutonic invaders had usually spared.   There indeed they found the most valuable booty — richly woven altar-cloths and sacred vessels of gold and silver.   Fearful stories were told of their cruelty, and one of the prayers in the Church service in the tenth century came to be, "From the fury of the Northmen, O Lord, deliver us."

By the year 1000 the many little tribes of Northmen had grown into three nations in their own homes — Sweden, Norway, and

THRONE OF CHARLEMAGNE in the Cathedral at Aachen.

Denmark — and were ruled by strong kings.   Missionaries from the south carried Christianity to them, and they became a part of the one great Church of Western Europe. Then their savage raids stopped, though they were still famous seamen and voyagers.

But while the raids had been going on, **many Northmen had settled on the coasts of different parts of Europe.**   Some of them had seized a district in the north of France.   The Franks turned their name *Northman* into *Norman*, and their new home came to be known as *Normandy*, a name which that region still has.   Other Northmen had settled in eastern England, where, after long wars, they became united

with the other people who lived there.   Others had made
settlements in Russia and were finally to start a strong
kingdom there.   Still others seized upon parts of eastern
Ireland and the little islands north of Scotland, like the
Shetlands, and even upon parts of southern Italy.   They
also discovered and col-

onized Iceland and the
coast of Greenland.

About the year 1000,
some of the Vikings from
Iceland on their way to
Greenland (led by a cer-
tain *Leif*, son of Eric
the Red) were driven
southward by a storm
and discovered America.
Afterward they made
several voyages there.
But they stayed only a
few years and did not
know that they had

This boat (the *Leif Ericson*) was built in Norway in
1925, to be a copy of the Viking ship that discovered
America in the year 1000.   It is 42 feet long, 13 feet
wide, and 6 feet deep, and at each end a small sleeping cabin is roofed over.   In the stormy spring of
1926 a Norwegian crew crossed the Atlantic in this
boat, from Bergen to Boston, by way of Iceland.

found a great continent.   Other European nations did not
hear about their find, and it was soon forgotten, though
some of the old Norse poems told about it.   America was left
to be really discovered several hundred years later.

NEW WORDS

steward   Viking   pirate   raid

THINGS TO DO

1. Make your own summary for this chapter.

2. Show Charlemagne's Empire on an outline map.   Mark the
part to which he spread civilization.   Name the modern countries
that were parts of his Empire.

3. Can you make a model of a Viking boat?   Study the picture
of one on this page.   Perhaps you can find larger ones.

4. Mark on a map the places where the Vikings settled.

5. Write the story of a Viking raid.   You might imagine yourself one of the Vikings, or one of those living in a raided settlement.

6. Compare Charlemagne as a conqueror and as a ruler with Alexander and with Cæsar.

7. In later times many legends grew up about the court of Charlemagne.   Some of these are told in Baldwin's *Story of Roland*. You would also enjoy Church's *Stories of Charlemagne*.   Report on some of these stories to the class, and also on the story of the Norse settlement in America, as they are told in Hall's *Viking Tales*, Johnston's *Our Little Viking Cousin*, Stuart's *Boy through the Ages*, and Tappan's *European Hero Stories*.

CHAPTER XVII

HOW BRITAIN BECAME ENGLAND

(*449–900* A.D.)

While the Franks were slowly changing Gaul into *France*
and other Teutonic tribes across the Rhine were becoming
a German people, the *Angles* and *Saxons* were changing
Britain into *England*.   To see how that happened we must
go back to the beginning of the Dark Ages

Even before the year 400, the coasts of Roman Britain had
been raided, year after year, by savage *Angles* and *Saxons*
(page 141).   One of these names became our name *English*
and it is convenient to call all of these raiders English.

The pirates who came most to Britain lived in the country
just south of Denmark — a land of dark forests, gloomy
marshes, and bare sandhills.   They had no wealth but their
swords and armor and long light boats.   The fruit-laden
orchards of Roman Britain, the ripe yellow grain in its wide
and fertile fields, the herds of fat cattle, the gold and silver
of its splendid villas, seemed tempting booty, worth any
risk.

Roman warships patrolled the coast, to keep them off, and
every little way along the shore there was a strong garrison
of Roman troops.   Often the ships caught the frail pirate
boats at sea and destroyed them.   But if a band were lucky,
it might slip past the ships on a stormy night.   Then it
might ravage a few farms, or even a rich villa, and, after
sacrificing some of the captives to Woden, it would carry
off the others for slaves, with the rest of the booty.

Sometimes, of course, even when the sea-rovers had reached Britain safely, the Roman soldiers in some garrison in the neighborhood were warned by signal fires or messengers, and caught them at their bloody work. Then would follow a fierce and merciless struggle, from which few raiders could expect to escape alive. But the reckless English found their highest joy in fighting, and welcomed death in battle. So they never stopped coming. A Roman poet wrote of them:

" Foes are they, fierce beyond all others, and as cunning as they are fierce. The sea is their school, and the storm their friend. They are the wolves of the sea, and they prey on all the world."

Then, in 408 A.D., the Roman soldiers in Britain were all ordered to Italy to meet the invasion of that land by Alaric's Goths (page 140). So the peaceful Britons were left to defend themselves against enemies on every side. At first the greatest peril seemed to come from the north, for the wild Picts and Scots of the highlands now swept down across the undefended Roman wall (page 116). **In 449 A.D. the Britons called in a band of sea-rovers** to fight against this enemy, *promising them rich lands for pay.*

So began the Teutonic conquest of this part of the old Roman world. The English easily drove back the Picts, but then they seized for themselves much more land than had been promised. And when their kinsmen across the North Sea heard how easy this was, they too began to come in many little bands, to seize homes for themselves in different parts of Britain.

The invaders had to come by water, in their long, open, fifty-oared boats, bringing women and children with them. So the conquest was slow, though steady. A little expedition of a few hundred would seize as much land as it could use, driving out or killing the Britons, except a few perhaps who might be kept for slaves. They even destroyed the churches and monasteries. (For this, you remember, was three centuries before Charlemagne began to Christianize the Saxons.) The next year these English might welcome a new band of kinsmen from the continent, and pass them on through their little territory, to win a home for themselves from the Britons farther inland.

It took nearly two hundred years of constant little wars to make Britain into Angle-land, or England; but in the end the job was done thoroughly. All the eastern part of the island was taken up with little English settlements, and these grew together slowly into several small English kingdoms (map opposite). In all these *the language was English* — which was a Teutonic speech, like German and Norwegian. There are many Latin words in our English of to-day, but these came in later. Those early pirates brought to Britain the main foundation of our English speech.

On the other hand, the Franks and Goths and Lombards had settled down finally among the old Roman peoples in Gaul and Spain and Italy, and for the most part adopted their language. So to-day French and Spanish and Italian are more like Latin than they are like any Teutonic speech.

For a time the English in their new homes in England lived much as all the early Teutons had done (page 135). In the old Roman towns the ruins of stone buildings still stood, but there was no one to live in them. The English called one of the deserted towns *London* — which was as near as they could come to pronouncing its old Roman name — and some other Roman place-names were kept, just as Indian names for lakes and rivers are often kept by us. But there was little else to show that Roman civilization had ever possessed the land.

Most of the Britons that had not been killed or made slaves **had fled to the woods and mountains of western**

BRITAIN
about 600 A.D.

Scots and Piets

IRELAND

R. Forth

NORTHUMBRIA

Jarrow

Whitby

York

R. Humber

Chester

MERCIANS
(West Angles)

Boston

(North Folk)

EAST
ANGLES

EAST
SAXONS

(South Folk)

MIDDLE
ANGLES

London

St Albans

Runnymede

SURREY

Canterbury

KENT

SOUTH
SAXONS

Hastings

Bristol
Bath
(Wessex)
Winchester

WEST SAXONS

WELSH

Severn

BRITISH

(Cornwall)

BAPTISM OF A HEATHEN SAXON KING CONQUERED BY CHARLEMAGNE (page 157), as a modern painter represents it. The tall figure looking on (leaning on his sword) is Charlemagne. Some Teutonic rulers in Britain were converted in much the same way by conquering kings who had already become "Christians," —after Augustine began his work (page 168).

Britain. Their descendants are the *Welsh* of to-day. For several centuries the Welsh kept themselves independent of the English kings, — as did the Scots also in the north of the island.

The Welsh lost most of their old Roman way of living during the hundreds of years of fighting, but they **did keep their Christian religion. So, too, did the Irish,** who had

ROMAN BATH (as it looks to-day) in the city of Bath.   Many more Roman remains are found in good condition in the *west* of England (where Bath is located) than in the eastern part of the island.   Can you think of a reason for this?

been converted in Roman days by the good missionary *St. Patrick.* For three hundred years after the English invaded Britain, there was more civilization in Ireland than in Britain. Indeed the Irish sent missionaries to try to convert the heathen English, and even started a few monasteries in the north of England. But the monks who finally converted the English to Christianity came from Rome.

An interesting story is told of how the Christian religion was brought to the new English kingdoms. Some English boys had been carried off by pirates and were finally offered for sale in the great slave market in Rome. Their yellow hair and fair faces drew much notice among the dark Italians ; and a good monk *Gregory*, passing by, asked, " From what people do those fair child slaves come ? " " They are Angles," said the slave dealer. " Alas," exclaimed the kind monk, " they look more like Angels." And, as he went his way,

St. Martin's Church, near Canterbury. — From a photograph. Parts of the building are very old, and may have belonged to a church of the Roman period. At all events, on this site was the first Christian church in Britain used by Augustine and fellow missionaries. A tomb, said to be Queen Bertha's (page 169), is shown in the church. About three miles to the west you see the later Cathedral, rising above the city of Canterbury.

he pondered whether he might not find some way to carry the teachings of Jesus to such fair-looking heathen.

Gregory himself never found time to do this. But later he became Pope (page 150). Then he remembered the fair slave boys, and **sent the monk *Augustine*, with** forty companions, **to carry the Christian religion to the English.**

This was in *597* A.D. Augustine landed in the little kingdom of Kent (map facing 166). The king there had married a princess of the Franks, who was already a Christian. This Queen Bertha persuaded her husband to listen to the good monks. Finally he consented, though he refused to hear them inside a building, for fear their strange god might work some magic upon him and his people. So he gathered his officials together on a hill near *Canterbury* to meet the monks.

Augustine came before him, bearing high the cross and followed by the procession of monks in their long robes, chanting a hymn of the Church. Then Augustine explained Christ's teachings of mercy and love. "All this that you say may be true," said the king at last, "but it sounds strangely different from the religion of my fathers. I will take time to consider it." But he did give the monks permission to use an old Roman church near by, and soon he and his people were all baptized as Christians.

This beautiful marble relief was carved above the door of St. Augustine College at Canterbury by a famous English sculptor, about sixty years ago, to represent Augustine preaching before the heathen king of Kent.

This was a good beginning. **It took a hundred years more to carry the Christian religion to all the English kingdoms in the island.** Sometimes even after a kingdom had seemed converted, a new king would drive out the priests and set up the old worship of Woden again. But in the end Christianity won, and the archbishop of Canterbury became archbishop of all England.

The English now began to be more civilized. Priests and monks came to them from Rome, and some of the English visited Rome and other lands. Soon they began even to build small towns in England. Many monasteries, too, grew up, and some of them came to have fine schools. You remember that when Charlemagne was looking for an especially good teacher for his Palace School, he found one in England.

One of the famous English teachers and writers of this time was a monk named *Bede,* who taught in a monastery in the north of England. He wrote a history of England and many other learned books in Latin, and he also put some of the Bible stories into English verse. Hard as it was to travel, scholars came from many lands to learn from him. At one time, there were sixty of them gathered about him. Even as he lay dying, his scholars sat near him, listening eagerly to the words that fell from his lips, writing them down as he spoke, though they were weeping bitterly at the thought of losing their master and friend.

A little after the time of Charlemagne (look at your time line), **all the English kingdoms in the island became united into one.** Soon after that, one of the greatest of all English kings, *Alfred the Great,* ruled England for thirty years (871–901).

Alfred's grandfather, *Egbert,* had been king at first only in *Wessex;* but he was a wise and powerful ruler, and finally all the other Teutonic kings in England accepted him as head-king. Then (827 A.D.) he took a new title—"King of the English," which his son kept after him.

This second "king of the English" had four sons. The mother of these boys was an unusual woman. She could read; and she wanted her children to have some learning, even though they were princes! An interesting story tells how one day she showed them a beautiful book, such as the most skillful monks made. It had many pen-drawn pictures, delicately colored in red and blue and gold; and almost

A Page from the Wingfield Horae.

A manuscript made for the first Duke of Buckingham. This is a fine illustration of the elaborate way the medieval monks illuminated their manuscripts.

every paragraph began with a bright-colored letter. (You can see a page of a book of that sort facing page 170.) The boys admired it greatly, and the mother promised to give it to the one who first learned to read and repeat certain poems in it. But the older boys were too busy with their sports and in learning to use sword and shield; so Alfred, who was only four years old, won the prize.

ALFRED being scolded by the cowherd's wife. See page 172.

But as Alfred grew up, it became necessary for him, too, for a long time to give all his attention to sword and shield. Danish Vikings had begun to attack England in huge fleets, and Alfred helped his brothers fight them. The Danes managed to conquer all the English part of the island except Wessex. Then, in 871 A.D., came a great battle in which they killed King Ethelred, Alfred's brother.

His other brothers were already dead; so **Alfred became king. The first half of his reign was taken up with war** to rescue his people from the terrible invaders. The Danes were now overrunning Wessex itself. At one time Alfred was left with only a handful of followers.

Many stories are told of Alfred's adventures in those days. Once he had to hide all alone in the hut of a friendly Saxon cowherd. The man's wife did not know who the guest was, and she rather grudged him his food from her scanty store. As Alfred sat by the fire one day, while she was baking the flat cakes of bread before it, she ordered him crossly to watch the cakes while she went on an errand. The king was busy making plans to defeat the Danes, and forgot the cakes. The woman smelled them burning, and came running in to save them. She scolded him sharply for his carelessness, saying, — " You eat enough of them I notice, when *I* take care of them! "

Another time, it is said, Alfred disguised himself as a minstrel, and went into the chief Danish camp to learn its strength and how to attack it. He even sang before the Danish king, and was able to learn the enemy's plans. Then, finally getting away from the Danes, who very much wanted to keep such a singer of sweet songs in their camp, he gathered some faithful Saxon farmers and nobles, and attacked the enemy.

This time, Alfred was victorious. The Danes were defeated and shut up in their camp, so that they could not escape to the sea or to other parts of England. Finally they agreed to leave Wessex for the north of England and to be baptized as Christians. New struggles broke out at once, however, and Alfred won more victories. Finally a treaty of peace was made in 886. It was agreed that the Danes should possess the northeastern half of England (all north of the Roman Road, Watling Street; map facing page 166), but in return their king was to obey Alfred as head-king.

The Danes were not much different from the English anyway. They had come from the same part of Europe as the old English pirates, only they had remained heathen and savage three hundred years after the English had gone away. Now that they became Christians, it was easy for them to mix with the English into one people.

The rest of his life Alfred spent in good works for his people. To prevent new attacks by heathen Vikings from

Denmark, he built the first real English navy, making his ships on a new plan, much larger than the Danish boats. He rebuilt the towns that had been burned and also many churches and monasteries. He made it easier for his people to know what the laws were by writing them down in a simple *code*. (Do you remember where we used and explained this word?)

Alfred did this modestly. He selected from the old laws what seemed to him " most right," and added only a few new laws. Said he, " I durst not set down in writing *much of my own*, for it was not known to me what of it would prove pleasing to those who should come after me." But the king was firm in making all the people *obey* the law. Rich men and nobles could not escape punishment if they were guilty of doing wrong, and the poor were sure to get justice.

More than anything else, Alfred wished to build up schools. He hunted out learned men and skillful teachers from other countries. This was necessary, because during the Danish invasions the schools that had started up in England (page 170) had been almost wholly destroyed. Alfred said that when he became king, there was not a priest in the kingdom who could understand the *meaning* of the Latin church service, though they could repeat the *words*.

He wanted his schools to teach not only in Latin but also *in English*. There were no textbooks at all in English; so the busy king wrote four with his own hand. He did this mainly by turning into English some famous old Latin books, but he added many thoughts of his own. These were the first books of *English prose*.

One of the books that Alfred put into English was the history of England that the good monk Bede had written in Latin. Another was a Roman history of the world. To this volume Alfred added a story of his own about two Viking voyages to Iceland in his own day, with a description of the frozen seas of the north and the strange beasts, like the walrus, that were found there.

Every one was amazed at the king's tireless industry. He had no time for idleness or even for play. He planned buildings on a larger and better scale, as well as ships and forts. He wished his people to build up trade again with other parts of the world, and so he offered a prize to any trader who made three voyages to the Mediterranean. He taught goldsmiths how to work better in their precious metals than they had ever known before in England.

OLD ENGLISH LANTERN
with horn sides.

Alfred himself made new and useful inventions. He taught the monks how to count the hours in their services, by using candles that would burn just four hours each. That is, he made candles of such a length that six of them, burning one after another, would last from sunrise to sunrise. But you know that a candle burns faster than usual if a draft blows upon it. So Alfred invented a lantern with sides of thin transparent horn, so that a candle would give light all the time and yet burn *evenly*. Such a light, too, could be carried from place to place, even in a high wind, without being blown out. (No one had yet learned to use *glass* sides for a lantern.)

Alfred saw carefully, too, to the training of his children, and they became great and good rulers after him. In his own time the English people called him " Alfred the Truthteller," and after his death he was spoken of as " England's Darling." Surely few men have so well earned the title " the Great," which also is often given him. He seems to have been as good as he was wise and brave. Toward the end of his life he once said, " It has ever been my wish to live worthily while I live, and to leave to those who shall come after me a memory of me in good works."

New Words

navy　　*prose*　　*poetry*　　*heathen*　　*treaty*　　*verse*

Thought Questions and Things to Do

1. Make your own summary for this chapter and mark two dates from it on your time line. Who came first, Alfred or Charlemagne? Augustine or Alcuin?

2. In what ways do you find Charlemagne and Alfred alike? How were they *unlike?* Charlemagne ruled over much the greater territory: do you think that made him the greater king?

3. Read Longfellow's poem, *The Discoverer of the North Cape.*

Before beginning the next chapter, let us stop to explain some "time names."

The first part of this book told the story of what we call *Ancient Times.* It is usual to say that Ancient Times *ended* when the Teutons broke into the Roman World — about 400 A.D. Those Teutonic invasions, as you have seen, also *began* what we call the " Dark Ages " — from 400 to about 800 A.D. The five centuries after 800 are called the " Feudal Age." That Feudal Age, with the two centuries after it and the Dark Ages before it, make all together what we call the *Middle Ages.* That name, then, belongs to the centuries between 400 A.D. and 1500 A.D., or between Ancient Times and *Modern Times.* (Sometimes we call the Middle Ages " Medieval Times.")

Of course no one could ever say at any one moment, " Now the Dark Ages are just over and the Feudal Age has begun," or " Last week we finished the Feudal Age." But it is convenient to have names for these great groups of centuries, even if they do not always fit exactly.

A LORD AND VASSALS HOLDING COURT (page 183),
as shown in an old German woodcut.

CHAPTER XVIII

THE FEUDAL AGE: THE FIGHTERS

We have read about the men of peace in the Dark Ages (chapter xv). But the people who made the most noise in the world at that time, and in the Feudal Age afterward, were the men of war. In fact, through all the Middle Ages **the fighting men owned all the land and nearly all the fine buildings and other property.** They were the " nobles," the " lords," and the rulers.

To be sure, there were good reasons why fighting men were so important at that time. After Charlemagne there was hardly anywhere a strong king to keep order, and the common people did not yet know how to protect themselves by joining together in a government of their own. Life became unsafe because of the new barbarian invaders and the great numbers of bandits and robbers. **So, during this time of violence and disorder, there grew up a curious way of living which we call** *feudalism.*

In every part of the country, each strong man took what he wanted, if he was strong enough, and kept it if he was stronger than other men who wanted it. Every brave and strong leader would gather together a band of fighters and fortify his buildings. Then he could protect his lands and make invaders and greedy neighbors think it best to leave him alone.

Before long, some of the weaker neighbors of such a leader would be glad to get him to protect them, too. They called him their *overlord*, or *liege*, and they became his *vassals*. They hadn't any money to pay for this protection, so they paid in *services*. They would always offer to give up their lands to the lord ; but he would let the vassal keep the land, only now it was not quite his own. It became what was called a *fief*.

The vassal then became a sort of *tenant* on his old land, and paid a queer kind of *rent* for it. He had to be faithful to his lord, and to make him gifts at certain times, and especially to *come to his aid*, when needed, with a certain number of armed men. The more land he had, the more men he must bring. This *military service* was the most important part of the payment he made for being protected. And the more vassals a lord had, the more powerful he was and the better able to protect them all.

If one of the vassals had land enough, then he, in turn, might give out parts of it to trusty followers. These men then became *his* vassals, and he became their liege. His own overlord, too, was almost always the vassal of the king of the country or of some other lord more powerful than himself. So, you see, **most of these fighting landowners were both lords and vassals at the same time,** and every vassal "did homage" to some higher lord. (See cut facing page 190.) Finally it came to be understood that the king of a country was the chief landlord and the liege lord over all landholders in his kingdom. But sometimes a vassal grew powerful enough to defy his lord, and perhaps to wage war against him, even if that lord were the king.

Both lords and vassals were "nobles." That is, they *paid for their land by military service*. A noble was not supposed to do any useful work. All the labor on the lands of lords and vassals was done by serfs or servants. Of course, a noble had to keep bands of soldiers, or " men-at-arms." Such fighters were not noble (unless they owned land), but they, too, despised all workers.

Sometimes one of these rough soldiers might save a noble's life in battle or do him some other great service, so that the noble would reward him with a fief. Then that fighter, too, became a vassal and a noble.

When a vassal died, his fief passed to his oldest son or other nearest heir. If that heir were a woman, she had to take a husband at once, so that there would be a vassal to do the military service for the fief. The husband was usually picked out by the liege lord, not by the lady. Indeed, a lord could force any of his women vassals to take any husband he chose for her, or else to give up her fief and go into a convent.

In order to be safe at all during the feudal age, **every noble had to have a fortified house, or** *castle.* At first this was usually a wooden blockhouse in an open space, surrounded by a stockade and ditch. But in the tenth and eleventh centuries, the nobles forced their serfs to build for them enormous buildings of massive stone. Such castles stood at every ford and above each mountain pass and on every hill-top that commanded a fertile plain.

If you ever visit England or Germany or France, you will see many of these castles. To-day they are only interesting, ivy-covered ruins. In the Middle Ages, each of them was the home and the fort of some powerful lord. In its under-ground dungeons he kept his prisoners, loaded with rusty chains. In the halls above, almost as dark and gloomy, he lived with his family and his troops of armed followers and servants. From its gates he rode forth across the draw-bridge, at the head of a band of iron-clad men-at-arms, to drive off invaders or to attack the castle of some rival.

The outer wall often inclosed a good many acres (twenty or more). Much of this was open space, or *courtyards*. Here the lord's serfs might take refuge with their cattle and their few other possessions if it was known in time that a hostile raid was on the way.

The wall was perhaps twenty feet high and six or eight feet thick. The top of the wall was called the *battlements*. It was left level — so that people might walk around it; but the outer edge was raised, about a man's height, above this walk, and every little way in this raised edge there were openings through which the garrison could shoot arrows at their foes, or hurl great rocks or boiling pitch down upon them, if they tried to place ladders against the wall.

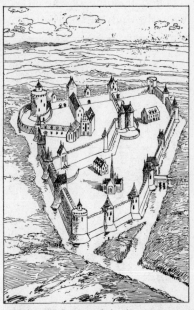

MEDIEVAL CASTLE of the larger sort, as "reconstructed" in Gautier's *La Chevalerie*. Why did the towers stand out farther than the rest of the wall? Compare with the picture of the earlier wooden stronghold facing 143, to see likeness in plan.

An attacking force, indeed, did not find it easy to reach the wall. Outside it, all around the castle, ran usually a wide, deep ditch, or *moat*, filled with water. The bridge from the castle gate across this moat was a *drawbridge*, which could be drawn up against the castle wall by strong chains. At night, and always in time of danger, the drawbridge was kept up.

If the enemy did manage to cross the moat, he found his troubles just begun. The gate was a mighty door, several inches thick, of solid oak sheeted with iron and held in place by iron bars. Behind it was a heavy iron grating (the *portcullis*) which could be dropped from above. (You can see part of the portcullis in its *raised* position in the picture just below.)

Then if some of the attacking force lived to make their way through all these defenses, they found that they were

DRAWBRIDGE AND PORTCULLIS. — From Gautier's *La Chevalerie*.

only in the outer courtyard. Here were no buildings but the stables and the homes of some of the servants. Another wall, just as stubborn, shut them from the *inner* court, where the important buildings and supplies were.

And if this wall, too, were passed, there remained the inner " keep." This was a mighty stone tower. It was where the lord's family lived in times of danger, and it was always the strongest part of the castle. Its walls were enormously thick, and the upper stories could be reached only by a narrow, dimly lighted winding stairway, built sometimes *in* the wall. On this stairway, not more than two or three men could possibly fight at one time.

In the keep the survivors of a defeated garrison would make a last stand, retreating slowly from story to story, until the last two or three wounded knights were flung over the battlements by the victors. Possibly, when it was plain that the castle was going to be taken, the lord's family escaped through a small *postern* gate or by an underground tunnel from the dungeons, running beneath the moat.

But castles were not often taken by assault. An enemy might destroy the crops outside and burn the miserable huts of the serfs; but the castle itself, until the days of gunpowder, could usually hold out against anything but surprise or famine or treachery in the garrison.

After all, you see, **the fighting nobles** didn't take many chances. When they fought outside the castles, their bodies **were covered with iron armor** that hardly any weapon could pierce.

The first feudal armor was made of *leather covered with iron scales*. (That is the kind you see in the picture on page 241.) About 1100 A.D. close-fitting suits of *chain-mail* came in. Such a suit was made of overlapping rings of iron,

FRENCH KNIGHT (wearing *chain-mail* under his coat), followed by his squire (page 191). — From a manuscript of the 12th century.

joined together loosely. There was also an iron hood that could be pulled over the head. Then, a little later still, came *plate armor*, such as you can see to-day in museums. A suit of this is shown on the next page. This plate armor had a helmet with a *visor*, which could be pulled down in battle, so that the only openings were the small slits to see through.

A suit of plate armor weighed about fifty pounds — or more if it was made for a large man. The noble had to carry also his heavy shield and a long two-handed sword and a lance. Accordingly, except inside a castle, he always fought on horseback. In such armor it would have been impossible to march far, or fight long, on foot. Of course, it took a strong horse to carry the weight, — especially as the horse too had its body protected with plates of iron. This was necessary, because, if his horse was killed or wounded, the noble was helpless.

It was the castle and the armor and the horse that gave the noble his high place above common men. He could ride down a mob of footmen without danger to himself. His bands of men-at-arms, too, wore armor almost as complete as his own, and also fought on horseback. A feudal army was made up of *cavalry*. To be sure, a noble might order his serfs and other villagers to follow him to battle on foot, armed with poles and pitchforks, without even shields to protect their bodies. But such men could do little more than kill the wounded and plunder the dead. When the barbarian invasions first began, the Teutons, like the Romans, fought on foot. But before long, footmen came to be called *infantry*: that is, boys, or "infants." For several hundred years the castle and the armed horsemen ruled Europe.

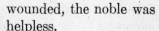

KNIGHT AND HORSE in plate armor. — From a model in the Metropolitan Museum, New York.

For the nobles, then, fighting was an exciting game, but not very dangerous. **On the least excuse, two lords would**

wage a " private war " with each other. It was the useful
workers who suffered in these wars of their lords, without
getting any of the fun. One noble raided the lands of the
other, tortured and murdered the miserable serfs, burned
their houses, ruined their crops. This might hurt the pride
of the lord whose lands were invaded, but it did not hurt him
greatly in any other way. Perhaps he with his men-at-arms
rode out to " get even " by a battle with the invader, in
which both sides shattered a few spears on each other's
armor. And perhaps he got further revenge afterward by
making a raid in his turn and burning and torturing and
plundering his rival's serfs.

Feudalism seems to us a very bad kind of government ;
but it **was better than no government at all.** For a long time
it was the only kind possible. Each noble *was* the government, so far as his fief was concerned. Each fief was a little
state, ruled by its lord. The lord held regular courts, to
which his vassals came. There they gave advice about ruling the fief and acted as judges in settling quarrels among
themselves or between one of them and the lord. (Look
back at the picture at the head of page 176.)

*For hundreds of years, people could not imagine any other
sort of government.* Not only the vassals, but the serfs as
well, looked upon the lord of the fief with love and admira-
tion. They felt for the fief much the same sort of patriotism
that we feel for our country. Many of the nobles, too, were
good men, anxious to do right, as they saw the right, and to
rule their vassals and even their serfs with justice and kindness.

**One reason why the nobles went to war with one an-
other so much was that there was no other very good way
to settle a dispute.** Some kinds of disputes, it is true,
were taken care of in Church courts ; but ordinary courts
settled most cases in ways that seem very strange to us.

No witnesses were brought before these courts to show that either side was right. Instead, the man who was accused of doing wrong was put to certain tests, in which, it was believed, God would show whether he were innocent or not.

One of these tests was the *ordeal by water*. In this kind of trial, the accused man or woman was tied up and then thrown into water. If he sank, he was believed to be innocent — because pure water, men thought, would not receive a guilty person — but the decision might not do him much good then.

RELIGIOUS CEREMONY BEFORE A JUDICIAL COMBAT. Each party is swearing (on Bible and Cross) that his cause is just. — From a fifteenth century manuscript reproduced in LaCroix's *Chevalerie*.

Or perhaps the accused person chose the *ordeal by fire*. Then he plunged his arm into boiling water, or walked over red-hot plowshares. After some days his flesh was examined by the priests who had charge of these "appeals to God," and if it was uninjured, he was declared innocent.

Sometimes a friend would stand those tests, in place of the accused man. That is how we come to say of a man that he is "ready to go through fire and water for a friend."

The fighting nobles did not often use either the "trial by water" or the "trial by fire." They preferred to trust to their weapons and armor, and liked another kind of test called *ordeal by battle*. This was a sort of duel, in which God was asked by the court and the Church to "show the right." The person who won in such a combat was declared innocent. A woman might have a *champion* to fight in her place.

Summary

The feudal age was a time of violence and disorder. Any man who was strong enough protected himself and his weaker neighbors, if they became his vassals. The lords and vassals were nobles. They built strong castles, and fought on horseback, covered with iron armor, waging many "private wars" among themselves. The useful work was done by serfs who were scorned by the nobles and their men-at-arms. The best excuse for the private wars was that there were not any good ways for settling disputes.

Thought Questions and Things to Do

Trial by Combat ("In the lists"). Companion piece to the picture on the opposite page.

1. Perhaps you are not ready to read all of Scott's *Ivanhoe*, though you would certainly enjoy *hearing* it read, but you yourself might read the story there of a capture of a feudal castle (chapters xxv–xxxi), and perhaps you could read the story of a trial by battle farther on in the same book (chapter xliii).

2. We have told about many things in this chapter which we do not have anything to do with to-day, though we still see them mentioned often in books we read. *Make a list of words* in this chapter that have to do with feudalism, and mark with a check those of them that we still use.

3. The class will find it interesting to build a model of a feudal castle. (The hardest thing to understand fully in the description on page 179 is the passage about the "battlements." The picture at the top of page 224 will show how battlements looked from outside the wall.)

4. What are some of the things you would miss if you could be suddenly carried back a thousand years to live in a feudal castle? What are some of the things you would find there that you do not have in your homes to-day? Why not?

5. Ruins of feudal castles are sometimes very beautiful: are you sorry that we have no such beautiful ruins in this country?

REAPING. — From an English manuscript of the 14th century. Compare with page 20. Then try to find a picture of harvesting to-day.

CHAPTER XIX

HOW PEOPLE LIVED IN FEUDAL TIMES

In the Castle

Life in the castle in time of peace was rather stupid, or at least it would have seemed stupid to us. Near the keep, in the inner courtyard, were the pleasantest living-quarters, in a large building called the *hall*. Here, at one end of the main room, the lord slept in a high-posted bed shut off by curtains that might be drawn together around it. In this same room he received his vassals when they visited him, and his stewards when they came to make reports about crops or buildings or about his dogs or falcons. Here, too, in some deep window or before a great fireplace, he played chess or backgammon with his priestly secretary — and, if the priest were wise, the lord won most of the games.

In this same hall, the lord and his household and guests feasted. **Meals were the gayest hours of the day,** — especially the mid-day and the long evening meal. The end of the hall where the lord's table stood was a step or two higher than the rest. There he sat with his family and his most honored guests. Down the length of the room stretched other long tables. At the farthest end sat the lowest servants of the household. Between, according to rank, came officers and stewards and upper servants, and perhaps some traveling jugglers or minstrels, who would later pay for their meal by songs or acrobatic feats or sleight-of-hand tricks.

Near the hall, across part of the courtyard, was the kitchen. From this the serving men carried course after course of food to the tables in the hall. Whole roast peacocks, swans, wild boars (or at least boar heads), and huge

INSIDE THE HALL OF A GREAT LORD IN THE THIRTEENTH CENTURY, as a famous modern scholar (Parmentier) imagines it.

venison pies were common dishes. Sometimes a skillful cook would surprise and delight his masters by a vast pie, which, when cut into, let live birds escape (like the four-and-twenty blackbirds of the Mother Goose rhyme), to be hunted down amid the rafters by falcons.

There were no forks and of course no napkins. Each guest cut slices from the roasts with the knife from his own belt, and dipped his hand into the huge meat-pies, carrying the dripping food directly to his mouth. There were hunks of bread at his place; and some of these he crumbed up and rolled in his hand, to wipe off the gravy, and then he threw them to the dogs under the tables. Between the courses, servants passed much-needed basins of water, with towels.

These times of waiting were filled with story-telling and song and with rude jokes by the lord's "fool," or perhaps with news of far-off districts from some traveling guest. The upper end of the table had plenty of wine, and often the drinking continued late, after the ladies had left the

JUGGLERS IN SWORD DANCE, as shown in a thirteenth century manuscript.

room, until most of the company fell under the table with the dogs. At the lower tables it was not so easy to get drunk, because the wine there was usually weakened with water.

None of these people, except some of the servants, had much to do. They knew nothing of our fine pleasures. They had almost no books, and could not have read them if they had had them. The ladies spent most of their time making embroideries and tapestries. The gruff men-at-arms found life even duller. Lounging in the courtyard, they could only polish their arms, or practice with spear and sword, and yawn

A COURT "FOOL."—From a medieval manuscript, where the picture is in brilliant reds and blues and yellows.

out their hopes for a war or at least for a raid on some neighboring village. **The favorite sport of the nobles** was a

sort of mock battle, called a *tournament*.   Next to this, they
enjoyed the *hunt*.   There was much more forest in Western
Europe then than there had been in Roman times (page
143), so of course there were plenty of wild animals.   At
times these even became a danger to the serfs and their
crops.   The noble kept down such danger — and, in return,
he claimed that he alone had
the *right to hunt* in his domain.
If a common man (below the
rank of noble) were found with
a haunch of venison, or even
with a hare, the lord might cut
off his hands or burn out his
eyes.

**Hunting was business as
well as sport.**   It brought in a
large part of the food of every
castle.   Large animals, like
bear, deer, and wild boars, the
hunters chased with trained
dogs to bring them to bay, and
then slew with spear or sword.
Such sport was often quite as
dangerous as fighting.   Smaller
game — herons, wild ducks,
rabbits — were hunted with
trained hawks.

HUNTING with falcons and dogs.   The
lady (seemingly a queen) has just
" cast off " at a bird that has appeared
in the sky.   (This picture is reproduced in Parmentier's *Album* from a
fourteenth century manuscript.)   Why
do lady and attendant both wear long
gloves on the left hand when they use
none on the right ?

This last kind of hunting was called *falconry*.   In every
castle one of the most important servants was a falconer.
This man's business was to catch young hawks and train
them to fly at game and bring it to the master.   Ladies as
well as lords were fond of falconry.   Even when making a
long journey, a lady always rode with her pet falcon on her
wrist, ready to " cast off," the moment a game bird rose
beside the road.

A famous feudal structure (*Conway Castle*) in North Britain to-day.
(What one thing would tell you that this is a modern picture?)

Doing Homage (page 177). — The kneeling noble, in return for a grant
of lands or for a promise of protection, is swearing to be a faithful vassal
to the higher lord standing before him.

Part of the Training of Boys of Noble Families in the Feudal Age, as pictured in a medieval manuscript. The boys ride in turn at the wooden figure. If the rider strikes the shield squarely in the center, it is well. If he hits only a glancing blow, the wooden figure swings on its foot and whacks him with its club as he passes. Near the tents stand the lord of the castle and some of his knights, looking on.

After about 1100, every young man of noble family felt that he must become a _knight_. There were three stages in the training for this honor :

1. When a boy noble was seven years old, his father sent him away from home to be trained in the household of an overlord or of some friend. Here the child served the lord and lady of the castle as a _page_, waiting on them at table and running their errands. Usually some lady of the castle had particular charge over each page, and taught him courtesy and obedience and loyalty to those above him, and a knight's duty to the Church and to ladies.

The pages dressed in gay-colored velvets ; and while waiting in the outer halls, or in their spare hours, they played games with one another, — backgammon, dominos, or tennis in the outer courts. (They were not afraid of breaking windows, for, until 1300, window glass was little used.) Those boys who were big enough and strong enough to wear light armor (that is, those who were nine or ten years of age) were trained each day by some old man-at-arms to ride, and, while on horseback, to manage spear and sword. (Look at the picture of this training on the opposite page.)

2. At fourteen or fifteen, the page became a _squire_ to the lord of the castle or to some other noble. He cleaned his lord's shining armor, and kept it bright and put it on him when it was wanted. He went with the lord to battle or to the hunt, and had special care for his safety. He saw that the lord's horse was cared for properly, and he led a spare one for him in battle.

3. At twenty, perhaps, the squire had " earned his spurs " and was ready to become a _knight_. Sometimes a noble won his knighthood in battle. If he was able to do some daring deed, perhaps his lord or some still greater leader rewarded him with the desired honor. The lord would order him to kneel, and, drawing a sword, would strike him lightly over

the shoulder with the flat of it, saying, — " In the name of God and of St. Michael, I dub you knight."

At other times there was a much longer ceremony. First came a bath. This was not merely to clean the body : it stood for the idea of purifying the soul from evil thoughts and desires. Then the youth " watched his arms " in a church or chapel, praying and fasting all night, standing or kneeling before the altar, on which rested his armor.

In the morning, he made solemn confession of his sins, and then listened to a sermon from some holy priest on the duties of a knight. By this time the household and many guests had gathered in the courtyard. There the squire knelt before the lord of the castle and took the vows of knighthood. He promised to be brave and to be gentle ; to defend the Church ; to protect ladies ; and to give help to widows and orphans and to others in trouble.

Next, the ladies of the castle put his new armor upon the young man, gave him his sword, and buckled golden spurs upon his feet. Then he knelt again before the lord and received the gentle stroke of the sword that dubbed him knight. A fine horse, which some servant had been holding ready, was then presented to him for his charger, and he was expected to leap into the saddle and give a show of his horsemanship by making the steed bound and gallop about the court. Games and friendly contests to show skill in arms followed, and feasting and exchange of gifts closed the exercises.

Knighthood, you must remember, with its fine ideas of gentleness and courtesy, did not belong to the Dark Ages. It began about 1100. Even then, of course, the ideas were not practiced by all knights. Still there were as many perfect knights, perhaps, as there are perfect gentlemen to-day. Our ideas of how a gentleman should behave come very largely from knighthood. But in one way they are a great deal better. A modern gentleman is supposed to be kind and courteous to

every one, rich or poor.   But when a knight of the Middle
Ages promised to protect widows and orphans and to be
courteous to ladies, he always had in mind only women and
children of his own *noble* class: *peasant* women were not
thought of in such promises, any more than cows were.

IN THE VILLAGE

We have read now about the praying men and the fighting
men of Feudal times.   But after all, even taken together,
these did not make
up a tenth of the peo-
ple.   **It took several
*peasants,*** or working
men, **to support one
priest, and a great
many more to sup-
port a noble.**   Out-
side the monasteries,
the peasants were the
only people who did
much useful work.

AN ENGLISH MANOR HOUSE of the 12th century.
Note the walls inclosing open courts and different
buildings.

There was little town life yet, you remember, in Western
Europe; so almost the only work was farm work.

The word *peasant* is used to mean the serfs and also other
men who farmed their *own* small plots of ground with their
own hands.   That name is used, too, for small farmers in
Europe to-day.

**A village of those workers, with its lands about it, was
called a *manor.*** The poorest noble owned at least one
manor, and great lords owned hundreds of them, scattered
in different parts of the country.

At some distance from the other buildings of the village
there was always a *manor house.*   This might be a lordly

castle, the home of a noble; or it might be only the home of the lord's steward, and so not much better than the houses of the peasants. Near the manor house, toward one end of the village, stood the *village church* in its church yard where rested the dead. Then came the village itself, much as you may still see it in some parts of Europe.

Usually there was only one narrow and crooked street, with ten or perhaps twenty houses on each side. These were low, one-room hovels, built out of sticks, or rough pieces of wood, plastered together with mud and thatched with straw. They had dirt floors and no chimney. Usually the only opening was the door. This often was made in two parts (as you sometimes see the doors of barns now), so that the upper part might be left open, to let out smoke from the fire, while the lower part was closed to keep out the pigs and other animals in the street. Behind each house there was a low stable (often under the same roof with the living room of the family) and also a small vegetable garden. All the dirt and refuse from the houses was thrown out into the street, and, after a rain the road was sometimes knee-deep in muddy filth. In this the hogs rooted, and the children played.

HALL OF AN EARLY ENGLISH MANOR HOUSE. — From a manuscript of the 13th century. Notice the small window-panes (just then coming into use), the timbered ceiling, and the bundles of rushes ready to be spread on the floor.

Each manor had its smithy, of course, and its mill, and its

bake-oven; but these were all the lord's property, and the peasant had to pay for using them. Out of each lot of his grain ground at the mill, he had to leave a measure for the lord; and he had to leave a loaf of bread out of each baking that the baker made for him. The smith and miller were rather better off than the other villagers, and lived in somewhat better huts.

The business of a village was to raise food — some for itself and much more for the master. So it had to have wide stretches of land round about it.

There was usually a large piece of *woodland*. The dead trees and fallen branches there furnished fuel for the peasants' fires, and the nuts and acorns furnished food for the people and for droves of pigs.

ENGLISH PEASANTS threshing grain with flails, as shown in a manuscript of the 14th century. No better way was known anywhere until about a century ago. See also page 21.

There were also *meadows* for hay; and after the hay had been cut, this land was good pasture for cattle. The meadows were "common" lands, and each peasant was allowed to pasture there his few geese and his pig and cow, or, if he was better off than the rest of them, his oxen. Of course, the lord's much larger herds fed there also.

The plow land **was divided into three large fields.** One was seeded to wheat or rye, or some other grain that had to be sown *in the fall*. ("Winter" wheat was the only kind of wheat men knew about then.) The second field was seeded *in the spring* to oats, or some other spring grain. The third field, which had been in oats the year before, was *left idle*, so that it might grow fertile again during a year's rest.

The next year, this " idle " field would be seeded to wheat, and the old wheat field, to oats ; while the old oat field would be the fallow (or idle) field. And so on, year after year, each field lying fallow one year in three.

This was a very crude kind of " rotation of crops " ; but it was vastly better than to wear out the soil by raising the same crop on a piece of land year after year. If you have lived on a farm, you will know that we have better ways to-day for rotating crops and keeping the soil fertile. But that old way of the Feudal Age, wasteful as it was, was the best kind of farming that Europe knew about until a hundred and fifty years ago.

There was another strange thing about that farming. Each plowed field was divided into a great many long, narrow strips, separated from one another by narrow lines of sod. Every peasant had several of these strips *in each field* (probably from ten to thirty acres in all) ; but his strips, even in one field, were scattered about, instead of lying next to one another.

About half of all the plow land was tilled by the peasants for the lord of the manor, under the orders of the lord's steward. Most of this land also lay in strips scattered through the three fields, just as the land of the peasants did.

All this meant poor farming. A peasant wasted a lot of time in going so often from one strip to another, and you would hardly expect serfs to be very clever or ambitious workers anyway. So, instead of getting a harvest of twenty or forty or sixty bushels of grain for two bushels of seed, as we do now, a peasant was lucky if he got four bushels or six.

The vegetable gardens (page 194) were poorer than those of Egyptian or Roman times. Potatoes, of course, were not yet known. (Do you know when they came into Europe?) There were turnips, cabbages, carrots, beans, and peas ; but

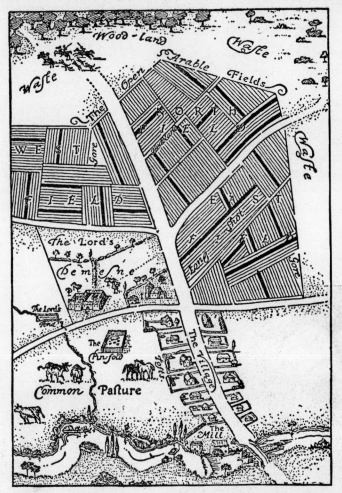

PLAN OF A MEDIEVAL MANOR. — A photo from an old drawing. Certain strips are blackened to show that they all belonged to the same peasant. "Arable Fields" means *plow-land*, and "Lord's Demesne" is an old form for *Lord's Domain*, or the Lord's personal holdings.

HALL OF A LARGE MANOR HOUSE. — From an English manuscript of the fifteenth century. The lord is drying his feet at the fireplace before joining his lady at the table.

BODIAM CASTLE TO-DAY — a well-preserved medieval structure in England. Unfortunately, many feudal customs lasted on in Europe, almost as long as the feudal castles, with even less reason.

these last were not the delicious things that we eat.   Instead they were a " field pea," such as we sometimes feed to cattle, and indeed they were fed then to horses as well as to people.

It was hard to get fodder enough to feed many cattle through the winter. Some had to be kept, of course, to do the next year's farm work and to raise young.   The rest were killed off in the fall; and (since there was no cold storage) the meat had to be salted down.   Large amounts of salt meat do not make a good diet.   Besides, salt was costly, and often too little of it was used to keep the meat properly. This large use of salt meat, or of spoiled meat, and the small amount of vege-

PEASANT GIRLS PLAYING ''BOB-CHERRY'' with a hanging apple (as girls still play every Halloween). — From an English manuscript of the 14th century.

tables, along with other faults in the way people lived, caused many diseases.

The chief table luxury was honey.   Sugar had never been used in Europe except by the rich (page 122), and since the barbarian invasions its use had been wholly forgotten; but well-to-do peasants always had a hive of bees in the garden. The wax of the honey was wanted, also, for candles to light church buildings and to keep burning before the shrines of saints.

Besides the payments that a serf had to make to the lord and the work he had to do on the lord's land (page 128), he had also to make payments to the Church — every tenth sheaf of grain from his little harvest, every tenth egg, tenth chicken, tenth lamb and pig and calf.   This did not leave him much to live on, especially as he might have to leave his own farm work at any moment to work on the lord's roads, place the huge stones of a new castle wall, or dig a ditch for the lord.

Each village was a little world by itself. Even the different villages of the same lord had nothing to do with one another. The lord's steward bought from the outside world the salt, the mill stones, and the iron necessary for plow shares and tools. Otherwise, except for a hostile raid or for the visit of some strange lord to the castle, a village hardly knew that there was any outside world.

From an English picture of the 14th century.

Almost never did a village have a shop to sell goods. In each home the women wove rough cloth for their clothing (one garment usually was all a woman wore) ; and the man prepared the leather from which the women made his heavy clothing. Commonly a peasant wore the same garment, night and day and year after year, until it was in shreds. Of course, the peasants were filthy. For that matter, few of the lords and ladies were what we should call clean.

There was one very bad side to this way in which each village kept to itself. If a crop failed in even a small district, the people were likely to die of hunger, though other districts near by might have plenty. Roads were bad, and there was no trade. One village might have more food than it could use, and no good way to sell it ; while in others, not more than a hundred miles away, the people might be eating roots from the forest and bark from the trees. Children died in great numbers from such food ; and sometimes whole villages were swept away.

From an English picture of the 14th century.

In spite of all this, **the peasants managed to find bright spots in their hard, drab lives.** They thought it a great treat to watch the gay procession of knights and ladies ride out from the castle gates for a hunt or a journey.   Sometimes a group of jugglers, on the way to the castle, stopped in the village and showed their tricks. And best of all were the festival times and holy days of the Church, when the peasants were free from work and could take part in games and merry-making, such as dancing and singing round a May pole.

FRENCH PEASANTS DANCING AROUND A MAY-POLE. — From a miniature of the 14th century, now in a public library in Paris.

SUMMARY

Life in a feudal castle would seem dull and uncomfortable to us. When not fighting, the lords passed their time chiefly in feasting, hunting, and playing at war. Every young noble was trained to become a knight. Life in the village was even less comfortable and more dirty and unsanitary than in the castle. The peasants farmed poorly and raised only small crops. They had to pay the Church and the landlord both by services and by part of their crop. Each village had only what it raised itself. There was almost no trade.

NEW WORDS

tournament	*page*	*peasant*	*crop-rotation*	*fallow*
knight	*squire*	*manor*	*steward*	*falconry*

THINGS TO DO

1. If you have not read any stories of the Feudal Age, you should do so now. Some of the best for young people are: Robert Louis Stevenson's *The Black Arrow*, Howard Pyle's *Men*

of Iron and *Robin Hood*, Charlotte Yong's *The Little Duke*, Frank
Stockton's *Story of Viteau*, Eva M. Tappan's *When Knights Were
Bold*, and Hall's *Boy's Book of Chivalry*. Martineau's *Prince and
Peasant* shows the bad side of Feudalism. So
does Mark Twain's *Connecticut Yankee at King
Arthur's Court* — a book which you would en-
joy *hearing* read. And you should be sure to
read *Gilbert the Page* in Jane Andrews' *Ten
Boys*.

2. King Arthur was supposed to have been
a Christian British king who during a glorious
reign held back the heathen English when they
invaded Britain. During the Feudal Age,
many fine stories were written about him and
his knights of the Round Table. The knights
and ladies of that time were particularly fond
of having those legends read aloud to them.
The things, however, that Arthur and his
knights are made to say and do in those books
did not belong to the fifth century, when he
was supposed to have lived, but to the twelfth
or thirteenth when the legends were written
out. Lanier's *Boys' King Arthur* is made up
from those old books and will give you a good

A JUGGLER AT WORK.
— As pictured in a
manuscript of the 14th
century.

idea of what lords and ladies of the feudal age
thought the best way to behave.

3. If you have made a model of a feudal
castle (page 186), can you now make one of
the fields and village of a manor, to go with it? Then, with your
model of a monastery (page 155), you will have the most important buildings of early feudal times.

4. This would be a good place to add to your scrap-book.

5. Each one of the class might write a *story* of the Feudal Age.
Imagine yourself a peasant or a noble, and tell your adventures.

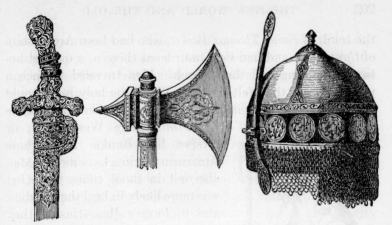

SARACEN SWORD, BATTLE-AX, AND HELMET — with gold-inlay on the steel.

CHAPTER XX

WHY THE CRUSADES BEGAN

In the Feudal Age Many People Went To the Holy Land as *Pilgrims*

The picture on the following page shows a common sight during the Feudal Age. Many people went on long journeys as *pilgrims*. Indeed, except for royal messengers and armies, there were almost no other travelers during much of the Middle Ages.

In those days each country and each district of a country had its favorite *shrine*, or holy place, where some saint had lived. In England the most famous was

AN ENGLISH INN OF ABOUT 1300 A.D. — Commonly the inn then had one large sleeping room with many beds crowded into it, in each of which at least two men were expected to sleep. Finicky travelers complained that often their bed-mates were vilely dirty and that the straw (rarely changed) on the inn floors was often swarming with fleas. About 1400, conditions improved rapidly.

201

must *obey* the will of God — which they must learn from Mohammed, whom God had chosen for his prophet.

Other teachings came to Mohammed from time to time in dreams and visions. Many of them were much like the teachings of Christianity and of the Hebrew prophets, but some things were like the old Arab ways. Mohammed said that Moses and Christ were both true prophets, but that he himself was the last and greatest prophet.

The Arab word for God is *Allah;* and the followers of the new religion had for their slogan: "*Great is Allah, and Mohammed is his prophet.*" Mohammed could not write; but some of his followers wrote down all his teachings in a book called the *Koran,* which is the Mohammedan bible. In Mohammedan lands to-day school boys are expected to learn the Koran by heart.

At first no one believed in Mohammed except his wife and a few faithful servants. The people of his town refused to listen to him, and he even had to flee to the desert to save his life. There, however, he converted some of the wandering tribes; and with their help, he conquered Mecca and forced it to accept his religion. "The sword," said he, "is the key of Heaven." He taught, too, that if a man died in battle for the new faith, all his sins would be forgiven. His fierce followers won battle after battle with other tribes, and **before Mohammed's death (in 632 A.D.) all the Arabs had been united into a mighty Mohammedan nation.**

Then the Mohammedans began to conquer other nations also and force them all to accept Mohammedanism. In less than one man's lifetime, they overran all the old Roman Empire in Africa and Asia, except for the western part of Asia Minor where the Greek Empire (page 130) still stood. Indeed, they carried their conquests eastward farther than the Roman Empire or Christianity had reached, — farther even than the bounds of Alexander's Empire, — beyond

the Jaxartes and the Indus.   In all those lands most of the
people to-day still have the Koran for their sacred book.

**It looked for a time as if Christian Europe, too, would be
made Mohammedan.**   After fierce struggles the Greek
emperors at Constantinople at last drove back the Arabs
(or *Saracens*, as they are often called), and kept them from
getting into Europe at the eastern end until several centuries
later.   But when the Mohammedan Moors from Africa invaded Spain, the Visigoths could not turn them back.   They
overran that peninsula
quickly and then crossed
the Pyrenees into Gaul.

**But *at Tours*, the Mo-
hammedan Moors were
defeated and driven back
by the Franks, under
Charles the Hammer,**
grandfather of Charlemagne.

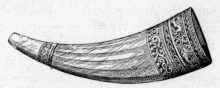

DRINKING-HORN, with Arabic gold-smith
work about the mouth, sent to Charlemagne
by Haroun-al-Raschid.

That was on an autumn day
in 732 A.D.   From dawn to dark the gallant, light-armed,
turbaned horsemen of the Moors hurled themselves in vain,
with frightful loss of life, against the stern wall of steel-clad
Franks.   That night they began to retreat beyond the
Pyrenees.   The battle of Tours saved most of Europe for
the Christian religion and for the new Teutonic nations.

Soon after this great battle, the Mohammedan world
broke into two parts, and so became less dangerous to
Europe.   The western part was ruled by the *Emir of
Cordova* in Spain.   The East was ruled by the *Caliph
of Bagdad*.   Some of you have read in the *Arabian
Nights* about the great *Caliph Haroun-al-Raschid*, but
you may not have understood that he was a real person.
He was, and he lived at the same time as Charlemagne.
By that time the Saracens were becoming more peace-
ful; and hard as travel was, those two mighty rulers,

so far apart, managed to exchange gifts. Haroun-al-Raschid sent to Charlemagne, among other presents, a white elephant and a curious water-clock that struck the hours. This last was an old invention of the Egyptians, you will remember, but it caused vast amazement at the court of Charlemagne.

The Mohammedan world had come to have a much higher civilization than Christian Europe then had. At first, to be sure, the Arab conquerors had destroyed some of the Roman civilization. When one conqueror seized Egypt, he burned the great library at Alexandria and so destroyed forever much priceless knowledge. Said he, " If all these books agree with the Koran, they are not needed ; and if they do not agree with the Koran, they are false and ought to be destroyed." (If a dozen of the greatest libraries in the world were burned to-day, it would cause less loss of knowledge than that fire did. Why?)

But soon the Saracens adopted the civilization of the East, and even began to add to it. They built many splendid cities while Western Europe had hardly any towns except stockaded villages. They used a new kind of *horse-shoe arch* in making their buildings, and decorated them with beautiful *domes* and *turrets* and graceful *minarets*, and much rich *ornament* carved upon the walls. Their manufactures in metal and in cloth were the finest in the world. Swords made in their city of *Toledo* in Spain were so much better than any that Christian Europe could turn out that we still speak of a particularly good weapon as a " Toledo blade." In like manner, we speak of " Morocco " leather. The first " muslins " came from Saracen *Mosul;* and at *Damascus* they made the wonderful cloth we still call " damasks." (Find these places on the map of the Mohammedan world. Can you find out which ones of them are still Mohammedan and whether they are still manufacturing cities?)

COURT OF LIONS, ALHAMBRA PALACE (GRANADA, SPAIN). — From a recent photo, but wholly Saracen in origin. Try to find here three of the special features of Saracen architecture that are named on page 206. Perhaps you can find two others in the pictures on pages 210 and 293.

In their farming, the Saracens used *fertilizers* and *irrigation* while Europe had only the wasteful three-year rotation plan (page 196). They produced also many *new varieties of fruits and flowers by grafting*, so that they had lovely gardens while Europeans were working from dawn to dark to raise barley and turnips enough to live on. And while Europe was still struggling along in the Dark Ages, the Saracens in Spain and in the East had come to have noble *universities*, with libraries containing hundreds of thousands of precious books. They began the science of *chemistry*. Indeed the word " chemistry " is Arabic. They carried the *study of the stars* farther even than the Babylonians and Greeks had done. (Most of the names on our star-maps are Arabic.) And from India *they brought* to Spain the *Arabic figures* and used them just as we do now, while Christian Europe still had only the clumsy Roman numerals.

During the Middle Ages a Mohammedan scholar wrote a Geography, in which he gives a full description of *Bagdad* in its day of glory (about 1200 A.D.).

The city was built on both banks of the river Tigris, in two huge semicircles, twelve miles across, and it contained about two million people ! Immense streets crossed the city dividing it into huge blocks. Each block was under an overseer who looked after its cleanliness and the comfort of the people.

Every household was plentifully supplied with water at all seasons by aqueducts; and the streets, gardens, and parks were swept and watered at regular times. All refuse was collected and carried off outside the city walls. At night the streets were lighted by lamps.

Both sides of the river for miles were fronted by the palaces, gardens, and parks of the rich merchants and nobles. Marble steps from each river-side garden led down to the water's edge, and the scene on the river was made brilliant by thousands of gondolas, decked with little flags and dancing like sunbeams on the waters, carrying the pleasure-loving people from one part of the city to another. Along the wide-stretching quays

CHAPTER XXI

THE CRUSADES AND THEIR RESULTS

First Came a Crusade by the Common People

The great lords who took the cross at Clermont had agreed
to get ready during the winter and set out together the following spring. But **vast companies of ignorant villagers started
at once from different parts of Europe to win back the Holy
Land.** They had almost no arms and no money to get food
and supplies. They were led only by a half-crazy monk,
Peter the Hermit, and by a reckless knight called *Walter
the Penniless.* These leaders could not keep order. The
ragged and hungry hordes of this " People's Crusade "
moved like a devouring plague down the valley of the Danube toward the place where, their leaders told them, lay
Constantinople. There they expected to get ships and arms
from the Greek Empire. They had no idea how far they
must go ; and whenever the church towers of a new town
were seen, many of them would cry out, " Is that Constantinople? "

Of course, great numbers perished on the road. They
seized food wherever they could get it ; so the inhabitants
of the countries through which they marched often attacked
them in battle. Thousands of the crusaders were killed
in this way, and still more died of disease and hunger. The
wonder is that any lived to reach Constantinople. A mul-

titude did get there, however; but the Greek Emperor got rid of them at once by passing them on into Asia Minor. There they were attacked by the Turks, and either killed or made slaves.

The First Real Crusade Started in 1096 A.D.

The real crusade of the great lords and knights the next summer was a very different thing. There were three hundred thousand of these crusaders, and they moved in five powerful armies, well-armed and with strict discipline. They had to pass over the same road that the " People's Crusade " had used, and so they found the country people along the way very unfriendly. But after many hardships they did at last reach Constantinople in good order.

The Greek Emperor was pleased at first at this splendid answer to his cry for help against the Turk, but he **soon began to fear the crusaders more than he did the Mohammedans.** They liked Constantinople so well that he was afraid they would try to seize it for themselves. The bold Western warriors had never dreamed of such a magnificent city or of wealth of so many kinds as they now saw spread about them, and they seemed in no hurry to move on.

At last the Emperor did get them off into Asia Minor. The Turks expected another easy victory, like the one they had won a few months before over the untrained mob of Peter the Hermit. But they soon learned that in a pitched battle their light horsemen were no match for feudal cavalry.

The crusaders won back all Asia Minor for the Greek Empire. Then they settled down to a stiff siege at *Antioch*. This lasted three months. While it was going on, a certain *Count Stephen* (a great French noble and a son-in-law of King William the Conqueror, of England, of whom we shall read later) wrote an interesting letter home to his " sweetest and most amiable wife." This letter shows us many things about how the crusaders felt.

" You may be sure, dearest, that my messenger leaves me before Antioch safe and unharmed, through God's grace. . . . We have been advancing continuously for twenty-three weeks toward the home of our Lord Jesus. You may know for certain, my beloved, that I have now twice as much of gold and silver and of many other kinds of riches as when I left you . . . You must have heard that we fought a great battle with the perfidious Turks, and, by God's aid, conquered them . . . Continually pursuing the wicked Turks, we drove them as far as the great river Euphrates . . . The whole army of God, having given due praise and thanks to the omnipotent Lord, then hastened with great joy to Antioch and besieged it. Very often we had conflicts with the Turks . . . In all these battles, by the aid of the Lord God, we conquered, and most assuredly killed a vast host of them. Many of our brethren and followers were killed also, and their souls were borne to the joys of Paradise.

" When the emir of Antioch — that is, its prince and lord — saw that he was hard pressed by us, he sent his son to the prince who holds Jerusalem, and to the prince of Damascus, and to three other princes. These five emirs, with 12,000 picked Turkish horsemen, suddenly came to aid the inhabitants of Antioch. We, ignorant of all this, had sent many of our soldiers away to the cities and fortresses; for there are 165 cities and fortresses throughout Syria which are in our power. But a little before they reached the city, we attacked them at three leagues' distance with 700 soldiers. God fought for us, His faithful. On that day we conquered them and killed countless multitudes; and we carried back to the army more than two hundred of their heads, in order that the people might rejoice on that account.

" These which I write you are only a few things, dearest, of the many which we have done. And because I am not able to tell you, dearest, what is in my mind, I charge you to do right, to watch over your land carefully, and to do your duty as you ought to your children and your vassals. . . ."

When Antioch was at last taken, the crusaders marched on to Jerusalem. There, too, the Mohammedan garrison held out bravely through a long siege, — during which the Christians also suffered terribly at times from lack of food, and still more from lack of water. " Many lay near the dried-up springs," says one old writer, " unable to make a sound with their swollen tongues, but stretching out piteous hands to any one who passed by." **Finally,** three years after the expedition set out from Europe, **the crusaders did capture the Holy City.** In a last desperate attack, they swarmed over the walls on their scaling ladders, and then for days they killed mercilessly, torturing and slaying even unarmed men and women and babes. These warlike pilgrims to the tomb of the merciful Christ thought it a pious deed to kill any Mohammedan.

The Crusades lasted till about 1300 A.D.

Of all the three hundred thousand knights that had started on the crusade only twenty thousand saw the capture of Jerusalem. Many of these turned homeward, now that the Holy City was again in Christian hands, but **new companies kept coming from Europe almost every month to take their place.**

New fighters were needed if the Christians were going to hold Jerusalem. For the Mohammedans soon began to win back the Holy Land. **This strange warfare between Europe and Asia went on for two centuries.** After about ninety years the Christians again lost Jerusalem ; but they kept some fortresses in the country and always hoped to capture the Holy City once more.

Little bands of knights were traveling from Europe to Asia, or from Asia back to Europe, all through that two hundred years ; and every thirty or forty years a really big expedition set out from Europe. **These large expeditions were given special names,** as the *First Crusade,* the *Second*

In the *Seventh Crusade* Louis IX of France (page 245) was a prisoner for some months — treated always with great courtesy except for one moment of peril from a mob of Arab soldiers, which is pictured thus by a modern French painter. (Seventy years after the crusade the story was dictated to a scribe by the young noble who stands just behind King Louis.)

Crusade, and so on.   The one we have just read about was the First Crusade, but the most famous of all was the Third.

The Third Crusade came in 1187, just after the Saracens, under their great leader, *Saladin*, had won back Jerusalem. The three most powerful kings in Europe then agreed to put away their quarrels with one another in order to join in driving back the foes of Christendom.   These three kings were *Richard the Lion-Hearted* of England, *Philip Augustus* of France, and *Frederick Barbarossa* (Frederick Red Beard) of Germany.

But Barbarossa was an old man ; and soon after reaching Asia Minor, he was drowned while swimming a river after a hot day's march.   The two other kings were bitterly jealous of each other, and soon their old quarrels broke out again. Before long, Philip returned home, so as to get the advantage in Europe while his rival was still in Palestine.   Richard worked mighty deeds of valor — so that Saracen mothers used his name for centuries to frighten naughty children. He could not take Jerusalem alone ; but he did make a treaty with Saladin which allowed Christian pilgrims to visit the holy places there.   Then dangers to his own kingdom called him home also.

Finally, about the year 1300, people began to lose interest in fighting Turks so far away, and found things to do at home which seemed more important.   So the crusades came to an end.   But during the two centuries that they had been going on, several millions of Christian knights had left their bones in Palestine.   At the end of that time the Holy Land was still in the hands of the Turks.

The Crusades Built up Shipping and Trade
And Trade Built Towns

In the Third Crusade, Richard and Philip did not lead their armies by land through Europe.   Instead they *sailed* directly to Palestine from France.   This brings us to some of the important results of the crusades.

The men of the First Crusade never even thought of going by sea, because in all Western Europe there were not then enough ships to carry them. But as soon as Christians reached Syria they began to need more food, armor, and horses from Europe — and those supplies could be brought most cheaply and quickly by boat.

Now the Italians and the southern Frenchmen had always had a few ships for their coasting trade, and they found this new business of carrying supplies to the crusaders in Palestine very profitable. So every year they built more and better ships — for the small vessels of that time could be built very quickly. Before long there were so many ships that it was possible on short notice to get hundreds of them together into a fleet large enough even to transport armies like those of Richard and Philip.

But it paid better to carry trade than to carry armies; and **the crusades led to more and more trade between Europe and Asia.** The very first crusaders had been surprised to find that the heathen Saracens knew how to make more useful and beautiful things than were made anywhere in Europe, and they wanted to take home as many as they could. As they found their way back to Germany or France or England, they brought with them some of those eastern products — Oriental tapestries and rugs for the walls and floors of their cold gloomy castles; jewels and skilled metal work in silver and gold and steel, such as only the Saracens then could turn out; fine cloths of silk and cotton and velvet, new to Western Europe; and also a great variety of new foods and plants, — lemons, rice, buckwheat, sugar and sugar cane, dates, apricots, melons, oils, and spices. The Roman Empire had known about some of these things (page 122), but for hundreds of years they had been completely forgotten in Western Europe.

All the nobles and rich churchmen in Europe were eager to buy such things. So Italian traders settled in the East, wherever the Europeans held a city there, and bought quantities of goods to send to Europe. Every little ship that brought to Palestine a band of crusaders, or a load of supplies for those already there, found it easy to get a rich cargo for the return voyage.

It cost a great deal to bring these articles so far, and so **their prices in Europe were very high.** But all well-to-do people wanted them. Indeed men soon began to think they *must* have these things in order to be comfortable at all. So working people in Western Europe began to try to make

some of them, because they could get better paid for doing that than for any other work. That is, **manufactures of many kinds grew up.**

CRAFTSMEN building a medieval cathedral. — From Parmentier's *Album* — reproduced from a book written by a monk.

In most feudal villages there had been a few skilled workers, such as shoemakers, tanners, and weavers, who often had learned their work from some neighboring monastery (page 152). But these people usually had not had much to do at their trades and had to make their living mainly, as the other peasants did, by working their strips of land.

But the men from among them who took up these *new* trades had to give all their time and attention to what they were making. They had to *buy* their food and the other things they needed. So they had to live near a market, — both to buy things for themselves and also to sell their own wares. *Merchants* and *lawyers* were soon needed, too, and money-lenders, or *bankers*. All such people found it more convenient to live near together.

This is how *towns* grew up. A few towns in Italy and southern France, you remember (page 142), had lived on from Roman times.   Now these grew larger.   And in northern France and in Germany and England, many little country villages grew slowly into new manufacturing and trading towns.   So during the two hundred years of the crusades, *Europe came to have a fourth class of people.*   Before, there had been only *churchmen, nobles,* and *peasants.*   But now, beside these three, appeared the bustling, energetic *townsmen.*

These town dwellers were prosperous, and were soon able to buy many of the new luxuries and comforts for themselves. This meant more trade ; and that in turn meant new and larger towns.   We shall read more about this when we come to the next chapter.

The Crusades Helped to Break down Feudalism and Serfdom

While the great lords were off fighting in Palestine, the kings in the European countries usually stayed at home, so they had a chance there to build up their power.   **Thus they grew much stronger than before.**   Then they were able to keep better order and to make even the big lords obey them.

The great lords lost power.   Their vassals no longer needed so much protection.   Besides, now that trade was bringing back money again, the vassals preferred to pay *money taxes* to the king for protection and to pay *money rents* to their landlord, instead of giving him all sorts of service whenever he might call for it.

At the same time, the peasants became more free.   They too refused to serve their masters any longer just for protection.   They began to demand wages in money, and they began to pay money rent for the land they used, instead of paying in labor.   Still they received such low wages that they remained very poor.   Even where they were no longer bound to the land as serfs, their lives went on much as before. But the lives of all the people except peasants were much changed.

The Crusades Started a New Age of Invention in Europe

Perhaps the most important effect of the crusades was the new ideas they brought to the people of Europe. There was hardly a little village anywhere that was not visited by men on the way to the crusades or on their return journey. So even very dull persons, who never left home themselves, began to understand that there was more to the world than they could see from the nearest hill — which was about all they had ever thought of before. They began now to be curious about what lay beyond. And you can see that soon the ambitious ones would probably find out a good deal.

Even at home, people were no longer content to go on just as they always had done, but began to try some of the strange Eastern ways that the crusaders told about. *Windmills,* for instance, were found to be very useful for many kinds of work, especially in places where there were no waterfalls to turn mill wheels, or where water had to be pumped continually, as in Holland. *Clocks* with pendulums, such as the Arabs had invented, were found much more convenient than the hour-glass or the sun-dial. And all the new ways of doing things brought on a new age of learning and of invention — which in the end led to the discovery of America.

You see it would be hard to make a list of all the important things that Western Europe gained from the Crusades. There were all the new *articles* themselves that made life more comfortable and more beautiful. There were the growth of *trade* and of *travel,* the new life in *cities,* the *freeing of the serfs* in parts of Europe, the *loss of power by the lords,* and the *better order kept by the kings.* And more important than all else would be the *new interest in learning,* and the desire to find better ways to do things, which led soon to a new advance in civilization.

SUMMARY

The crusades lasted about two centuries (**1100–1300** A.D.). The crusaders did not keep Palestine for Christians, but they learned many things that were useful to Europe and resulted in great changes there. The last paragraph of the chapter sums up those changes.

NEW WORDS

scaling ladder	*expedition*	*windmill*	*rent*
pendulum	*garrison*	*tapestry*	*manufactures*

THINGS TO DO

1. On the time line mark dates for the crusades and the growth of towns.

2. Imagine yourself a crusader taken prisoner and carried to the court of the Mohammedan rulers. Write your impressions of what you saw there.

3. Suppose posters had been used to advertise the crusades, as they would be in such a case now, can you make some fit for that purpose?

4. A very interesting account of a meeting of Richard the Lion-hearted and Saladin is given in Scott's *Talisman*, chapter xxvii. Other good stories of the crusades are Hewes' *Boy of the Lost Crusade*, Knapp's *Boy and the Barons*, Stein's *Our Little Crusader Cousin of Long Ago*, Yonge's *Prince and Page*. Tappan's *When Knights Were Bold* has a good chapter on the Crusades, and so has Van Loon's *Story of Mankind*.

5. Make a list of the ways in which the crusades might help the kings to build up their power, and so help do away with feudalism.

6. In 1918, during the World War, the British took Jerusalem from the Turks. That British expedition is sometimes called " the last crusade." Find out something about it and how it differed from earlier crusades. What people own Jerusalem to-day?

7. Find pictures of the Holy Land to-day for the class scrap-book.

PART OF THE OLD WALLS OF A TOWN in Southern France as they look to-day. This town won its first charter in 1246.

CHAPTER XXII

TOWNS IN THE MIDDLE AGES

The People of the Towns Had Won Freedom by Buying Charters or by Fighting for Them

The people in the towns won their freedom long before the peasants in the little villages. Sometimes a town *bought* its rights from a bishop or noble lord or king. Sometimes it got them by *fighting* for them. In any case, the townsmen found that *by working all together* they were strong enough to get many things that they wanted.

The crusades had helped the towns get their freedom. When King Richard of England was trying to beg or borrow or squeeze money from his subjects to pay for his crusade, the citizens of Norwich, a small English town, agreed to pay him about $10,000, in order, they said, " to have the town in our own hands." Then Richard gave the townsmen a charter — that is, a written statement of just what their rights were to be. The chief ones were :

1. The citizens were to have their own law courts ;
2. They were to elect their own mayor ;
3. The town treasury was to make to the king a small fixed payment of taxes each year, but no citizen was to be called on for any other tax.

though in Italy and Germany there were perhaps a dozen
that had from 30,000 to 50,000.   Even as late as the time
of Columbus, only two English towns (London and Bristol)
had as many as 12,000 people.   (How did such towns compare in size with Bagdad or Constantinople at that time?
How would they compare
with *your* town now?)

Each town was sur-
rounded by a strong wall,
and could be entered only
at guarded gates, like those
of a feudal castle.   You
have read enough about
Feudal times to understand
why this was so.   The town
had to be kept in as small
a space as possible, so that
the wall would not be too
long to defend.   For this
reason the streets were very
narrow.   Then the people
found that they could save
still more space by letting
the upper stories of the
houses jut out farther into
the street, so that the
streets sometimes were almost roofed over.   This made
them dark and damp.

Town Street as pictured in a manuscript of the 13th century, reproduced in
Parmentier's *Album*.

Still most of the better houses had small high-walled gardens at side or rear.   Each town, too, had at least one large
open square where markets and fairs were held.   Here was
the town well, about which the women gossiped as they
drew water for their households.   On one side was the town
hall — often a grand building even for to-day.   On another
side was the town's most magnificent church or cathedral.

The people of Northern Europe in the Middle Ages had come to use **a new style of building, called** *Gothic*. Gothic buildings had narrow *pointed* arches, instead of the old Roman *round* arches. They were much higher, too, with slender columns and tall spires pointing to the sky. The arches and doorways and tops of the columns were beautifully carved — sometimes so delicately that they looked more like lace work than like stone. The many windows were set with glass of the richest colors, which no modern glass workers have been able to copy. It took more than two centuries to finish building some of those cathedrals, and people to-day travel thousands of miles to see them.

Life in the towns had many new comforts. The old straw-thatched hovels with dirt floors gave way to stately homes. These were houses of two or three stories, and they were more like ours of to-day than any earlier houses had been, though their windows on the street side were always protected at night by iron shutters. The rooms began to have glass windows and were heated by fireplaces. They were furnished with heavy carved oak furniture; and the rich hung their walls with fine tapestries brought from the Orient.

Once or twice each year a town held a *fair*. Then for weeks it became one vast bustling bazaar. Along each important street, merchants from all parts of the land, and often from other lands also, set up their booths to show their goods; and from smaller towns, many miles in every direction, the wealthier people crowded in to buy. The town treasury charged every merchant a tax for the right to set up his booth — as we do at our fairs now — but it also spent much money at such times on gay festivals and feasts and pageants.

It cost the town a good deal, too, to protect the goods and money of the merchants against robbers. The watch at the

SIEGE OF A MEDIEVAL TOWN. — An officer of the attacking army is reading aloud the summons to surrender. Note that the drawbridge before the city gate is up, and the portcullis down.

ROBBER KNIGHTS plundering a merchant's caravan. — From a modern painting.

GOLDSMITH'S SHOP in Paris about 1500, — according to a copper engraving made by the smith himself.

A STREET SCENE DURING A FAIR IN THE MIDDLE AGES, — as imagined by a famous French scholar, Parmentier. Notice the crippled beggar in front and the band of jugglers in the background.

gates, and in the streets at night, was doubled at such times, and the garrison on the walls was strengthened. In particular the town had to keep out armed nobles, for such men were likely to think it right to plunder and steal from townsmen, even of their own country. Once when the English town of Boston was holding a fair, a band of armed nobles got past the watch at the gates by disguising themselves as play actors. Then at dark they began a horrible work of murder and plunder. They set fire to the booths (to cause confusion among the merchants), slaughtered those who tried to defend their wares, and hurried the rich booty to ships that they had ready at the quay.

The king of England at that time was the great Edward I (page 259) ; and he hunted down and hanged those " noble " murderers, with wise firmness. No English nobles ever tried such a raid again ; but on the continent such things went on for centuries longer. Indeed the common name for the lords of strong castles in some parts of Europe came to be " robber knights," because they made their living largely by raiding the towns or by attacking bands of merchants who were traveling from one fair to another.

With all its wealth and comfort, **the European city of the Middle Ages,** you see, **was far behind the old cities of the Roman Empire or the Arabian cities.** It had no street lighting, and no water supply except the well in the public square. (Do you suppose the water was always safe for drinking?) The town, too, had no drains for sewerage and no paving except rough cobble stones in a few streets.

The dark and narrow streets were never cleaned. All sorts of dirt from the houses were thrown out into them, to be scattered or heaped up by wind and rain. Even large cities let swine run loose in the streets and allowed pig-sties to be built out into them. Little wonder that a certain German king, welcomed joyously to a loyal city, just after a heavy rain, got stuck in slime and mud that almost drowned his horse under him.   And no wonder dreadful plagues killed off thousands of people, where so little was done to keep the cities clean.

There were other things in the life of even the most prosperous citizen that we should find most inconvenient.   He must cover his fire and put out all lights at eight or nine o'clock every evening — when the great bell in the town watchtower rang " curfew," or " cover fire."   This was necessary to guard against fire, when buildings of wood were so crowded together, and when there were no regular fire companies.   Each citizen, too, must take his turn every little while at serving on the town watch to guard the gates and to patrol the streets from dark to dawn.   In spite of such protection as the " watch " could give, many fights took place at night in the streets.   So no well-to-do citizen dreamed of stepping out of his door after dark except in armor and with a following of his own stout " apprentice " lads, carrying torches and swords.

The Workers of the Towns were Organized in Trade Gilds

If you were to wake up some morning and find yourself back in a town in the Middle Ages, and ask in what part of the town you were, you would be told that you were in the " Street of the Armorers " or the " Street of the Cloth Merchants " or the " Street of the Butchers."   And soon you would see that all the shops on that street were of one trade.   Even to-day in London you may find " Milk Street " and " Bread Street," though the fine modern buildings there have nothing to do now with dealers in bread or milk.

In the Middle Ages **all the workers in one trade had to belong to the same " gild,"** and most of them lived near each other in the same street — all leather workers in one, all goldsmiths in another, and so on.   Each town had its *merchant gild* (a " merchant " was a man who traded *outside*

the town), besides many *trade gilds*, or *craft gilds*. A large
city might have as many as fifty gilds.

You remember, the Roman workers had gilds (page 117).
Probably that is how the gilds of the Middle Ages started.

A gild was very different
from a modern union of
workers in one trade. It
contained employers as
well as workmen, and
kept up a good feeling
between them. There
were no "strikes" in the
gild days. The members
of a gild decided at what
price its goods should be
sold and what wages the
workmen should receive.
They also punished
sternly any shopkeeper
or workman who charged
more than the gild price,
or who put out poor arti-
cles, or who mixed poor
wool with good or gave
short weight. In all
ways possible, the gild
helped the worker to take
pride in doing a good job.

HALL OF THE CLOTHMAKERS' GILD AT YPRES
(Belgium). This beautiful example of Early
Gothic architecture (page 228) was begun in
1200 A. D. but not finished until 1364. To the
loss of the world, it was destroyed in the World
War when the Germans bombarded Ypres.

The gild also took
care of its members. It
buried a gild "brother"
if he died poor, and cared for his wife and children. It was
a social club, too, and gave great feasts for its members. In
many places the gilds came to be the city government. The
town hall was called the "gild hall," and the town council

was made up of "aldermen," one chosen by each of the leading gilds.

If you could have looked in at a shop in those days, you would have seen the "master," and perhaps his wife also, waiting on customers, or standing in the door, inviting people in to examine the goods that showed in the window. Inside there would be two or three skillful workmen, making the goods.   When not busy with customers, the master, also, worked with his tools, and it was a shame to him if he could not do the best job in the shop.   To each workman there

would be at least one boy, to run errands and do odd jobs — and meanwhile he would be learning the "mystery" of the trade. (The ways of the trade were kept a deep secret from all but the gild members.)

This game is shown in an English 14th-century book.   The gilds of a town often played against each other in such contests.

These boys were *apprentices*.   They were "bound out" by their parents to the "master" for several years, — ten, perhaps.   During all this time they received no wages — except a suit of plain clothes each year; but they were fed and lodged in the master's house, in the rooms above the shop, and were treated almost like members of his family.

When the ten years of an apprentice were up, he was examined by the older men of the gild, and if he did his work well, he "graduated" into the class of *journeymen*.   The graduating exercises of *our* colleges and schools grew up out of the way the gilds promoted apprentices.   The new journeyman's "diploma" certified that he was now fit to practice the "mystery" of his trade anywhere, and recommended him to all members of the gild in other towns.

For the next few years this new gild member did usually journey from town to town, and perhaps even from country to country, working for a few months or years under the most skillful masters he could find in different cities.   (After 1300, you see, with the growth of trade and of towns and gilds, travel had begun again ; and all sorts of people were on the move, — not merely pilgrims and soldiers, as two hundred years before.)

Then at last, if the journeyman was ambitious, and if he had saved his earnings, he might become a *master*. But first he had to let the gild masters in his town examine a piece of his best work (his " masterpiece "), to see whether he was fit to teach others his trade.   If they approved his work, and if they decided also that there was business enough in the town for another shop, he could open a shop of his own with journeymen and apprentices to work for him.

You cannot form any true picture in your mind of a medieval town unless you know about these gild customs.   *But you must not think that these customs were ever brought to America*.   The early Spanish and French colonies in this country had no manufactures.   The colonist, instead, *imported* all manufactured goods from the home land.   And in the sixteenth century, before any English colonies were founded, the English people gave up the gild system.

The English way of manufacturing that *was* transplanted to America was called the *Domestic system*.   It grew out of the break-up of the gilds.   Men still did their work by hand, because there was no machinery yet for manufacturing; and much of the work, too, was still carried on in some " master's " house.   The master still bought the materials and hired skilled workers to help him work them up into the finished goods for sale ; and he still had apprentices to work for board and lodging while they learned the trade.   But those who had learned it now sometimes carried the work to their own homes, to do it there.   *And there were no longer any gild rules*, even in the masters' houses, *to fix wages and prices and ways of doing the work.*

Instead, each master *competed* with other manufacturers — who now were not " brothers " but rivals. This Domestic system did not have all the good things about it that the old gilds had had, but it did give more freedom for a clever man to work in his own way, and so it led to more rapid changes in manufacturing.

In the New Towns, or Near Them, Groups of Scholars Built up Universities

Nowadays we think of a university as a group of buildings, but in the Middle Ages all that was needed was a group of teachers and students. The teachers and students would get a charter from the king of the country, to permit them to govern themselves, and they then carried on their work much after the way of a gild. The *professors* were the masters; the *young* students, the apprentices; and there were many *traveling scholars*, a little further on their studies, who went from university to university, as journeymen traveled from city to city.

Many of the greatest universities of to-day in all the countries of Western Europe were started in this way. One of the first grew up at *Paris*, just outside the walls. Students came there from every part of Europe to listen to the great teacher, **Abelard**. No hall was large enough to hold them, but they gathered eagerly about him on the banks of the Seine, kneeling on one knee and holding their writing tablets on the other, since they had no desks or chairs. Later, King Philip Augustus (page 218) took pity on the poor scholars and ordered that when the straw that carpeted the floors of his palace was changed (once a week or so), the old straw should be sent across the river and spread on the river banks — so that the students would not have to kneel in the mud or dust.

Some of the universities studied chiefly the teachings of the great churchmen. Others studied mainly medicine or law.

This picture shows something of how universities grew up in Europe (page 234). A learned scholar is lecturing in the basement (or "crypt") of a church. His pupils (some taking notes) are both young and old.

VENICE TO-DAY. — The building next the canal is the famous Palace of the Doges ("Dukes"). Beyond it is seen the dome and part of the rest of the Cathedral of St. Mark. Both palace and cathedral were built during the Middle Ages, in a style that is partly Roman, partly Gothic, and partly Saracenic.

GATE OF ST. GEORGE, ANTWERP, — as pictured in a Dutch woodcut of about 1550; reproduced in E. S. Bates' *Touring in 1600*, published by Houghton Mifflin Company, Boston, who kindly permit the use of the picture here. Note the skating and the "covered wagon."

(Roman law had been falling into neglect in Western Europe; but a Latin copy of Justinian's Code (page 130) was discovered at Bologna in Italy and used as a textbook in a university there. So a better knowledge of the old Roman Law soon spread over Europe again.)

Italian and German Cities Formed Strong Leagues

When the cities in Germany and Italy *did* finally win their freedom from their old lords (page 226), they soon became very independent indeed. They not only managed their own special affairs, as English and French towns did, but also they coined money, like kings, and had great fleets and armies.

A few of them, like Genoa and Venice, became very wealthy and ruled over wide empires of their own. These two cities were rivals for the rich trade of the Mediterranean, and fought many wars with each other to get sole control of it. One or the other of them did control most of the trade between Europe and the East till Vasco da Gama found new routes outside the Mediterranean (page 295). **These and some other cities remained free republics for centuries —** until about a hundred years ago.

Do you remember how Venice began? See page 146. After the crusades it became one of the most beautiful cities in Western Europe, as well as the richest. The long canals, winding between the many islands on which the city is built, served as its streets. They were lined by splendid public buildings and by marble palaces in which dwelt the wealthy Venetian merchants and bankers. Long black gondolas glided along the canals, as they do to-day, and carried the citizens about on business or for merry-making.

The cities had shown that they could fight when they had to, but they preferred peace because trade does not prosper in times of war and disorder. One way that they found very helpful to protect their trade was to form large and powerful *leagues* among themselves. About the year 1300 many North German cities united in a league of this sort, called *the Hanseatic League.* It came finally to contain fifty towns, and it was powerful enough to make treaties with great monarchs and to get safe trading stations for its merchants in almost every northern European country — in England, in the Netherlands, in Sweden, and far into Russia.

A New Kind of Clergy Grew Up
To meet New City Needs

The larger towns soon came to have many poor inhabitants. These were even worse off than the old peasants, in some ways, because they were so huddled together. Their misery aroused deep pity in a youth named *Francis,* who was the son of a rich merchant of the town of Assisi in Italy. Francis had been a gay, pleasure-loving boy, but, after a severe sickness, he suddenly turned away from all his former joys. He wished now to give himself entirely to caring for the poor and the suffering.

His father tried in vain to coax him back, and finally disinherited him. Then Francis wandered from town to town, begging from the rich and giving to the poor, and preaching to all the gospel of a good life. His aim seems to have been to live as nearly as possible as Jesus had lived on earth. Other young men who heard his preaching gathered about him to help in his work. These he sent out, two by two, wherever misery and sin were greatest. " Fear not," he said to them, " because you are small and seem foolish. Preach peace and patience; tend the wounded; relieve those who suffer; reclaim those who sin; bless them which persecute you."

Finally, " Saint Francis " gained approval for his work from Pope Innocent III. His followers were called " friars "

GOLDEN AGE OF CRAFTSMEN. — This picture is a reproduction in *The Survey* (XLIX, 572) of a woodcut in a Dutch "block book" of 1470. (The new invention of movable type had been made just a few years before, but an older and clumsier way of printing books had not wholly gone out of use. See page 280.) You can readily make out a goldsmith, painter, wood carver, organ maker, book decorator, clock maker (some of these with apprentices at work with them), besides the two who are employing a rest period in eating.

CENTRAL AISLE (*Nave*) OF AMIENS CATHEDRAL (France). — Notice the piles of chairs ready to be set out for worshipers at service hours. In the Middle Ages, when this "Early Gothic" building was constructed, no chairs were provided in any way. The high vaulted roof was entirely of stone. Our modern lofty buildings are reinforced with steel.

(from a Latin word which means " brothers "). They took vows like the monks, only instead of staying within a quiet monastery and caring only for those who came to them for help, they went forth into the world to *hunt out* the needy. They brought comfort and help to thousands of people in the new cities whom the priests and monks had not reached.

The Franciscan friars came to be known as the *Franciscan Order*. Soon there was organized also the *Dominican Order* of friars. These sterner " black friars " (clothed in black robes), it was said sometimes, worked more to save the souls of men, while the gentler, gray-robed Franciscans worked more to save their bodies. Soon after 1250 both gray friars and black friars were a common sight in every large town in Europe.

SUMMARY

The towns of the Feudal Age won charters from their lords either by paying money or by fighting. Life in the towns had many new pleasures and comforts, though still without many things that we now think necessary. The workers in each trade in a town were organized into a gild. Many Italian and German towns became free republics, and formed strong leagues among themselves to protect their trade. The Franciscan Order of Friars did much to make the life of the poorest townsmen happier and better.

NEW WORDS

cathedral	*fair*	*curfew*	*gild*	*gild master*
Gothic arch	*pageant*	*friar*	*apprentice*	*journeyman*

THOUGHT QUESTIONS AND THINGS TO DO

1. Find on some map the towns mentioned in this chapter.
2. What things did Bagdad have that cities in Western Europe in the Middle Ages did not have?
3. Imagine yourself a serf escaping to a town to get your free-

dom, and tell what happened to you.   Or tell about your life as an apprentice.

4. Could you draw and color a picture of a cathedral window?

5. Study the pictures of buildings of the Middle Ages and tell what things those buildings have that are different from Greek and Roman buildings.

6. Van Loon's *Story of Mankind,* chapter xxxv, tells in a very interesting way how cities got their freedom.   Other good accounts of town life are given in Stuart's *Boy through the Ages,* Tappan's *When Knights Were Bold,* Lamprey's *In the Days of the Guild* and *Masters of the Guild.*   A beautiful story of St. Francis for children is Jewett's *God's Troubadour.*

7. What reasons can you find why dreadful plagues swept over the towns of Europe in the Middle Ages?   What measures do we take to prevent such plagues to-day?

8. What towns in our country have grown chiefly because they were well placed for trade with foreign countries?

MEDIEVAL MUSICIANS. — From an old manuscript.

Town Hall at Audenarde (Belgium), built in the 16th century. Late Gothic style,

CATHEDRAL OF COLOGNE. — The building was interrupted for a long time, but when the structure was completed, in modern times, it was done in the medieval Gothic style in which the work had been begun.

KING'S MESSENGER. — From a manuscript of the 13th century.

CHAPTER XXIII

NEW NATIONS GROW UP IN EUROPE

Look at the map of Europe in 800 A.D. after page 158, and then at the map of Europe in 1500, after page 286. You will see at once that great changes took place during these seven hundred years and that many new nations grew up. The story of just how all this happened is too long to tell in this book. But we will tell some of the important things about the growth of those nations that afterward helped most in making a great nation of us.

Perhaps you have not thought before about **what the things are that make a group of people a nation.** The whole group must really feel like one people and must be willing to work together for the good of the whole group. It helps them to feel like one people if they are descended from *the same group of ancestors.* It helps, too, if they all have *the same language, the same religion, the same customs* (or ways of living), and *the same ideas* about such things as liberty and beauty and respect for law.

The people that form a nation must all be bound together, too, by *the same government.* The government keeps up an army to protect its people, and provides law courts to give justice and to prevent quarrels among them. It also provides roads for travel and trade, a coinage to make trade more convenient, and schools to educate the people.

Which of these things make the people of our country a nation? Does a group of people have to have *all* these things in order to be a nation? Do all people who speak the same language belong to the same nation? Do all that have the same religion? Which of these ties that unite people into a nation do you think the most important?

ENGLAND

The first country of Western Europe to grow into a strong nation was England. Look back over the chapters on how Britain became England and on the work of Alfred, and notice what the English had by 900 A.D. to make it easy for them to grow into a nation. We are especially interested in that growth because the United States afterward got its civilization more directly from England than from any other one country.

In 1066 A.D. Normans from France Conquered England And Built up a Strong Government

In the year 1042 a new king came to the throne in England. This ruler, called *Edward the Confessor*, was a descendant of Alfred, but he proved to be not much of an Englishman. His mother was a princess of Normandy (page 161) and he had spent his boyhood at the Norman court. The Normans had then been living in France more than a hundred years and they had become good Frenchmen. They spoke French and used the new French ways of living.

Edward, too, had grown to feel and live like a Frenchman. When he became king of England, he put Normans in all the high offices in the English church and in the government. And, though he was a good man, he was a weak king. He had to depend upon his Norman courtiers to advise him in

all important matters.   Moreover, he had no son to follow
him on the throne, and he wanted his cousin, *Duke William
of Normandy*, to be king of England after him.

The English people did not like this.   So, when King
Edward died, in 1066, a great meeting of nobles and people
chose for their next king a Saxon nobleman named *Harold*.

BATTLE OF HASTINGS — the final stand of Saxon Harold and his footmen against
Duke William and his Norman knights (see below). — From the *Bayeux Tapestry*, a
band of linen 20 inches wide and 230 feet long, on which William's wife and her
ladies embroidered seventy different scenes about the Conquest. (The border
shows vultures and wolves hurrying to feast on the dead.)

But Duke William then came to England with a great army
of heavy-armed feudal horsemen.   The English were still
fighting on foot, depending only on their tall shields to protect them against cavalry charges.   They made a stubborn
stand at *Hastings*, on the south coast, but they proved no
match for the mailed horsemen.   Harold himself was slain
in the battle.   **Then William quickly conquered all England,
and on Christmas Day, 1066 A.D., he was crowned King.**

William the Conqueror was a born fighter.   He was almost
a giant in body, — so tall and heavy that it was hard to find
a horse strong enough to carry him.   No one of his followers

was able to swing his mighty sword. Sometimes he would have terrible outbursts of anger that made his closest friends tremble. " Stark he was," says an English monk of the time, " and great fear men had of him ; so grim and cruel that no man dared withstand his will."

THE SHIP THAT BROUGHT WILLIAM THE CONQUEROR TO ENGLAND. — From the Bayeux Tapestry. Like the Viking ships (see page 162), this vessel was built before the crusades led men to use larger ships — such as the one on page 265.

But William was more than a mere fighter. He was a stern ruler, but also a wise one — so that the Norman Conquest proved a good thing for England. The same English monk who tells of William's cruelty, tells too of the " good peace " that he made, " so that a man might fare over his realm with a bosom full of gold." This strong and firm government was good for trade, and that helped towns to grow more rapidly. Besides, William, and his sons after him, were rulers of Normandy as well as of England ; and so Englishmen began to have more to do with France, and indeed with other European countries, than ever before since Roman times. This, too, helped trade, and brought new and better ways of living to the English people.

The most important thing about the Norman Conquest is that it gave England a stronger government than ever before. Wars between the different parts of the kingdom and between great lords came to an end. William did give big grants of land to his Norman followers, but he did not let them make war on one another, or coin money, or put their courts above the king's courts, as great lords did in France and Spain and Germany. The king had his own courts and his own officers in every part of the kingdom, to see that his laws were carried out. He appointed in each county, or *shire*, a special " shire-reeve " (a sort of king's steward) to represent the king's own power ; and these " sheriffs " were able to keep order among even the most powerful vassals. (What are the duties of *our* sheriffs?) Besides, every *free man in England* had to swear to be loyal to the king, and to go to his aid if called upon, *even if it were to fight against his own overlord.*

A NORMAN DOORWAY in the Cathedral of Ely, England ("the dean's door"). Notice the round arch and the simple ornament. The Saxons had not been good builders. Norman architecture in some ways was like the old Roman. (It came earlier than the Gothic, shown on pages 152, 231, and facing 237, 238, and 239.)

At the same time, under the Norman kings, **the people of each small division of the kingdom kept much of their old Saxon freedom.** The most important divisions were the *shires* and the *towns*. (The government of such *parts* of a nation we call *local* government, while the government of the *whole* nation is the *central* government.) Each shire kept its old folk-moot, which was now called the *county court.* The king's sheriff and the bishop presided over it, but all free men had a right to attend and to help decide matters.

On the continent most small farmers had long before become serfs, so there would not have been many people to go to such a meeting. In England, however, there were a good many of the common free men who had not become serfs, but had small farms of their own. They were called *yeomen.*

The Strong Norman Kings Built up Good Law Courts And Established a " Common Law " for All Their People

It had always been one of the chief duties of a king to see that his people got justice. (Do you remember the meaning of the name *Pharaoh* in Egypt?) Any man who felt himself wronged by another had the *right* to bring his case before the king and ask for justice against the wrong-doer. And almost any king would *try* to do justice. But it was not easy for a man who lived far from the royal court to get to the king,

CONRAD OF GERMANY answering calls for justice. — From a modern painting.

and it was not possible for the king to inquire into all the cases that needed attention. This is well shown by stories about great German and French kings in the Feudal Age.

A little while before the Norman Conquest of England, a certain *Conrad*, who loved justice, became king of the Germans. While he was passing to the church to be crowned king, in the midst of a splendid procession, three poor people pressed through the crowd, crying to him for justice. One was a widow, one a child, one a peasant. Conrad kept his procession waiting, while he listened to these people and righted their wrongs. His nobles, and the bishop who was to crown him, urged him not to stop so long; but he replied, — " Since I have been chosen king it is better to do my duty at once." But do you think the best of kings could really do justice among the great body of a nation if he depended upon ways like that?

One of the greatest and best French kings was Louis IX or *Saint Louis* (cut on page 217), who ruled two hundred years after the Norman Conquest. After the death of Louis, one of his officers had a priest write down this story about him :

" Sometimes I have seen him, in order to administer justice, come into the gardens of Paris, dressed in a green coat, a surcoat of woolen stuff without sleeves, his hair well combed, and a hat with white peacock feathers on his head. Carpets were spread; and all who had business to be disposed of stood before him. . . . Many a time it happened in summer that he would go sit in the wood of Vincennes [now a famous park in Paris] with his back to an oak, and make us take our seats around him. And all who had complaints to make came to him without interruption."

These stories show that Conrad and Louis were good men, but they show too that there was no regular court, no " king's justice," except where the king happened to be and only when he had time to spare for it from war and travel and other business. At other times there was nothing much better than the feudal courts of the nobles, and many unjust things were never set right. With feudal courts, too, each little district would have its own laws, often quite different from those of other districts near by. Indeed, less than two centuries ago a great French writer, journeying through his country, complained that he came under new laws every time he changed horses.

There was great need, then, in the new nations of Western Europe, of *regular* courts, which could be reached easily by any man and which would have one kind of law for all.   *England was the first country to get such courts.*   Henry I, the third Norman king, divided all England into a number of districts, or *circuits*.   In each district, one of his judges traveled from place to place, holding court for the king and seeing that justice was done.

These *circuit judges* could even try cases against great lords, and they all used the same kind of law, so that it came to be called the *Common Law* for all England.   Later on, *English colonists brought that English Common Law to America, and we still use it in the United States.*

Some of our most important rights come from the Common Law: our rights of *free speech*, of *meeting freely* in order to discuss public questions, and of *prompt trial* if arrested by an officer, instead of being left to die forgotten in prison without trial, as sometimes happened in France down to a hundred and fifty years ago. Above all, we get from that same Common Law *the right to be tried by a jury of our neighbors*, instead of being left to the mercy of some far-away official.   All these rights of ours grew up in England hundreds of years before any such liberties were known in France or Germany or Italy or Spain.

There is One more Reason why the Norman Conquest Was especially Important to *Us:* It Made the English Language Simpler and Richer

William the Conqueror and the other Norman kings after him brought many Norman nobles to England.   For a long time these victorious Normans scorned to speak anything but French, while on the other hand the conquered English clung even more stubbornly to their own language.   Gradually, however, the bitter hatred between English and Normans died out, and the two races mingled into one.   (If you stop to think where the ancestors of the English and of the Normans had come from, you will remember that they were near kinsmen anyway.) Then, when the two races had mingled, they had to speak one language, and it was the English language that conquered.

But after all it was a "*New* English" that the new English nation spoke. It had been made richer by many French and Latin words from the Norman speech. And while the Normans were learning the English speech, they dropped some of the old endings of words

CANTERBURY PILGRIMS, as pictured in a fourteenth-century manuscript. (See page 248.)

and also many of the harsh sounds. So the whole language became *simpler* and *smoother*, as well as *richer*.

All such changes are slow. It was not until 1362, three hundred years after the Conquest, that the king's courts were allowed to use English instead of French and Latin. About that same time arose a great writer who wrote in the New English language great poems that all English people might understand and love.

This first great "New English" poet was *Geoffrey Chaucer*. He was the son of a London wine merchant and was born in 1340. He became one of the most learned men of his time, but he was not a priest. He served the king both as a soldier and as a messenger to other lands. He had a brave and cheerful spirit. As he walked the roads in the beauty of the English spring he had a clear-seeing eye for bird and flower, and he knew and sympathized with all kinds of people.

His famous *Canterbury Tales* give us our best and most vivid picture of English life in that day. The poem is a collection of stories told (Chaucer pretends) by some pilgrims who have met at an inn on their way to worship at the shrine of the famous saint of Canterbury (page 202). Plowman, miller, lawyer, doctor, poor priest, monk, weaver, merchant, prioress, and " a verray parfit gentil knight " speak in turn, and so show us the manners and feelings of all classes of Englishmen. Perhaps you will read parts of this poem in your high school study of our language and its great poems. Some of the words look strange to us, and the spelling is quaint and sometimes difficult to understand; but you can read the poem with a very little help, while King Alfred's English is a foreign language, almost as much as German is.

NATIONS ON THE CONTINENT OF EUROPE

The *Germans* and the *Italians* did not become true nations until long after the Middle Ages. Neither of these countries had a strong central government during that time. Instead, they broke up into many little governments. In Italy the people of the little city republics (page 235) ruled themselves for a long time, but at last, in most cases, some military leader made himself master of the city and ruled it as he liked. In Germany, each feudal lord became a sort of despotic little king for his own territory — which sometimes was not much larger than a big farm. The German common people had no part in any of those governments, but in Germany, too, there were some " free cities."

The German nobles during this time did one important thing that had good results for the world. They always

wanted more land, and so little by little, they won territory
on the east from the heathen peoples there (Slavs and Avars
and Lithuanians).   Indeed they formed a union among themselves ,for this purpose, known as the *Teutonic Knights*,
with a government of its own.   In each district that they
won from the eastern barbarians, they founded little German
colonies, with churches and monasteries and trading centers.
Thus **they spread civilization farther and farther east,**
away beyond the limits of Charlemagne's empire, even on
the farther coasts of the Baltic Sea (map after page 286).

During the last part of the Middle Ages the other peoples
of Western Europe did become nations in different ways.
In some of the small countries, like Switzerland and
Holland and Norway, the common free men kept many
rights under the new governments.   But more commonly,
especially in the large nations, the king became a despot and
ruled just as he liked.

We shall soon see (page 253) how King Philip made himself master of lands in France that English kings had held
as his vassals.   Other French kings did much the same
thing with other vassals who had been almost independent
kings.   So at last it became easy for the king of France to
raise much larger armies than any of his vassals could.
Then he was able to destroy the castles of the most powerful
and dangerous feudal lords and to force them to keep the
peace.

The kings of France then made every one pay taxes —
instead of feudal dues — and with this money they kept up
a regular army of hired soldiers.   They also paid officers to
go through the country and see that the laws were obeyed.
Thus the kings of France finally got all the powers of government into their own hands.   The townsmen and other
common free men found this kind of government so much
more just and safe for them than the rule of the old feudal

lords had been that they welcomed it gladly. As for the poor peasants, most of them in nearly all countries remained serfs for a long time more. It made little difference to them, therefore, whether king or lords managed the government.

SUMMARY

Soon after the Norman Conquest of 1066, England became a strong nation with much liberty in local governments but with a firm central government and a Common Law for all the people. The language of the new nation, too, was a New English (in which Chaucer wrote), richer and with simpler forms than the Old English of Alfred.

Germany and Italy remained broken up into many little states until quite recent times; but, before the end of the Middle Ages, the other countries of Western Europe on the continent had become nations. All the larger ones among them were ruled by despotic kings, — whose government, however, proved better than that of countless little feudal tyrants.

NEW WORDS

nation	*sheriff*	*central government*	*Common Law*
custom	*shire*	*local government*	*circuit court*
court	*yeomen*	*courtiers*	*jury*

THOUGHT QUESTIONS AND THINGS TO DO

1. On the time line mark the date for the Norman Conquest. What other important date comes thirty years later?

2. List the ways in which the Norman Conquest helped to give England a stronger government. List other effects of the Conquest.

3. Make a list of rulers we have mentioned who tried to see that the people received justice. Give the reasons why circuit courts were a good way of giving justice. How do people get justice in countries that have no kings? What are the duties of *our* circuit courts? How do we get such courts?

4. Find out what you can about how we use trial by jury to-day. Your class might have a jury trial. Why is this a better kind of trial than the ones told about on page 184?

5. Can you find in this chapter two important things which our country learned from the English? You will find more in the next chapter. Be on the lookout for them.

6. There are good accounts of the Normans and the Norman Conquest in Church's *Stories from English History*, Harding's *Story of the Middle Ages*, Stuart's *Boy through the Ages*, Tappan's *European Hero Stories* and *In the Days of William the Conqueror*, and Stein's *Our Little Norman Cousin of Long Ago*. In chapter i of Scott's *Ivanhoe* there is given a conversation between two Saxon serfs which shows partly how the Normans changed the English language.

This building at West Deane in southern England was the home of an English village priest in the 14th century. It is a better house than such priests usually had at that early time, but it had been used earlier, it is said, by a *group* of religious men. The building is still standing — and indeed it is still the rectory, or home of the clergyman of the parish.

A Fourteenth-Century Bridge in a country road in England.

CHAPTER XXIV

THE ENGLISH PEOPLE WIN MORE FREEDOM

The English people had several advantages for winning freedom from their kings. In the first place, *England was an island,* and so less likely to be invaded by enemies than the countries on the continent were. The king, therefore, had no excuse for keeping up large armies of trained soldiers; and so it was not easy for him to put down the people when they rose against tyranny.

Besides, *there were two kinds of freedom-loving people in England not found in any large number in France or Germany or Italy.* (1) There were the *yeomen* (page 243) living on their own little farms. (2) There were also many men who owned more land than they could farm with their own hands, though they were not as rich as a noble had to be. Some of them were the younger sons of nobles; others were the descendants of Anglo-Saxon chieftains. In either case they were what the English called *country gentlemen.*

These two groups played a great part in winning freedom for England. Later, it was mainly their descendants who settled the English colonies in America and passed on to us the kind of free government that their fathers had invented and fought for in England.

The Great Charter

The *old* rights of Englishmen were *written down* in a " Great Charter " which the lords forced King John to sign in *1215 A.D.* This has been called " *the first document in the Bible of English liberty*," and it belongs to us here in the United States as well as to England.

Not all the Norman kings were good rulers. Some of them were weak and selfish men who tried to get all the power and wealth for themselves and cared nothing about ruling justly. **The worst of these kings was *John*, who came to the throne in 1199.**

John was a brother of Richard the Lion-Hearted (page 218), who, you remember, had sold many charters to English towns in order to get money for his crusade. Richard had been brave and strong, but fonder of fighting and adventure than of spending his time planning for the welfare of his people. Still he was generous and open-hearted; and the English became very proud of him. Perhaps you have read stories about him in your *Robin Hood* or in the *Talisman* or in *Ivanhoe*.

John was very different from his brother. He was not only a bad king and a cruel tyrant, but also a mean and cowardly man, who cared only for his own wicked and selfish pleasures. But it happened that **John's very wickedness and meanness helped to bring more liberty to England.**

In the first place, John got into trouble with the French king Philip Augustus (page 218). The kings of England now ruled not only England and Normandy, but also much more French territory (map opposite page 257). For these French lands they were vassals of the French king, and were bound to come to his court and to his aid when called (page 177). John refused to do this. So Philip made war against him and took Normandy and much more of his French lands away from him.

In the end this was a good thing for England. The people there for a long time afterward did not have to spend their time and money in fighting to keep their king's French lands for him, as they had had to do before, and the kings themselves began to give more of their attention to England. But at that time the English people were very angry at John, and they felt disgraced because the French had beaten their worthless king so easily.

John also quarreled with the Pope. He robbed the Church in England of some of its lands; and when the Pope appointed a new Archbishop of Canterbury, John would not let the man take his new office. Instead, John seized for himself all the money that should have gone to the Archbishop as head of the Church in England.

For a time, John seemed able to go his wicked way in this matter. He paid no attention to orders and threats from Rome. But at last the Pope put an " interdict " upon the kingdom, to force it to overthrow John. This was the most severe punishment a Pope could use. It forbade nearly all church services throughout the whole land. Church doors remained closed, and the church bells were silent. There could be no marriages, and the dead had to be buried without religious ceremonies and somewhere outside the hallowed churchyards.

This soon made the English people ready to accept even a French king in John's place, and the French raised an army to seize England. So, in order to keep his crown at all, John made peace with the Pope. He gave back the Church lands and allowed the Archbishop to take possession at Canterbury. *He even surrendered his kingdom to the Pope, and received it back as a fief.* That is, he became a vassal of the Pope, and had to pay him tribute at regular times.

But this did not please the English people either. They were obedient to the Pope in all Church matters, but they did not like to think of their country as a fief of *any* overlord.   Besides, their taxes were heavy already, and they did not wish to send more money to Rome.

Then John had a third and still more important quarrel.
This was with his own subjects in England.   He had been taxing them unjustly and imprisoning their leaders.   He had robbed many nobles of their lands and sometimes of their lives.   So now all England was ready to rebel against him.

A body of great nobles first came together at Canterbury. No one of them was strong enough in the first place to act alone against the tyrant; so they needed to make plans for acting together.   But it was not very safe even to hold a meeting.   So each noble pretended that he was merely going to Canterbury on a religious pilgrimage (page 202).

When these " pilgrims " got together, they bound themselves by a solemn oath to rise in arms *together*, in order to stop John's tyranny.   *Stephen Langton*, the new Archbishop, suggested a plan.   He brought out and read to the meeting an old " charter of liberties " that King Henry I (page 246) had given to the English people a hundred years before. Then the nobles agreed to force John to grant a new charter which they wrote out themselves, setting down clearly *all* the liberties of Englishmen which they believed no king could lawfully take away from them.   Indeed they wrote in the charter that the people would even have the *right to rebel* against a king if he should try to take away any of those liberties.

When John heard what he was expected to sign, he broke out in wrath : " Why don't they ask for my crown?   I will never grant liberties that will make me a slave ! "   So both parties prepared for war.   But everywhere the rebels were welcomed by all classes of people ; and when their army reached London (the only town of any great size then in England), the citizens opened the gates to them and joined them with all their own forces.

John had to depend on a small army of paid foreign troops. His camp was on the bank of the Thames a few miles west from London. The mighty army of England marched out against him, and camped on the opposite bank. It was plain that the king must yield or lose his crown. So, **June 15, 1215,** John met the leaders of the patriot army on a little meadow-like island, between the two armies, called **Runnymede.** **Here the king gave his consent to the Great Charter,** and took a solemn oath to keep its promises faithfully.

At the meeting, the king had kept a smiling face. But, once in his own room again, he threw himself down in a furious rage, gnashing his teeth, biting doglike at the reeds on the floor, and swearing vengeance on the lords who had forced him to give up so much power. He never meant to keep his promises. Instead he began to hire more soldiers from the continent and to prepare for war.

Fortunately, John died while these preparations were going on. **His young son, Henry III, was then made king;** *but first that young prince and his officers were made to sign the Great Charter.* During the next two centuries, English kings were obliged to " confirm " it, or renew it, thirty-two times. To-day its principles are part of the constitutions of every one of our states.

The Great Charter was written in Latin, and it **is often called by its Latin name,** *Magna Carta.* It states the chief facts about all the old English liberties. *It puts the law clearly above the king,* and says that he must obey it, like every one else. No king could keep this charter and be a tyrant.

One great passage in the Charter says, " No free man shall be seized or imprisoned or punished in any way, except by the lawful judgment of his peers (equals) and by the law of the land." Another says that justice shall not be sold or

KING JOHN SIGNING THE GREAT CHARTER, — as a modern artist pictures the scene. Some of the barons facing the king have pledged themselves to a crusade. (How can we tell that?) Should this have been some protection against the king's anger?

.Peasant's Cart, — as pictured in a fourteenth-century manuscript (now in the British Museum). Such carts were used mainly to carry farm crops. Very few peasants of that time owned a horse of any sort ; but even when a pony is pictured drawing the cart, there is almost always a man pushing, also.

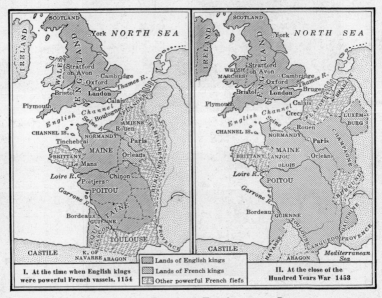

ENGLAND AND FRANCE AT TWO IMPORTANT DATES.

Only the first of these maps concerns the reign of John. That king lost the English possessions in France north of the Loire River. The French kings did not become masters of the other English territory in France until the later " Hundred Years' War " (page 260).

delayed. These two together meant that no king or king's officer could throw a man into prison and keep him there without a fair trial, as John had been doing, but that every man who was accused of wrong-doing had a right to a speedy trial according to the English law.

Another passage said that no man should ever lose his oxen or his plow by a fine in a law court. This protected even the poorest peasant. It meant that he was to be left at least the means of getting his living. *All these rules about getting justice and protection from the courts we keep to-day in our own courts.*

One of the important things the king promised in the Charter was to collect no money from his vassals (except certain regular gifts) unless a Great Council of his vassals voted that he might do so. This was the foundation for the famous idea in English law that **" Taxation without consent is tyranny."** More than six centuries later, an English government forgot to follow that principle in dealing with its colonies in America, and so brought on the war for American independence.

The Beginning of Parliament

In America, from the very beginning, we have had " representative government," and, during the past hundred years or so, nearly all the civilized world has at least imitated its forms. This kind of free government was first worked out in England during the century after Magna Carta was won. It is the greatest of all England's gifts to the world.

During the long reign of John's son, Henry III, a new kind of government grew up. Henry was a very small boy when he began to reign, and when he became a man, he proved to be a weak sort of king. He changed his mind often on important matters, and did not keep his promises, — not even those in the Great Charter. The kingdom fell into

great disorder. Henry refused to take advice from the
Great Council of nobles; and finally the nobles and the
people became so dissatisfied that they rebelled against him.

The leader of this rebellion was a great earl, *Simon* **of**
Montfort, whom the common people trusted and about
whom they chanted many songs of praise. Simon finally
beat the king in battle, and took him and his son Edward
prisoners. Then for a while the earl was the real head
of the kingdom.

Simon was a true English patriot, and he wished his rule
to stand for the will of the English people. **So** *in 1265,*
**when he called a meeting of the Great Council, he made it
a** *new sort of meeting.* He invited the great lords and church
officers who had always attended before; but he also asked
the gentlemen of each county to send two *representatives* to
speak for them all. These representatives were chosen in
county courts (page 243), and were " country gentlemen,"
not nobles.

Simon made another and even greater change. By this
time, several towns had grown up in England (page 242).
**Simon asked each of these towns also to send two of its
citizens** to the assembly to speak for the town. You see,
Earl Simon knew that he must have the support of all classes
of the people if his rebellion was to be successful.

These changes were exceedingly important. They made
this assembly of Simon's so different from the old Great
Council of nobles that it is given a different name. It is
called the first *Parliament.*

This Kind of *Parliament* became the Usual Thing and slowly Gained More and More Power

Simon's rule did not last long. Henry's son, the young
Prince Edward, escaped from his jailors and gathered the
royal forces once more. He managed to take Simon off his
guard. The great earl was defeated and slain, and Henry

came back to the throne. Soon after, however, he died, and Edward became king.

Edward I was one of England's greatest kings. In his youth he had been a pupil and warm admirer of Earl Simon, and soon he showed that he had learned a last great lesson from him. *In 1295* he called together a Parliament, formed just as Simon's Parliament had been. " It is right," said his proclamation, " that matters that concern all should be settled by those who can speak for all." Ever since that time England has had a *representative* Parliament. Our own State legislatures and our Congress at Washington grew up as copies of this plan of government.

After a while the representatives of the towns and counties came to sit in a room by themselves, where they could talk things over and make their decisions without being influenced by the great nobles. Their meeting then came to be called the *House of Commons*, and the meeting of nobles was called the *House of Lords*. The two together make up the English Parliament ; and it was not long before the House of Commons became quite as important as the House of Lords.

At first the king's chief reason for calling a Parliament was *to ask it for money*, in the form of taxes. (Do you remember *why* an English king could *not* get much money from his people without doing this?) But after a while the Parliament began to refuse to grant the requests for money *unless the king first gave his consent to the kind of laws they wanted.* A Parliament would draw up a long petition asking for a certain new law, and then it would almost force the king to agree to the petition by waiting until he had done so before voting him any taxes. When the king did agree to a petition of Parliament, that petition at once became a law. **So the Parliament,** which had been started as a new way of getting taxes for the king, **became the most important law-making part of the English government.** Finally it gained the right also to dismiss and to punish any of the king's officers whom it thought unjust or foolish.

We must not think that Parliament was able to win these important powers all at once. The kings remained stronger than Parliament for a long time, and some of them even tried to get along without any Parliament at all. They found it very hard, however, to collect taxes that Parliament had not voted. For the people would answer the demand of a king's officer for such taxes by saying, "Taxation without consent is tyranny," or, before long, by saying, **" No taxation without representation."** These are important sayings for us to remember, for they have played a great part in our own history.

One thing that helped the growth of Parliament was the cruel and wicked "Hundred Years' War." In 1338 an English king began a war with France, which was waged, off and on, for almost a century. The fighting was all in France, and greatly injured that country; but the English kings often had special need of grants of money from Parliament, and so got into the habit of granting its requests in return.

Other countries during the Middle Ages, *at times*, had assemblies somewhat like the English Parliament, but none of them became very important. About the year 1300 one of the greatest kings of France fell into a long and bitter quarrel with the Pope. To make sure that the French people would support him, the king then called together a *States General*, as it was called in France. In form this gathering was much like the Parliament that Edward I had just set up in England. But it never could do much except say " Yes " to the king's demands. And when the French kings no longer felt the need of its help, they stopped calling it together.

BATTLE OF CRÉCY (1346) during the Hundred Years' War. English footmen (mainly yeomen archers) repulsed charge after charge of splendid French feudal cavalry. Gunpowder, too, was used in this battle (see page 283), but is not noticed in this old picture because it was still so unimportant.

AN ENGLISH CARRIAGE, — as pictured in a fourteenth-century psalter and reproduced in Jusserand's *English Wayfaring Life*. Only the wealthiest nobles could afford such a luxury for their families, for it was worth as much as a thousand oxen. The lord himself and his men followed the carriage on horseback. This carriage was represented as drawn by five horses tandem, just to the right of the part of the picture shown here.

DINNER IN THE HOME OF AN ENGLISH GENTLEMAN, — as pictured in a fourteenth-century manuscript. Note the musicians, the dogs, and the beggar at whom the "fool" is poking some joke. The windows show that the Norman round arch has given way to the Gothic pointed arch.

The End of Serfdom in England

All the liberties we have been talking about were for *free* Englishmen. No one thought much about the serfs. Still at first after the Norman Conquest there were many times more serfs than free men. By the time Parliament began, two hundred years later, the use of money and the growth of towns had helped many of the serfs to become free, but it took almost two hundred years more of struggle and suffering to free all of them.

That struggle might have lasted even longer if it had not been for a dreadful disease called the **Black Death.** During the long French war, soldiers coming back from France brought this sickness with them. In those days people knew nothing about how to care for the sick; and, before this plague was over, **half the population of England had been swept away.**

The loss was greatest, of course, among the poor, because they had the least care and because they were the most crowded together in their little village hovels and in the towns. **This meant that labor became very scarce.** Landlords no longer had serfs enough on their lands to do the work. Some landlords began to offer high money wages to any laborers they could get. Then other landlords had to pay their serfs good wages, to keep them from running away to find better pay for their labor.

But Parliament, which then was almost entirely made up of landlords, **tried very hard to keep the serfs in their old place** and to stop their becoming free laborers. It made laws forbidding any landlord to offer high wages, and other laws forbidding any laborer to leave his old village. Severe punishment was ordered for any worker who disobeyed.

The peasants hated to obey such laws, but they **might not have been able to unite in a rebellion** against them **if**

it had not been for *John Wyclif*. Wyclif was a famous professor at the new University of Oxford. He had translated the Bible into English, so that more people could read it, and he taught that there ought not to be such great differences between rich and poor. Some of his followers, called " poor priests," went from village to village preaching to the people. One of them especially, named *John Ball*, urged the peasants

to get their rights from the " gentlemen " landlords, who, he told them, were only sons of Adam and Eve, just as they themselves were. Every peasant in England knew Ball's rhyme,

" When Adam delved and Eve span
Who was then the gentleman? "

Finally, in 1381, there did come a great "Peasant Rebellion." Seizing for weapons any tools they could find, like

JOHN BALL, as pictured in Froissart's *Chronicles*, in the 14th century.

scythes and pitchforks, the peasants marched from every direction upon London — each army growing like a rolling snowball as it moved. Their leader was a man known as *Wat the Tyler*, and their chief demand was that *all* the old labor rents should be changed to money rents. (Do you see how this change would make the serfs free men?)

On the way to London, some bands of peasants burned a few castles and manor houses and destroyed the lists of services that the serfs had to pay. But when they got to London, they hardly knew what more to do. You see they were used to working, not to fighting, and even their leaders were not soldiers. Besides they did not want to fight their king, the young Richard II. They believed he would get justice for them if they could tell him how badly they were treated by his officers and by their masters.

At London the king marched out with his troops to meet them. Wat the Tyler was murdered treacherously while he was telling the king what the peasants wanted. Then Wat's followers wanted to kill, in turn. But Richard rode over among them and promised to grant all their demands, and so persuaded them to go back to their homes as soon as his promises could be put in writing for them. It kept thirty clerks busy for days to write out all these promises in charters for the peasants to take back to their villages.

But when the peasant army had broken up, then Parliament declared that the king's charters were of no use, because (it said) he had no right to free the serfs from duties they owed their masters. The king was glad of this excuse to break his promise to mere peasants. He raised a mighty army of trained soldiers and marched through all England, from village to village, seizing back by force the charters he had given and putting to death the leaders of the peasants.

In all he killed about seven thousand in this treacherous way. We do not know even the names of most of them, but we do know the story of one. This was *Grindecobbe,* leader of the villagers of *St. Albans.* After this hero had been seized and condemned to die, the king's officers offered him his life if he would persuade his fellow villagers to give up their charters. Grindecobbe refused. Then he turned to his comrades and bade them hold firm their rights. " I shall die for the freedom we have won," he said, " and I count myself happy to end my life by such a martyrdom."

The memory of brave leaders like this gave the peasants new courage in their long struggle for freedom. They did not give up meekly, and go back to serfdom again. Instead, they kept on stubbornly demanding their rights; and, as the long wars with France continued to make labor scarce, the landlords finally had to listen to them. **By 1450, serfdom had passed away from England forever** — much sooner than from any other large country of Europe.

SUMMARY

For several reasons the English people found it easier than other European nations did to win freedom from their kings without losing the firm government that was needed to keep order. (Name some of the reasons.) The most important steps in winning freedom, during the Middle Ages, were: the winning of Magna Carta from the tyrant John; the beginning of Parliaments, under Simon and Edward; the division of Parliament into House of Commons and House of Lords; the establishment of the principle, " No taxation without representation " ; and the rise of the serfs into free farmers or laborers.

NEW WORDS

*interdict   rebellion   peers   Parliament   petition   representatives
House of Commons   Magna Carta   country gentleman*

THOUGHT QUESTIONS AND THINGS TO DO

1. Put the three most important dates in this chapter on your time line. Notice that the two centuries during which England was building a strong government, in which all free men had a share, were the two centuries of the crusades.

2. Imagine that you are a serf, and write of your part in the Peasant Rebellion.

3. Plan and act scenes from the story of King John.

4. Write a statement of how the right to grant taxes grew into the power to make laws.

5. Imagine yourself one of the county or town representatives in the first Parliament, and tell what happened there and what you thought and felt.

6. Make a list of important men mentioned in the last two

chapters, and write a short sentence about each one, telling why we should remember him.   What one of them all would you like best to find in a list of your own ancestors?

7. Without looking up the matter at all, arrange these events in the order in which they happened; then look at your time line and see whether your arrangement is correct: Magna Carta, Norman Conquest, beginning of circuit courts, Edward's Parliament, Simon's Parliament, the Peasant Rebellion.

8. Good accounts of the rise of English freedom can be read in Church's *Stories from English History*, Tappan's *European Hero Stories*, and O'Neill's *The World's Story*.   Interesting stories are Bolton's *The King's Minstrel*, Gandy's *In the Days of Richard the Lion-Heart*, and Marshall's *Cedric the Forester*.

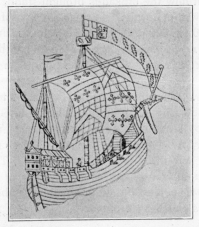

TYPICAL 15TH-CENTURY SHIP — *before* the discovery of America.   (See also cut on page 290.)   The growth of trade after the crusades had caused a marked advance in sailing vessels (page 219) as compared with those of earlier times.   But voyages across the Atlantic soon brought further advance — as may be seen by comparing this picture with pictures of ships just a little later, on page 310 and facing pages 2 and 321.

A SCHOOL FOR ADVANCED PUPILS. — From an engraving in an Italian book printed in 1495. Notice the motto " Silence " (*Silentium*) on the wall.

CHAPTER XXV

EUROPE WAKES UP: 1300–1500

We have seen how the crusades brought trade, and how trade brought the growth of towns. During that Age of the Crusades, too (or from 1100 to 1300), the nations of our own times had begun to grow up, and new ideas that the crusaders had brought back to Europe had started a new age of invention. Europe had *begun* to wake up.

During the next two hundred years (from 1300 to 1500) Europe *fully* woke up. Much of the old learning of the Greeks was discovered again, by studying old manuscripts; and new inventions changed the way men lived and worked. New continents were discovered, and our own Modern Age began. These two centuries of very rapid change are called *the Age of the Rebirth of Europe*. The two peoples that did most to bring about this rebirth were the *Italians* and the *Germans*.

The Growth of Towns Helped Learning

For nearly a thousand years the only learned men had been priests and monks, and almost the only schools had been monastery schools for training more priests and monks. But when towns and trade started, the merchants and gildmasters and their clerks found that they needed to know how to read and write and keep accounts, and how to figure out problems about profits and losses in their business. They had to learn, too, about the different parts of the world with which they traded. **So the towns began to set up** *trade schools* **for the common townsfolk.** In these schools the teaching was not in Latin, but in the language used by the people of the town.

Then, too, as trade heaped up riches, **more people could take time for study and books,** instead of having to work all the time for a living. In the earlier times, if a son of a tradesman cared more for books than for fighting or trade, he probably became a priest or monk; but now he might follow his own kind of life without doing that. We have already told about the English poet Chaucer (page 247), who was one of this new class of scholars and writers.

This new learning started in Italy. More of the old Roman towns had lived on there than in any other part of Western Europe. In those towns, locked up in moldy chests or hidden away in damp cellars, were a good many old Greek and Latin books. Some of them had been written by the great scholars of the University of Alexandria in the days of its glory (page 74) and contained all the Greeks knew about science. Others contained the works of the great Greek and Roman poets and philosophers.

All scholars of Western Europe in the Middle Ages knew Latin, because that was the language of the Church, but they had not much wanted to read the books of the *old* Romans who lived before the days of Christianity. As for the Greek books, for a thousand years there had been almost no one in Western Europe who *could* read them. So the old knowledge was about completely lost. When a monk did find a bundle of these old manuscripts (or " hand-written books "), he didn't stop to think about the learning that might be in them. He would erase the Greek writing from the costly papyrus or parchment, so that he might write upon it the legend of some Christian saint or a story of his monastery. (Western Europe, you see, couldn't get papyrus any more, and it had become hard to get enough material of any kind to write upon, even for the needs of those days.)

The man who did most to save what could still be saved of those old books was an Italian poet named *Petrarch*.

PETRARCH. — A portrait sculpture in marble.

He saw clearly that the best way to advance learning was to get back once more the *foundations* that had been laid by Greek scholars and then to build up from that.

Petrarch's father wanted him to become a lawyer, and once he threw the boy's books of poetry and philosophy into the fire. But, one way and another, the young Petrarch managed to carry out his plans, and it became the main work of his life to hunt out and study old manuscripts and to get other scholars to do the same thing.

Petrarch never had a chance to learn Greek himself; but he talked and wrote so much about how important it was that he made the study of Greek fashionable. Rich Italian nobles (who themselves perhaps could hardly read in their own language) began to offer fabulous sums for old Greek books and to pay large salaries to secretaries who could translate them. Many a young scholar from Constantinople made a fortune by bringing the works of some ancient Greek writer (like Aristotle or Archimedes) to sell in Italy, and by offering himself as a secretary or a teacher of Greek to some Italian prince. It became quite fashionable to form *clubs* for the study of Greek, much as our people sometimes have French clubs to-day.

Then, in 1453, Constantinople was captured by the Turks. At last the Mohammedans had entered Europe from the East. They quickly conquered westward through old Greece and northward to beyond the Danube ; and even to-day, after six hundred years, they keep a small foothold in southeastern Europe.

This Turkish victory drove more Greek learning from Constantinople to Italy. Hundreds of Greek scholars fled there, carrying with them their precious books. Then the universities began to teach Greek, and before long the scholars of Western Europe knew all that had been saved from the learning of ancient Greece. Soon, indeed, these scholars began to translate

ERASMUS (1466–1536), a Dutch scholar who spent much of his life in England. — From a portrait painted by a Dutch artist, Holbein. Erasmus stood to the "Rebirth" in Northern Europe much as Petrarch did in Italy, but he was a greater scholar. His kindly but keen wit did much to do away with old and foolish ideas.

part of that old learning into the languages of the different countries so that still more people could understand it.

And we must not think that people were content with just the *old* learning. Now that it had waked them up, they started to do things for themselves, and all their ways of working and even of thinking were much changed.

For one thing, **in each country many writers began to write poems and plays and stories in the language spoken**

by their own people. We have seen that Chaucer wrote in English. A century earlier than that, Petrarch wrote *his* lovely poems in Italian, and writers in other countries followed his example. Petrarch even invented a new way of arranging lines of verse, called the *sonnet*, which many of our poets use. (Books of *science*, it is true, were still all written in Latin. Can you see why?)

The Rebirth of Europe was Marked By a Famous Growth in Art

The only artists of the earlier Middle Ages had been monks, and you remember that monks thought it wrong to mingle with the world around them very closely. They were expected to go about all their work with eyes cast downward and their thoughts on heavenly things. So, though the saints and angels that they painted had very lovely faces, the bodies were usually out of true proportion and looked as flat as the parchment they were pictured on.

But the people of awakened Europe began to look for beauty in the world about them, as the Greeks had done. Then, first in Italy and soon in Holland and Germany and Spain, **new artists learned to paint lovelier pictures than the world had ever seen.** They gave their saints and angels glorious bodies as well as beautiful faces. They spent years in studying how to make their pictures lifelike, practicing sketch after sketch, so that not a hand or a foot or a muscle or a fold of drapery should be badly drawn. They learned to show *distance* in their pictures, and they tried different kinds of paint, so as to get the softest and most brilliant colors and those that would last the longest.

There were many rich merchants in these Italian towns, ready to spend money freely for beautiful paintings as well as for Greek manuscripts. Popes and bishops ordered lovely carvings and paintings for the new churches that were being built. Kings and princes invited artists to their courts to paint portraits of the royal family or perhaps religious pictures for the palace chapel. The common people of the towns, too, not only in Italy but also in Holland and Germany, loved beautiful things, and often they voted large sums from the town treasury to get some famous artist to come and adorn their town hall or their church with paintings. Sometimes, when such a painting was finished, the whole town would turn out in a great procession to see it and to do honor to the artist.

Until after the year 1400, all large paintings in Europe had been *frescoes*. That is, they had always been painted directly on the plastered walls or ceilings of churches or palaces. But **in the fifteenth century the *Van Eyck* brothers in Holland invented a new way to prepare *oil* paints so that artists could paint on canvas.** This made it much easier to preserve a great painting century after century.

To-day most of the works of the " Old Masters " (as the painters of the Rebirth period are called) are hanging in the art galleries of Europe, where people from all over the world go to see them. Some of them, indeed, have been bought, for thousands of dollars, by wealthy Americans and have come to be the most precious possessions of famous art galleries in our own large cities. *Copies* of the most famous of these paintings, or at least *photographs* of them, hang in many of our schools and homes.

Just the names of famous painters of that Rebirth period would fill more than one page of this book. One of the earliest was the " angelic painter," *Fra Angelico*. Perhaps you have seen colored copies of some of the glorious forms of angels that he was particularly fond of painting as he knelt at his work.

A later painter, and one of the greatest, was *Raphael*. Raphael was not a monk. He liked to paint what he saw in the streets of the Italian cities where he lived. His saints and madonnas were real Italian girls, and his little angels were real children.

Raphael had so many friends that he was called " the Beloved Painter." His friends told many stories about him.

COOPER SHOP. — From an engraving of the early 16th century. It was in some such place, according to the story, that Raphael painted the " Madonna of the Chair." Such shops were common in the United States until new kinds of machinery did away with them about sixty years ago.

Those tales may not be exactly true, but they do show how he was always looking for what was beautiful in life around him. Once, said one story, Raphael saw two beggar children gazing longingly into a baker's window. He hurried to his studio and painted them into a picture of the Madonna and Christ Child which he was just then working on. (Can you find them in the *Sistine Madonna* facing page 276?)

Another story tells how he came to paint the *Madonna of the Chair,* — a picture that many of you must know. While walking with friends in the country, he passed the open gate of a cooper's yard. The cooper was busy at his work of making casks, and his wife and children were looking on. The young peasant mother with her two beautiful boys made so lovely a group that Raphael caught up his brushes and oils and painted them at once on one of the round barrel-heads lying at hand.

Raphael was finally called to Rome by the Pope, to paint part of the decorations of the great *Cathedral of St. Peter's,*

which was then being built and which is still one of the
most famous buildings of the world.   The architect was
Michel Angelo of Florence.   His paintings on the ceiling
of the Sistine Chapel are more famous even than any of
Raphael's.

**And Michel Angelo was also the greatest sculptor of his
time.**   Another sculptor had spoiled (as every one thought)

St. Peter's (Rome) To-day.

a huge block of splendid marble — chipping off parts of it
clumsily and leaving an ill-shaped mass of which it seemed
impossible to make any good use.   But Michel Angelo
begged for a chance to work at it.   He had a closed wooden
tower built around the marble, so that he might work unseen
and undisturbed ; and when that tower was at last removed,
all the city marveled at the beauty and strength of a statue
of the young *David* (page 274) which he had created.

The Newly Awakened Europe Felt also Great Interest in Science

Michel Angelo was great not only as architect and painter and sculptor but also as poet and as engineer. Another Italian artist, **Leonardo da Vinci,** was great in all those ways and besides **was the best scientist of his day.** His writings show that he knew more about botany, chemis-

try, and physics than any man who followed him for a hundred years. He was also a famous inventor. Many of his new ideas he worked out into useful tools. Perhaps the one you know best is the humble wheel barrow ; but, even in that early time, he *tried* to make steam engines and flying machines. But the tools that he had to work with were still too clumsy,

HEAD OF MICHEL ANGELO'S DAVID.

and his materials were not light enough or strong enough. Men had much still to learn before the airplane could be a success. Leonardo, however, did succeed in making a flying toy — a " machine bird " that could be wound up for short flights. (Leonardo liked to study a book written more than two hundred years earlier by *Roger Bacon*, an English friar, who prophesied then that men would learn to fly. And see cut opposite.)

That Roger Bacon was the most interesting of all the early scientists. He lived and studied in a small round tower that stood, until a few years ago, on a bridge across the River Thames at Oxford. But for fourteen precious years he was shut up in dungeons, because the government thought his teachings dangerous ; and at many other times his work had to stop for months or years because he could not find, or could not afford to buy, some necessary book.

There is an old legend in Spain that the Moors there did invent a flying machine about 1100 A.D. — nearly two centuries before Roger Bacon. This modern painting represents the supposed inventor explaining his model to the Saracen ruler of Spain. Roger Bacon got many ideas, we know, from learned Moors,

Bacon experimented with an *explosive powder* much like our gun-powder. The Chinese had used something of that kind for many centuries in their " fire-crackers," and Bacon had learned about the powder in some way — probably from some statement in a Greek book. At all events he wrote that if a man wished to make a big flash and a loud noise, he could do so by mixing together saltpeter and charcoal and sulphur, and then touching fire to it. He experimented also with *steam*. In time to come, he said, wagons and ships would move " with unbelievable speed " without help from horses or sails. In the year 1258 an Italian friar visited Friar Bacon and wrote back to a friend in Italy as follows :

" Among other things he showed me a black, ugly stone called a magnet, which has the surprising quality of drawing iron to it; and if a needle be rubbed upon it and afterward fastened to a straw, so that it will swim upon water, it will instantly turn to the pole star. . . . Therefore, be the night never so dark, neither moon or stars visible, yet shall the sailor by help of this needle be able to steer his vessel aright. This discovery, so useful to all who travel by sea, must remain concealed until other times, because no master mariner dare use it, lest he be suspected of being a magician ; nor would sailors put to sea with one who carried an instrument so surely constructed by the devil."

Bacon had learned in some of his books that sailors in China used *the magnetic needle*, but it was more than a century later before European sailors really began to use it. (Do you know what we call that instrument to-day ?)

Bacon died just at the beginning of the Rebirth of Europe. He lived too soon for his own happiness. He left no followers, and was despised during his life by all except a few humble scholars. But he came nearer being a true scientist than any other man between the Fall of Rome and the beginning of Modern Times.

This painting by a modern German artist (now in the Corcoran Art Gallery at Washington) represents Pope Julius II showing to a group of friends a glorious marble statue (the Apollo Belvedere) dug up not long before in Italy. Among the company are Michel Angelo (on the far left) and the youthful Raphael on the far right.

THE SISTINE MADONNA, — a painting by Raphael (page 271); now in a
Dresden art gallery.

In the early Middle Ages it had been a dangerous thing to know much. A little science had found its way into Europe from the universities of the Saracens in Spain; and here and there some lonely scholar had tried to experiment with chemicals and medical drugs. But men of that kind who lived before 1400 were likely to be put to death as wizards. At least, when they showed themselves on the streets, they and their families were often stoned by boys. Ignorant people said that such a man practiced " Black Art." How could he know so much more than other people, they reasoned, unless he had paid the Devil to teach him? And if a serious and fatal explosion happened in his laboratory, then the neighbors were sure they had seen the Devil come for his soul, with thunder and lightning, leaving the smell of brimstone behind him.

Roger Bacon had to fight against such ignorant fears and hatreds all his life, fears that were found even among the rulers of his time. But when Leonardo was born (1454), such superstition was fading away.

When Europe's Rebirth Began
Men were beginning to Wonder
About Far-off Parts of the World

From a French friar, *Rubruk*, who had traveled far into central Asia on business for the French king, Roger Bacon had heard a report of an *open ocean* east of Asia. This seemed amazing, because all Europeans of that time thought that Asia extended endlessly into some sort of impassable swamp or desert, inhabited by horrible monsters. Bacon had already come to believe that the earth was round, as the Greeks had taught; and now he began to wonder whether that ocean east of Asia (if there really *were* such an ocean) might not be the same as the Atlantic ocean west of Europe. If it were, he argued, men might reach Asia by sailing west! All that Bacon wrote about this was copied (nearly a hundred and fifty years later) into a book which, later still, fell into the hands of Christopher Columbus.

And during the last years that Roger Bacon was studying and experimenting in his tower on the Thames bridge, **three Venetian merchants gave the world other important new facts about geography.** Two brothers of the Polo family, with a young son of one of them named *Marco*, journeyed from Venice through central Asia to the court of the " Great Khan," ruler of China and of much of the rest of Asia. There they traded for more than twenty years, winning vast riches. Indeed, they became trusted and favorite officers of the Great Khan. But when they asked his permission to return to their homes, he was unwilling to let them go.

Finally, however, he gave his consent in this fashion. His daughter was to be sent as a bride to the King of Persia. But the route by land was thousands of miles long, with mighty mountain ranges and desolate deserts to be crossed, and it was unsafe because of wars among savage tribes along the way. Even a sea voyage to so distant a land as Persia seemed full of dangers, though the Khan did know of a route that no European knew anything about. Such a voyage called for the best seamen to be found anywhere. The Khan had heard of the fame of Venice as a great sea-power, and he had learned to trust the word of the Polos. So now he told them that if they would take charge of the expedition, and deliver his daughter safely to the King of Persia, they might then go on from Persia to their home in Europe.

This they did. The company took ship at Peking, sailed south along the coast of China, passed through the straits into the Indian Ocean, and, at the end of a two-year trip, arrived at the head of the Persian Gulf, in territory that many Europeans had visited by caravan.

You see, this voyage *proved* what Friar Rubruk had *heard* long before about the ocean east of China. And it proved, too, that one could sail from this ocean into the Indian Ocean, which Europeans had known about ever since the days of Alexander (page 74), but which they had thought a lake.

Back at Venice the Polos found themselves long-since given up for dead and almost forgotten. The rich Venetian merchants did not like the strangers' shabby and ragged Chinese clothing, and no one was quite sure that the three men really were the Polos. But the travelers managed at last to get some of their old friends to come to a splendid feast. There they appeared in rich Venetian robes; and, after the meal, they brought out the ragged coats they had worn home, and, ripping open the seams, poured forth on the table piles of flashing diamonds and glowing rubies and other precious gems.

This was in the same year that Roger Bacon died. He never heard of this remarkable voyage. (If he had, it would have made him still more hopeful that a ship might sail west from England and reach Asia.) But for that matter, in spite of the stir that the Polos made in Venice, few people anywhere else knew much about their voyages for several years. Vague rumors floated about that someone had *heard* a strange and unbelievable story from someone else — who had said that he had *heard* it from someone else, and so on. No one knew just how much to believe. In those days you see, merchants and travelers did not write out full accounts of their discoveries.

But, by a happy accident, a few years later, **Marco Polo** *did* **get his story into writing.** Venice and Genoa were fighting each other for the control of the trade through the Mediterranean (page 235). In one of the battles, Marco Polo was taken prisoner. He was kept some time in Genoa.

There he amused and entertained his fellow prisoners with long accounts of his adventures in Asia. The stories were so interesting that one of the prisoners, who was a writer, wrote them down as Polo told them.

Soon the Invention of *Printing* Spread the New Learning

For more than a hundred years only a few scholars saw Marco Polo's book. Then came a new invention which made it impossible ever again to lose the memory of such

stories. This was **the invention of printing.**

Long before, the Chinese had printed books from blocks, — *one block for a page*. A printer took a block of wood, the size of the page he wanted, and cut out on its face the words and sentences, just as, later, men cut wooden blocks to make the kind of pictures that we call woodcuts. The wood was cut

BOY A-COCKHORSE. — From a woodcut of 1549.

away from the letters, you see, so that they were left *raised*. Then ink could be spread on this block, and if a page of paper were pressed down upon it, the page would be " printed."

Sometime during the fourteenth century, this kind of printing reached Europe. It was better than making books by pen and ink, because quite a number of copies of a page could be made from one block. But when the printer had run off all the copies he wanted, the *very costly block was good for nothing more*. It could not be used in printing any other book, where the words were arranged differently, because *it was all one piece.*

But about 1450 a German block-printer, **John Gutenberg**, thought out a better way. He **cut out** *each letter separately;*

then he bound these very small blocks together in words, enough to fill a page. When he had printed as many copies of this page as were wanted, he separated all these little letter-blocks again and used them *over and over*, in new combinations, for other pages or to print other books.

These *letter-blocks* were called *type*. But the *wooden* type were hard to carve, and they wore out quickly. So, next, Gutenberg learned to " cast " his type out of *metal*, by running melted metal into molds that he had cut. These metal type were much better than the wooden type; and they were cheaper, because many of them could be made from one mold.

Then the ingenious Gutenberg completed his work by taking one more step. At first, after he had set up a page of type, he had to press a sheet of paper upon it *by hand*, taking the greatest care to see that every part of the sheet touched the type in just the right way. But soon he invented a " printing press," to press the paper evenly and quickly upon the page of type. This press was worked up and down by a " screw," much like the press used by Benjamin Franklin in America three centuries later.

Perhaps you noticed that we have just been talking about " paper " instead of papyrus. Even Gutenberg's inventions would have been of little use, if, just before, men had not found how to make a cheap paper. After papyrus became hard to get, the monks had begun to use what we call *parchment* and *vellum* (made from sheep skin and calf skin), such as school diplomas are still sometimes printed on. Such stuff, however, was very costly and no one could possibly get a great deal of it. But about the year 1400, Europe had learned (from the Saracens in Spain) how to make paper from cloth and old rags.

The invention of printing and of paper came just in time to *spread* the old Greek learning, as it was recovered, and also all the new knowledge. Within a few years every city in

Europe had its printing shop. In 1474, *William Caxton*, an Englishman who had been studying in Germany, brought one to England, and among his first books was an edition of Chaucer's *Canterbury Tales*. Before the year 1500, at Venice alone, three thousand different books had been printed, — probably a thousand copies of each book; and Europe had

GUTENBERG examining his first printed sheet, as pictured by a modern German painter (C. Reichert). His assistant still grasps the lever that has been working the screw of the press. On the further side of Gutenberg stands his partner, John Faust. This Faust sold the first printed books and came to be looked upon as a wizard and a dealer in " black art," because people could not understand how he got so many copies of a book so quickly unless the Devil helped him.

millions of books, where, fifty years before, it had only hundreds. A volume cost only about a twentieth as much, too, as the written manuscript had cost in earlier days; and so knowledge of all sorts soon reached people who before could not have afforded it.

Among the first books printed was *The Book of Ser Marco Polo*. This was widely read, and it became a favorite book of Christopher Columbus. It told marvelous stories, some of them rather exaggerated, about Japan with its golden palaces, and about the huge Empire of Cathay (China), with its stores of jewels and gold, its rich and populous cities many times larger than any that Europe knew about, and its huge fleets for trading with the " twelve thousand seven hundred islands " that lay in the open ocean south and west.

At Nearly the Same Time Several Other Inventions Changed the Way of Living and Working

When the early experimenters mixed saltpeter and charcoal and sulphur in their laboratories (page 276), they did not think of the mixture as *gun*-powder, for as yet there was no gun. But they did know that the powder had a strange power to scatter things by its explosion. Then, some fifty years after Bacon died, it occurred to some forgotten genius that if this powder could only be put at the *closed* end of a strong tube, and exploded *there*, its power might drive an iron or stone ball out of the open end with great violence — and so make an altogether new kind of " hurling engine " for war.

A BOMBARD OF 1500 A. D. — From an old German woodcut.

This unknown inventor made a sort of big " gun," or small " cannon," in which to use the powder. In 1346, in the *Battle of Crécy* in France during the " Hundred Years War," the English used " several small bombards," said a writer of that day, " which, with fire and noise like God's thunder, threw little iron balls *to frighten the horses* " of the French nobles.

These first cannon were made by fastening bars of iron

together with hoops; and the powder was still very weak. But about a century later there were cannon good enough to batter down the walls of feudal castles.   It was the use of cannon that made it possible for the kings to destroy the castles of the feudal lords (page 249).   From this time on, kings and lords stopped building the old kind of castles. Instead they built spacious *palaces*, with broad galleries and richly decorated rooms lighted by many windows.

Keystone Photo.

A Spinning Wheel was found in every American home when George Washington was President.   This photo shows one still in use in a country district of Norway.

(Compare the buildings facing pages 358 and 359 with the castle facing page 197.)

Then, somewhat later still, troops on foot (or infantry) had muskets that would send bullets through any iron armor.   The peasant, so armed, was a match for the noblest knight. Roger Bacon and the later unknown inventors of "bombards" and muskets had done more to end feudalism, and to make the common man the equal of nobles, than the crusades had done.   Gunpowder, too, made it easy, a few years later, for small bands of Europeans to conquer America from the Indians.

Two other new inventions made certain kinds of work easier than before.

1. *Sawmills* were first used, so far as we know, in Germany soon after 1300.   That is, men then first found how to drive a saw through wood *by water-power* instead of by hand.

This invention has a special interest for *us*. Very few saw-
mills were built in Europe for three hundred years after the
invention. But almost as soon as Englishmen settled in
America, lumber became one of the chief things they found
it paid to send back to England (because the English forests
were giving out); and so sawmills were built quickly on
every stream in New England.

2. The other invention had to do with the work of women.
This was the *spinning wheel*, which was to be important for
hundreds of years for Europe and America alike. A spinning wheel now seems to us a very slow way to get thread
and yarn. But it was much better and quicker than the
older ways of twisting and stretching the thread *by hand*
(page 50), and the busy housewife soon found it much easier
than before to keep her family clothed.

Another remarkable invention, a little later, was the
telescope. Roger Bacon is said to have made a small "far-
seeing" tool; but anyway about 1600 A.D. scientists had
learned how to make very good ones — though nowhere
near so good or large as ours now. Then scholars were
able very soon to learn more about the sun and moon and
stars than the Greeks had ever known, and to find out
just how the earth and the other planets move around
the sun.

SUMMARY

The "Rebirth" of Europe began in Italy soon after 1300.
Petrarch especially helped to make the study of the old Greek
learning fashionable. The "Rebirth" was marked by great
artists (especially in Italy and Germany and later in Holland and
Spain); by new advances in science; and by many inventions
(name five or six) that helped to overthrow feudalism, spread
knowledge, and make life easier for many people. Europeans, too,
began to be deeply interested in distant lands, by the printed
stories of travelers like the Polos.

New Words

manuscript	wizard	type	musket	architect
parchment	scientist	printing press	telescope	fresco
artist	magnet	palace	engineer	studio

Thought Questions and Things to Do

1. Write down all the reasons you can why the new learning *started* in Italy instead of in Germany or England.

2. Put the important dates on your time line.

3. What things had the Greeks written in their books that the world could not afford to lose?

4. A famous writer once said, " Gunpowder made all men the same height." Can you explain what he meant?

5. What do we have now that make it unnecessary for our homes to have spinning wheels?

6. List the countries on the map following this page which are not found on any earlier map in this book. Notice how the countries on this map compare with those of Europe to-day (map after 378).

7. Dramatize scenes from the life of Marco Polo. A good book about him is Brooks' *Story of Marco Polo.*

8. Other books which tell about the new learning and inventions are Stuart's *The Boy through the Ages*, Tappan's *European Hero Stories*, O'Neill's *The World's Story*, and Van Loon's *The Story of Mankind.*

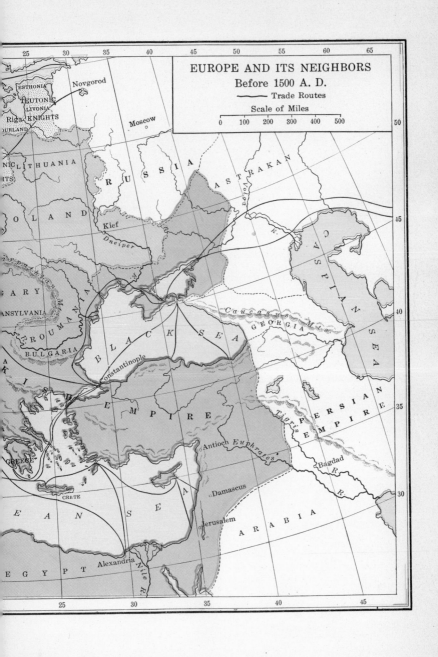

EUROPE AND ITS NEIGHBORS
Before 1500 A. D.
——— Trade Routes
Scale of Miles
0   100   200   300   400   500

25   30   35   40   45   50   55   60   65

ESTHONIA
TEUTONIC
LIVONIA
Riga KNIGHTS
COURLAND

NIC LITHUANIA
ITS

Novgorod

Moscow

RUSSIA

ASTRAKAN

Volga R.

50

45

POLAND

Kief

Dnieper

CASPIAN

GARY

ANSYLVANIA

ROUMANIA

BULGARIA

BLACK   SEA

Caucasus Mts.

GEORGIA

SEA

40

Constantinople

KISH   EMPIRE

Tigris

PERSIAN   EMPIRE

35

GREECE

Antioch Euphrates

Bagdad

CRETE

Damascus

30

EAN   SEA

Jerusalem

ARABIA

EGYPT   Alexandria

Nile R.

25   30   35   40   45

CHAPTER XXVI

EUROPE FINDS AMERICA

The nations of Western Europe had long wanted some cheaper way of trading with the East, and the stories of Marco Polo made thinkers believe that some easier route could be found to those regions. Besides, that trade was growing more important all the time.

You remember that European towns had learned to manufacture many of the new luxuries and comforts that the crusaders brought home (page 220). But some of the Eastern products that people wanted most had still to be brought from Asia. Towns had grown so much larger and richer, too, that many more people were able to buy such things. So year by year there was more of this trade with the East.

Chief among the things that still had to be brought from the Far East were *spices*. The Europeans had come to value these above all other articles of trade. Cloves, cin-

287

namon, nutmeg, and pepper, were used both to preserve
foods — as we use them still in pickling — and also to keep
people from noticing strong tastes and disagreeable odors
of other food that we should consider quite spoiled and unfit to eat.

So kings gave pepper to their favorites as the choicest of
presents, and wealthy merchants sometimes left small
boxes of it to their friends in their wills. Then after a while,
people stopped looking upon spices as luxuries but came
instead to think them necessities, as we do and even more
than we do, though they still cost vastly more than such
things cost us.

To get these goods from the East was hard and dangerous.
Englishmen and Frenchmen did not themselves go to India
or China to buy them. **The merchants of northern Europe
bought their spices from the Italians.** The Italians got them
from Greek, Turkish, or Saracen merchants in Constantinople, Egypt, or Palestine. These merchants, in turn, had
first to import them from India or from the more distant
Cathay. Indeed, the spices came, as they still do for the
most part, from a group of islands in the ocean southeast
of China, known later as the Spice Islands. But it was not
until after the time of the Polos that Europeans had any idea
just where those islands were.

Of course **the Eastern trade was beset with perils.** Caravans of camels crossing the deserts were often attacked
by hostile tribes, and could not carry large amounts of goods
at one time anyway. The Turks, through whose lands they
had to come, demanded high tolls. Even after the goods
reached the Black Sea or the Red Sea, they had to be carried
hundreds of miles farther in what we should think very frail
and small ships. These were often lost in storms or captured
by pirates. Then when they reached the Mediterranean,
the precious goods had to be unloaded and reshipped for
another long voyage to Italy. Even from that land to

France or England or Spain, the journey was long and dangerous, whether the goods were carried by land or sea.

All this made the goods from the East extremely costly; so Europeans now began to look eagerly for safer and cheaper routes by which to get them. This was why men were so deeply interested in the stories of Friar Rubruk and the Polos and of other travelers of a century later, who printed books about the East and made maps to show as nearly as they could how the land lay. There was hardly a village now that had not been visited by some merchant or traveling scholar, who told marvelous tales about distant lands.

The New Learning Now Showed Europeans How to Find Better Ways to the East

Ever since the days of the old Greeks, **a few wise men had believed that the earth was round;** and now that the Greek learning was being spread by the printing press, more and more people believed it. Scholars gave the same reasons for thinking so that we find in our geographies to-day. But no one had actually gone around the earth or even tried to do so; and many scholars who believed it was round did not believe that men could really travel around it.

Before the time of the Polos most people had thought that China could not be reached from the *east,* because of vast impassable regions where no man could live (page 277). And they had feared, too, that if a ship sailed *west* out into the Atlantic from Europe, it might fall off the earth when it got to the other side. At least, many men argued, after the ship had gone " down hill " the first half of the way round, it could never climb " up hill " again. Still others feared that, as they approached the other side on such a voyage, they might find themselves in a land of ice, or in boiling seas, or in a misty " Sea of Darkness," or that strange and horrible sea monsters would swallow up their ships.

It is no wonder that the unknown oceans terrified sailors in that day. Their tiny ships were not a hundredth as large as our ordinary ocean steamers; and, until about 1450 (page 276), they had no way to tell directions when out of sight of land, except by sun or stars. **But after sailors**

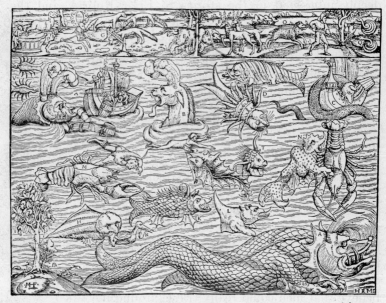

DANGERS LIKELY TO BE MET IN DISTANT SEAS, as a German artist pictured them in a woodcut of 1575. One ship has just been seized by a monstrous sea-serpent. Floating casks hint that another has been sunk or devoured. And a third would seem to have little chance to escape.

The picture is reproduced from an old German book in E. S. Bates' *Touring in 1600*, published by Houghton Mifflin, Boston; and, through the courtesy of those publishers, its use is permitted here.

finally took Friar Bacon's compass as a trusted guide, long voyages out of sight of land were at last possible.

Master mariners and skillful ship captains had learned also how to find, when out at sea, how far north or south they were. They had found that on a voyage to Iceland, for instance, or on the coasts of Norway, the North Star was much higher in the heavens than it was when they sailed in the Mediterranean. And rude instruments had been invented to *measure* such differences though not so exactly as it can be done now.

And now that men could measure directions at sea better than before, they could also make better maps. Several scholars tried to make maps of the world that would fit the reports of sailors and the stories of travelers. A good deal of every such map, of course, had to be guesswork still, and some parts of the world that we think very important were left out. Still these maps gave more courage to sailors and helped in the finding of America.

The New Nations were very Unwilling
To Leave all the Rich Eastern Trade to Italy

When you look at the map after page 286, you can see why the Italian cities had carried on most of the trade with the East as long as it went by the old routes through the Mediterranean. But **the countries on the Atlantic were getting tired of paying Italian merchants double prices for Oriental goods.** They themselves had good ports and able seamen. For centuries they had been sending forth daring sailors in trading and fishing fleets along the northern and western coasts. *Why could they not find a way to the Spice Islands and to India and Cathay by some new route that Venice and Genoa could not control?*

The *rulers* of the new nations that had been growing up in those Western lands also wished to get that rich trade for themselves and their own people. How could they better become wealthy and famous than by finding some new way to Cathay? What if the wild guess of Friar Bacon about a *western* route there by way of the Atlantic should be true? The first country to find that route would perhaps be able to set up a *monopoly*, — allowing no other country to use it, or charging well for its use, as Venice and Genoa were doing for the routes through the Mediterranean to Egypt and Asia. So the kings of Western Europe came to be interested in geography and became rivals for trade routes — as European countries have continued to be down to the present time.

The Two Countries that Led in the Search Were Portugal and Spain

For many hundred years the Christian peoples of the Spanish peninsula had been busy driving the Mohammedan Moors back to Africa. (The Arabs who conquered Spain had already mixed with the people of North Africa, and were called *Moors*.) Some of the old Visigothic chieftains had not surrendered, at the time of the Mohammedan conquest (page 205), but instead had fled with their followers to mountain strongholds in the northwest. There they gathered bands of Christian Spaniards about them and began the slow work of winning back their land.

Each band, under a king of its own, would win a little district for itself. These small Christian kingdoms fought among themselves almost as much as they fought the Moors. But as time went on, some of them conquered others, and some became joined together in other ways. The Moors still kept some rich provinces in the south; but, soon after the year 1400, the rest of the peninsula had become united into three Christian kingdoms — *Portugal*, *Castile*, and *Aragon*.

For a while, all these three countries had strong rulers, who built up firm governments and kept the feudal lords in order. Finally the brilliant and charming *Queen Isabella of Castile* married the soldier and statesman, *King Ferdinand of Aragon*. Then, in the year 1492, by making use of the new European inventions of gunpowder and cannon, these two monarchs were able to capture the last Moorish stronghold, at *Granada*, and drive out the Mohammedans altogether. This left only two countries in the peninsula:

CATHEDRAL OF SEVILLE (Spain). Spanish architecture keeps many traces of Moorish influence. (See page 206.) Near every Mohammedan mosque, or place of worship, rose a tall separate building (like the Bell Tower, or Giralda, in this picture), from which the religious criers called forth to the people each hour of prayer. The tower in this picture was built originally by the Moors for this purpose (though the smaller part at the top was added later by Christian architects), but it was used afterward to carry the bells of the Christian cathedral.

big *Spain*, as Isabella and Ferdinand called their kingdom, and little *Portugal*.

For some time Portugal had already been building up an empire *outside* the peninsula. This was largely the work of the king's brother, Prince Henry, who was also called *Henry the Navigator*. In his youth this prince had gained fame and glory by fighting the Moors, but he came to believe that his country could grow great sooner by trade than by war. So he built himself a high tower on a rocky cape looking out over the sea, and invited famous geographers and map-makers from foreign countries to join him there. He set up a school, too, to train sea-captains in the use of the new instruments and in the best way to manage their ships. Then finally **he began to send expeditions down the coast of Africa to try to find a way around its southern end** into the Indian Ocean — and so on **to Cathay.**

These expeditions discovered the Cape Verde islands and the Azores (which are still Portuguese colonies) and learned much about the west coast of Africa. Each expedition ventured a little farther south than the earlier ones. Before very long, they reached the Gold Coast, and loaded their ships with ivory, gold, and slaves. Then the people who had made fun of Prince Henry began to be much interested in his expeditions and to think it quite worthwhile to train sailors and fit out ships. So when Henry died soon afterward, the expeditions kept on.

Finally, *in 1486*, *Bartholomew Diaz*, one of the Portuguese explorers, sailed around the southern end of Africa, and found himself going northward as he followed the coast, keeping it still on his left hand. Of course he could not be *sure* that he really had got around Africa, because, for all he knew, the shore might sweep south again; but he went north far enough to feel quite certain that he was in the

The map *in black* on the other side was drawn about 1490 by an Italian geographer named Toscanelli. It is supposed that Columbus had this map with him on his first voyage. Toscanelli got his ideas from a careful study of the reports of European traders who had visited parts of Asia and had heard stories about more distant parts.

Our map-maker has drawn in the *true outline* of the continents and islands in *red*. (Asia is too far east to show at all on this true map.)

Does Toscanelli's map show you why Columbus was sure he had reached India? You should compare it not only with the true map here, but also with the European maps that were made soon after Columbus' voyages (after page 296).

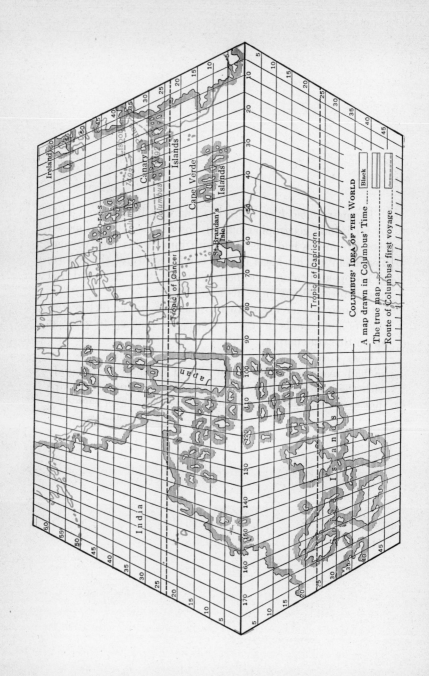

COLUMBUS' IDEA OF THE WORLD

A map drawn in Columbus' Time ..... [Black]

The true map .....

Route of Columbus' first voyage .....

Ireland

Azores

Canary Islands

Cape Verde Islands

St. Brandan's Isle

Tropic of Cancer

Tropic of Capricorn

Japan

India

Islands

Indian Ocean. Then he wanted to sail on and try to reach India, but his sailors were frightened and forced him to turn back to Portugal. (See map facing page 305.)

There the king rejoiced at the news Diaz brought, and ordered that the southernmost cape should be called " Cape of Good Hope." A few years later the " good hope " was fulfilled. **Vasco da Gama sailed around the Cape in 1498 and kept on to Calicut in India.**

But a few years before this, an Italian sailor had made a still more daring and more important voyage, not creeping along any coast, but **heading out into the open Atlantic westward.** This man was *Christopher Columbus.* He knew about Friar Bacon's guess that perhaps a man might reach Asia by sailing west (page 277). He had read Marco Polo's account of the sea east of China, and had studied the latest maps of Italian and German map-makers. He had also sailed north to Iceland, and there perhaps he had heard legends that had grown up about Leif Ericson's voyage of five hundred years before. And he had thought about all these things until he had come to believe firmly that a man could reach Asia by sailing west. Anyway he was bound to risk his life in trying to do so.

At first Columbus had tried to interest the king of Portugal in his plan, but the Portuguese cared only for their new route around Africa, which seemed pretty sure by that time to be successful. So Columbus tried the court of Spain, — for no poor sailor could possibly fit out such an expedition unless he could find some powerful prince to furnish the large sums of money that were needed. For a while Ferdinand and Isabella were too busy fighting the Moors to give much attention to his plans. But at last Granada, the last stronghold of the Moors, fell, and they had time for other things.

Even then at first they thought his ideas wild and impossible. But finally, as he was leaving Spain in despair,

Isabella sent messengers after him, and his dream came true. He was given his chance to find the East by sailing west. A few months later, his three little ships left the harbor of Palos, and on **October 12, 1492, Columbus landed on San Salvador in the West Indies.** Europe had found America.

Summary

Europeans needed spices from the East. To get them was hard and dangerous, and the Italian merchants who brought them charged high prices. New inventions were making it easier to venture far out to sea, and the printing press spread new knowledge of great oceans east of Cathay. The new nations on the Atlantic shores wished to find new trade routes. Portuguese sailors found one to the East around Africa; and Columbus, trying to reach the East by sailing west, found America.

New Words

spices	*necessities*	*tolls*	*monopoly*
luxuries	*caravan*	*compass*	*navigator*

Thought Questions and Things to Do

1. Study the four maps following this page, and see how men's knowledge of the earth had grown since early times. Which countries had done the most to add to that knowledge?

2. Put in important dates on the time line.

3. Let the class make an *illustrated chronology*, making a sketch for each century or each two or three centuries, to show the most important events with pictures, using pyramids for Egypt, ships for Phoenicia, and so on.

4. Look back over the part of this book that tells the story of the Middle Ages, and make a list of what was contributed to our civilization by each of the peoples mentioned in those chapters.

5. Make a list of the chief events that led to the discovery of America. Did Columbus plan to find America? If not, why does he deserve credit?

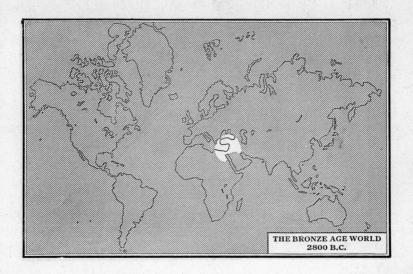

THE BRONZE AGE WORLD
2800 B.C.

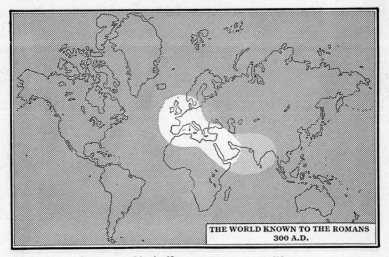

THE WORLD KNOWN TO THE ROMANS
300 A.D.

Growth of Man's Knowledge about the World.

The parts known to civilized men are made white. The lightly shaded parts were known by vague rumors. Maps on the back of this page show further advance.

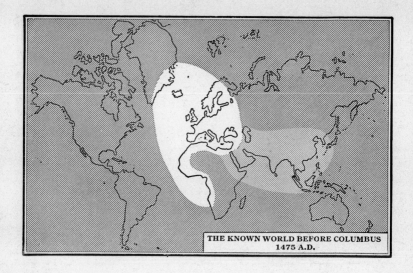

THE KNOWN WORLD BEFORE COLUMBUS
1475 A.D.

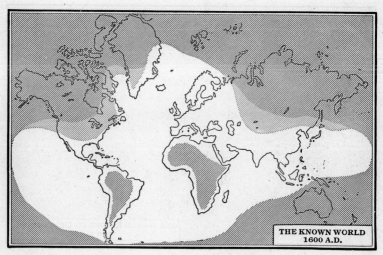

THE KNOWN WORLD
1600 A.D.

GROWTH OF MAN'S KNOWLEDGE ABOUT THE WORLD (*continued*). — See first the maps on the other side of this page. If we made such a map for to-day, what parts would be left dark or shaded?

6. Study a map of the world to-day, and see how much of her empire Portugal has left.

7. Imagine yourself a sailor on one of these expeditions and relate what happened to you.

8. Read about the explorers in McMurry's *Pioneers on Land and Sea*, Tappan's *European Hero Stories*, and West and West's *The Story of Our Country*. Good stories of the time are told by Padraic Colum in *The Voyagers*.

Before beginning the next chapter, turn back and read the passage about "time names" on page 175. We have come now to the point where we are concerned especially with one of those names:

Our story has finished with the Middle Ages and is about to begin *Modern Times* — the period since the discovery of America, or since about 1500 A.D.

In the very beginning of that period European countries began to found the colonies in the New World that have grown into the great free nations of America. We shall not tell *much* of the story of the colonies here, because you will read that in another book. Instead, in the following chapters we shall try to tell you some of the things that were happening in the rest of the world while the colonies were growing up — in particular, things that were happening in the countries from which the most colonists came.

As you read, watch for the things: (1) which made men want to leave the Old World for the New; and (2) which help to explain their ways of living and thinking after they came to America.

Wide World Photo.

OLDEST BRIDGE IN AMERICA, — built by early Spanish conquerors near Panama City.

CHAPTER XXVII

SPAIN CLAIMS THE NEW WORLD

France and England Failed, for a Long Time, To Make Strong Claims to any Part of America; So Spain Claimed All of It

As soon as Columbus' voyage had shown that the Atlantic *could* be crossed, other navigators wanted to cross it, too, and see what they could find on the other side. And kings now were glad to fit out expeditions; for each country felt that it could claim for its own all the new lands that its sailors discovered.

So in 1497, King Henry VII of England sent out *John Cabot*, an Italian sea captain who was living in England. Cabot sailed nearly straight west, and in a few weeks he reached what he thought at first was the coast of China but what really must have been Labrador or Newfoundland. He was disappointed to find no rich cities and neither gold nor spices; but he did report great quantities of fish off the coasts — so many that his small ship sometimes could hardly make its way through them.

It was not long before fleets of little English fishing boats, and French fishing boats, too, began to visit

those coasts every year, where they quickly loaded up
with profitable cargoes of fish. Even to-day the
" Banks " of New Foundland are one of the most
famous fishing grounds in the world.

When Cabot got back from his voyage of discovery, he
was hailed as a great admiral. An Italian living in London
wrote home about him: " He dresses in silk, and every one
runs after him like mad." But King Henry lost interest
in expeditions that brought him neither gold nor spices, and
for a long time England took no further part in the discoveries. Still, eighty years later, when the English wanted
a share in the New World, they claimed a right to it because
of Cabot's voyage.

The French, too, were disappointed when their first
explorers found no gold. **So, for a time, both France and
England left the New World to Spain.**

Little by Little, Men Learned More
About the Shape and Size of America

Columbus made three more voyages across the Atlantic,
but he never learned that he had discovered a New World.
He died broken-hearted at his failure to find the rich cities
of Cathay.

The Spanish people, too, were bitterly disappointed, and
envied the Portuguese who were now using the new route
around Africa and were growing rich from their trade with
India and the Spice Islands. But since Portugal was careful
to keep this route for herself, the Spaniards kept on hunting
for a way to the East by sailing West.

The first Spanish explorers felt sure, just as Columbus had
done, that they *had* reached Asia. When it became plain
that they had not done that, men thought that the new
lands must be *islands* near the coast of Asia, and kept on
trying to find a way through them or around them.

Then came a man with a new and truer idea. This was *Americus Vespucius,* an Italian map-maker and geographer. Vespucius had sailed with several Spanish and Portuguese explorations, and had coasted what we now call South America for a long distance — until he **made up his mind that the new lands formed a great continent.** He wrote interesting letters about his voyages, and soon map-makers took up his idea and called the new continent AMERICA in his honor.

It was some time more before men knew that there were *two* new continents, or what was their shape and size, and still longer before they found out that Asia lay much farther west, beyond another great ocean. But, **little by little, scholars learned more and more about the new parts of the world.** Look at the three maps following this page, and see how ideas changed as explorers brought back new reports.

One of the most important of the early explorers was ·*Magellan,* a Portuguese sailor in the service of Spain. **Magellan made up his mind to finish the work of Columbus and sail all the way around the world.** The voyage took three years. Magellan himself died on the way, but not until he had taken his ships around the southern point of South America, through the stormy straits that we call by his name, and across the wide Pacific.

In crossing the Pacific, his men nearly died of hunger and thirst. For three months and twenty days after leaving the Straits of Magellan they saw no land except two little rocky islands, which furnished neither food nor water. At last they found inhabited islands and claimed them for Spain. One group of these islands was afterward named the Philippines, after the Spanish King Philip. (Do you know anything about those islands to-day?)

Magellan had sailed with five ships; but only one of them found its way back, around Africa, to Spain. From the

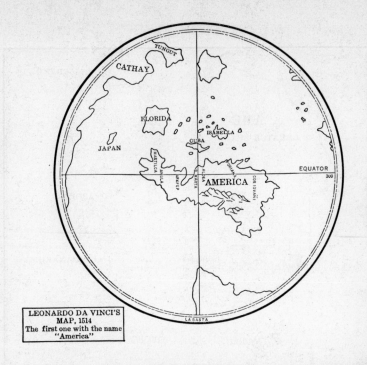

LEONARDO DA VINCI'S
MAP, 1514
The first one with the name
"America"

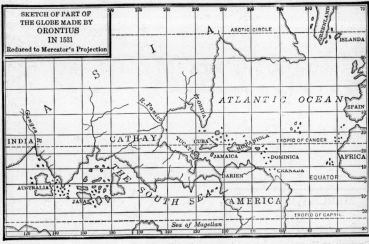

SKETCH OF PART OF
THE GLOBE MADE BY
ORONTIUS
IN 1531
Reduced to Mercator's Projection

GROWTH OF KNOWLEDGE ABOUT AMERICA. — The first map made South America and Florida islands. The second made South America in a truer form, but joined it (and Florida) to Asia. See also over the page, and compare these maps with the one facing page 295 and with maps in your geographies.

ICELAND

AME-
GREATER SPAIN

FLORIDA

AZORES

NEW
SPAIN

CUBA

HISPANIOLA

CANARIES

YUCATAN COSUMELLA

TRINIDAD

PERU

RICA

(Sometimes called
New India)

PACIFIC

OCEAN

Straits of Magellan

**MERCATOR'S MAP
1541**

GROWTH OF KNOWLEDGE ABOUT AMERICA (*continued*). But notice how narrow North
America was thought to be.

Spice Islands it brought twenty-six tons of cloves — a very rich cargo. What was still more important, its voyage proved beyond any doubt that the world is really round, and that the East *can* be reached by sailing west. It proved, too, that Vespucius was right and that America is a continent, with a vast ocean lying between it and Asia.

Magellan's voyage, however, did not open up a new trade route from Europe to the East. The distance his ship had had to travel was too great for the route to be used for trade in that century. (Name all the reasons you can why that is no longer true.)

> Spain's first colonies were in the West Indies. Later, the Spaniards made many settlements in both North and South America. Some of those in North America were to become important parts of the United States, and the rest of them have grown into nations with whom we have more and more to do each year.

On his second voyage, in 1493, Columbus planted the first European colony in America. He sailed from Spain with seventeen ships and fifteen hundred men, bringing also horses, cattle, sheep, seeds of grain and of vegetables, sugar cane, and shoots of grapevines and fruit trees — oranges and lemons among them. He started a town, called Isabella, on the island of Santo Domingo — or of *Little Spain* as he called it. The town was laid out on a grand scale, and its public buildings were made of stone. The private houses, however, were built of wood or even of straw. Most of the Spaniards who came were not willing to do the work necessary in starting a colony. They had come to find riches and adventure, not to toil harder than in their old homes. So they made slaves of the Indians, and forced them to do the hard work.

Within a few years, Spanish colonies were begun on most of the islands of the West Indies. (Do you see how those islands got that name?) Plantations were started, and mines were opened up. But everywhere Indian slaves did the heavy work. The poor Indians were not used to this sort of labor. Many of them, too, were treated very cruelly, and in some islands nearly all of them grew sick and died. Then the Spaniards brought in Negro slaves from Africa to take their places.

In all the colonies there were many people who tried to save the Indians from slavery or at least to have them treated kindly. Chief among such men was a good monk named *Las Casas*. He did get better treatment for both Indian and Negro slaves, but he could not persuade the planters to free them.

The Spaniards soon Found Riches in Mexico and Peru And then Hunted for More in North America

Meantime, many expeditions were fitted out, both in Spain and in the West Indies, to explore farther *on the main-land*. The adventurers were looking for two things in particular: for a water route to India shorter than Magellan's, and for gold. The water route they did not find, though they explored every wide stream they came to in the hope that it might lead to the Pacific. But gold they did find in such quantities that Spain soon became the richest country in Europe.

The first Spaniard to discover great amounts of gold was *Hernando Cortez*. In 1519, the same year that Magellan started around the world, Cortez set out from Cuba with eleven ships, six hundred men, and a few horses and small cannons. On the coast of Mexico he started the settlement of *Vera Cruz* and made it his headquarters. The natives near the coast told him that they were forced to pay tribute of gold and human beings to a strong league of three tribes called *Aztecs*, who lived farther inland and whose chief was *Montezuma*. Messengers from this king soon reached

Cortez with rich gifts — shields, helmets, and ornaments of gold.

The Aztecs hoped the white men would be satisfied with these presents and go away. But the sight of so much gold only made the Spaniards eager for more. To make sure that his men should not lose courage and change their minds, Cortez sank his ships. Then he began a long hard march inland.

When the Spaniards reached the Aztec capital (where Mexico City now stands), they were filled with wonder at its beauty. It was built on an island in the middle of a lake, and was reached by roads, twenty feet wide, built up from the bottom of the lake on high walls of solid masonry. One of the men with Cortez wrote that the white-plastered houses of the city, its floating gardens, and its temples and towers, rose out of the water " like the enchanted castles in old tales."

Montezuma decided to let the Spaniards enter the city peaceably, and he gave them the great council house to stay in. They fortified that place at once, and kept Montezuma there with them, as a sort of half guest, half prisoner. The Aztecs were angry at this, and at the way the Spaniards plundered their temples; so they got their forces ready in secret and surprised Cortez completely by a fierce attack. Cortez sent Montezuma out on the battlements to order them to stop fighting, but the unhappy king was killed by stones and arrows of his own people.

After a week of ceaseless fighting, the Spaniards had to retreat from the city. That was no easy thing to do. They lost nearly two-thirds of their men in crossing the long causeway back to the mainland. After that " sad night," as it is called in Spanish history, Cortez bowed his face upon his hands and wept bitterly.

But now Cortez got the help of other Mexican tribes who hated the rule of the Aztecs, and, after long fighting, he took the city again. The Aztecs were punished with cruel slaughter. Then the Spaniards quickly conquered all the rest of Mexico. The whole story is one of fearful cruelty on both sides. But, on the whole, the Mexican tribes were better off under Spanish rule than they had been before. They no longer had to send young men and maidens every year to be offered up as sacrifices to the Aztec gods. Still they did have to serve stern Spanish masters.

Mexico proved to be a country of tremendous wealth, and shiploads of its gold and silver were carried back to Spain. **Just a few years afterward another Spanish adventurer, _Pizarro_, conquered Peru, and discovered even greater wealth there.** Then the young King Charles of Spain found himself surrounded by adventurous nobles begging him to let them hunt through America for more rich mines and heaped-up treasure. Two of the explorers that the king sent out are especially interesting to us, because they were the first white men to travel through much of the country that later became the United States. These two men were _Fernando de Soto_ and _Francisco de Coronado_.

1. **De Soto** set out from Cuba with a large company of armed knights. Many of these had sold all their lands and houses in Spain to get money for the expedition. They brought with them carpenters and shipbuilders and a doctor with his medicines. They brought smiths, too, with their forges, to mend armor and make new weapons and to fasten chains and iron collars on Indian captives. There were also many priests and friars, in their long robes. The nine ships carried two hundred horses, a drove of hogs (to be taken along to furnish food), and a number of bloodhounds to help in capturing Indians for guides and porters.

The expedition landed on the coast of Florida and at once set out, with banners flying, to march through the swamps and tangled forests of that region, where even to-day it is hard for men to make a way. Mosquitoes bit the adven-

An Early French Explorer (*Jean Nicollet*) landing in Wisconsin in 1634. — From a wall painting in the Milwaukee Public Museum. With some friendly Canadian Indians, Nicollet had paddled up the St. Lawrence from the early French settlement at Quebec. He had hoped to find China (page 333), and so he wore a gorgeous Chinese robe embroidered with flowers and beasts. Instead of civilized Chinamen, he found only savage Winnebagoes. To put them in awe, he discharged his pistols, and so won from the amazed Indians (who had never seen a white man before) the name, " The-wonderful-man-who-speaks-with-smoke-and-thunder."

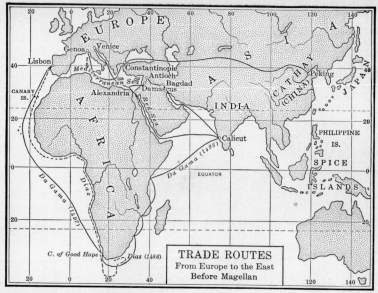

For Portuguese voyages, see page 294. For Magellan, see page 300. There was no canal in those times through the isthmus that joined Africa to Asia; so goods from the Red Sea had to be carried across by caravan and then re-shipped.

CORONADO'S EXPEDITION ON THE MARCH (page 305) in what we now call New Mexico. — From a modern painting.

turers until, as one of them said, blood streamed down their bodies. Indians shot arrows at them from ambush along their march. Once Indians set fire to the camp at night, and the Spaniards lost most of their clothing, so that they had to make themselves coverings of bark and plaited reeds and skins of animals.

After wandering for two years in the wilderness, the expedition came to a great river — which we know as the Mississippi. It was May, and the stream rolled in a yellow flood toward the Gulf, carrying along masses of floating trees and logs. The Spaniards managed to cross in big barges that they built on the shore. Then they explored the land toward the northwest. After a year more of this exploration, De Soto died of a fever. Fearing to let the natives know of their leader's death, his followers buried his body at night in the river. Hoping now only for a safe return to their homes, the discouraged Spaniards hurriedly built boats and floated down the river to the Gulf. Then they coasted the shore westward till they reached Spanish settlements in Mexico.

2. At the same time that De Soto was pushing his way through the damp and tangled forests of the southeast of North America, **Coronado was exploring the burning plains of the southwest.** He had heard stories from the Indians about seven wonderful cities far inland, whose houses were built of gold and had doorways set with precious jewels. Instead he found only clay pueblos, ornamented with colored pebbles. For meat the Spaniards found huge herds of " hump-backed cows," as they called the buffalo, and the Indians furnished them with corn. But the expedition at times suffered agonies of thirst. The farther north they got, the poorer grew the villages, until finally they turned back and, after terrible suffering, found their way to Mexico again.

At one time, Coronado and De Soto must have come very near meeting — somewhere in what is now Kansas. It is certain that De Soto's men captured an Indian woman who had escaped from Coronado only a few days before.

The Spanish Established Colonies From Mexico to La Plata

These expeditions taught the Spaniards something about the vast size of North America, and, though they had found no gold north of Mexico, they made up their minds to hold the country. The first town in what is now the United States was built by them at *St. Augustine* in Florida *in 1565*, to drive off the French who had tried to start a colony near there. Before many years, another Spanish settlement was begun at *Sante Fe*, in what is now our New Mexico. So you see the two oldest cities in the United States are Spanish.

Farther south, there were many more Spanish towns, and some much grander ones. **By the year 1600 there were more than two hundred of them, scattered all the way from Mexico and Florida in North America to Chile and La Plata River in South America** — except that Brazil belonged to Portugal because a Portuguese sea-captain had been the first to discover its coasts.

The Spaniards ruled also over thousands of Indian villages. The Spanish government by this time had forbidden the colonists to make slaves of the natives, but they did still make the Indian villagers work for them much as serfs in Europe worked for their masters. In the country districts wealthy Spanish landlords farmed vast estates by the labor of hundreds of Indian workers, growing corn and sugar cane and raising immense herds of horses, cattle, and sheep.

In the towns, where most of the Spanish colonists settled, the Spanish officials and their families, and many other well-to-do colonists, lived much the same life that they had lived at home. They had fine public buildings, beautiful churches, and good colleges and universities.

The common soldiers and the workmen among the Spanish colonists often married Indian wives. Great numbers of the people of the Spanish-American countries to-day are of mixed Indian and Spanish blood. And the Spanish language is still spoken (except in Brazil) from the Rio Grande River (south of Texas) to the Straits of Magellan.

The king of Spain and his council made the laws for all the Spanish colonies and appointed the governors and officials to carry them out. **The people in the colonies had nothing to do with the government.** They could not even build a church for themselves, or any public building, without the consent of the king or his officials. One-fifth of all the wealth taken from the mines went to the king's treasury. The king also collected high taxes on trade, and forbade his colonists to trade at all with any country except Spain.

West Front of Cathedral of Zucatecas (Mexico) ; begun in 1612.

The people who did most to teach the Indians better ways to live were the friars and monks and village priests. From the beginning, some Spaniards had wanted to explore America mainly so that they might make Christians of the Indians. Wherever explorers went, priests and friars went, too, learning to speak the languages of the natives and teaching them the Christian religion.

A little group of four or five friars would start a mission near an Indian village. There they would teach the Indians to speak Spanish, to sing hymns and to pray, and to live peaceful, busy, and happy lives. They taught also better ways of farming and the trades of weaving, shoemaking, blacksmithing, and building. Most of the famous old Mission buildings in America were built by willing Indians, and even decorated by them — for the Indians loved to

SAN LUIS REY, near San Diego, — one of the oldest missions in California. Its various buildings surrounded a large open space, and the church (with its strong walls and small windows) could easily be turned into a fort.

paint and often became skillful artists. On the whole the Spaniards did much more to civilize the Indians than the later English colonists were able to do.

SUMMARY

Other explorers followed Columbus. John Cabot sailed along the northern coasts of North America and gave England her claim to that region. But, on the whole, the New World was left to Spain through the sixteenth century. It took the Spanish explorers many years to learn the true shape and size of the new lands. The first man to teach that they formed a continent was Americus Vespucius. The first expedition to sail around the world was Magel-

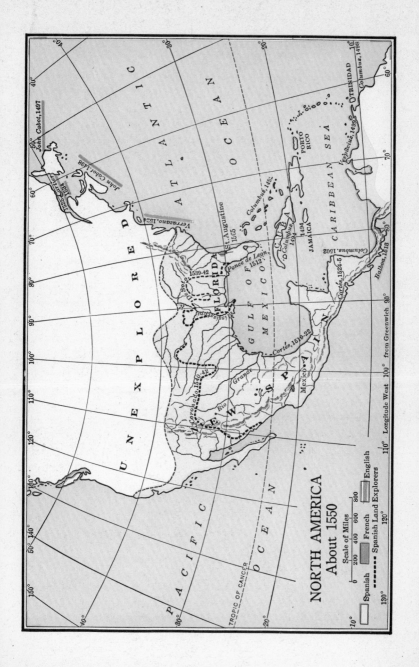

NORTH AMERICA
About 1550

Scale of Miles

0   200 400 600 800

Spanish   French   English
- - - - - Spanish Land Explorers

lan's. In Mexico and Peru the Spaniards found rich mines of gold and silver, and soon they established colonies in the West Indies and on both continents. The hard work in the Spanish colonies was done by the Indians, who were at first slaves and later became a kind of serf. The priests and friars Christianized and civilized the Indians, and taught them many kinds of useful work.

New Words

continent   *pueblo*   *human sacrifice*   *mission*

Thought Questions and Things to Do

1. Put the chief events of this chapter in their proper places on the time line. Which of the new dates ought to be remembered?

2. Make a list of scenes for a pageant of American exploration, and name some of the characters that should appear in each scene. Make a class collection of pictures that would be useful in helping plan scenes and costumes.

3. Make posters urging men of the sixteenth century to go on an exploring expedition in the New World. Are there any explorations going on in the world to-day? Where?

4. On a map of North America show the land claimed by Spain because of Spanish explorations. Which of these lands are now part of the United States? In what parts of the United States are there many people of Spanish descent? Start a collection of pictures of Spanish buildings in the United States.

5. In your geographies, or in the *National Geographic Magazine,* find pictures of famous buildings in South American cities.

6. Good accounts of the explorers can be read in McMurry's *Pioneers on Land and Sea* and in Tappan's *European Hero Stories.* There is a longer story of Magellan in West and West's *Story of Our Country.*

THE BLACK PINESS, which brought Sir Philip Sidney's body back to England (page 319). — From a copper engraving by a Dutch artist in 1587.

CHAPTER XXVIII

SPAIN'S RIVALS — IN EUROPE

Toward the year 1600, **other Western European countries** besides Spain **began to get anxious for a share in America.** They hoped to find gold, as Spain had done, and to get rich by trading with the Indians for furs. They wanted also to found colonies that might soon be able to send them goods like silks and spices, which could not be made in Europe. And they still believed that somewhere toward the north they would find a shorter water-road to India than Spain's long route around South America.

But Spain would not let ships from any other country even visit any coast of America, if her great navy knew about it. She meant to keep all the New World for herself, as she had had it for almost a hundred years. So this rivalry about trade and colonies led finally to many long and terrible wars in Europe; and these wars were the more savage because the quarrels between the different nations became mixed up, for a long time, with bitter disputes about religion. First, then, it is necessary to understand how those disputes about religion grew up.

Soon after 1500 A.D. Little Groups of People Began Protestant Churches

You remember that in the Middle Ages all Western Europe belonged to one church, called the *Catholic Church,* with the Pope at Rome for its head.   During all those centuries it was not thought right to teach anything different from what the Church taught.   But by 1500 a good many people were learning to read the books that came from the new printing presses (page 282).   One of the first books to be put into print was the Bible; and, as more people read this book for themselves, some began to explain parts of it in ways different from those given by the Church.

In Germany, especially, **a bitter quarrel arose about the teachings of a man named** *Martin Luther.*   Luther translated the Bible from Latin into German, so that still more people could read it.   He also printed many new ideas of his own about its meaning.   He would have been put to death for this, except that some of the German princes took up his ideas and protected him.   These followers of his were called *Lutherans.*   They *protested* when an assembly of great clergy and princes ordered Luther to be punished; so they were also called *Protestants.*   **And soon that name came to be used for all Christians who differed from the Catholic Church.**

Nowadays we are used to having many kinds of churches in our towns.   It does not seem necessary to us, or even natural, that all should think alike about religion.   Our Constitution says, — ' Congress shall make no law respecting an establishment of religion or prohibiting the free exercise thereof.''   That is, our government may not favor one church more than another, or forbid people to belong to any church they like.   We call this '' freedom of religion.''

In those old days there was no freedom of religion. **Governments thought it their right and duty to tell their**

people what to believe. If a ruler remained a Catholic, none of his subjects could belong to any Protestant church. But if he took up any of the new ideas about religion, he would at once order every one in his country to adopt them, too, — and then all his people had to pay taxes to support the church he had chosen. In every country of Europe thousands of people were shut up in prison or put to death for refusing to belong to what was called " the state church " — the church of the government of that country.

Soon All Western Europe Was Divided By Bloody Quarrels and Wars about Religion

In Germany, from time to time for more than a century, Protestants and Catholics fought terrible wars with each other. The last and worst of these struggles is called *the Thirty Years' War.* Most European countries joined in on one side or the other — even the far-northern lands of Denmark and Sweden, which had become Lutheran. But all the fighting and destruction was in Germany itself. When the war stopped, in 1648, half the population of that country had been swept away by slaughter or disease. Large cities had shrunk to small villages, and thousands of prosperous little villages had disappeared altogether or had become the haunts of wolves. Neither party had won, but both were worn out. Most of the princes (and their people) in northern Germany remained Protestant, and most of those in southern Germany remained Catholic.

At one time it had seemed as though the Protestants were going to be completely crushed in this struggle; but just at that moment the king of Sweden, *Gustavus Adolphus*, came to their aid. Gustavus stands out from all the other commanders who took part in this war as a great and good man. Wherever his army of tall, light-haired Swedes marched, the people received it with joy, because Gustavus (alone of all the generals on either side) ordered his men not to rob the poor peasants and townsmen, but to pay fairly for every thing they took.

Gustavus, too, was a splendid general, and he soon won great victories over the most famous commanders that were sent against him. His army was probably the best-drilled of all in the world at that time. Soldiers were beginning now to use muskets, instead of spears and bows, but those early guns were still very clumsy weapons. Gustavus trained his men so well that they could fire three shots to one from the enemy. But at his last battle of *Lützen*, in a heavy fog, while he was pressing too eagerly to the front, he became separated from his own men and rode into the enemy's lines, where he was killed.

Before sailing for Germany, Gustavus had bidden farewell to a great assembly of nobles and freemen in Sweden. Holding his little four-year-old daughter, Christina, in his arms, he asked his people to be loyal to her if he should fail to return home; and to them all he said earnestly, — " I wish for you that your little cottages may grow into big stone houses, and your little fishing boats into great ships. I wish that your fields may bring forth fruit and that your comfort may increase so that you may do your work in joy and not in sighing."

It is pleasant to remember that this victorious king loved peace rather than war. Before getting into the German war, he had already made Sweden one of the greatest and strongest states in Europe. Very eagerly he had worked for the welfare of his people, building towns, giving help to universities and schools, and aiding his country to increase its trade with other lands. He planned to build a mighty Swedish empire around the

Baltic Sea and even to plant colonies in the New World. If it had not been for this Thirty Years' War and for his early death, Sweden might have been one of the leading countries in colonizing North America. As things were, there came to be only one Swedish colony, small and short-lived, about which you will read a few pages further on. Swedes and Norwegians and Danes do now make a large part of the people of the United States, but nearly all of them are from families who came here two hundred years later.

In France, too, there was much fighting between Catholic and Protestant lords. There the Catholics won; but they had to agree to give the Huguenots (as French Protestants were called) certain French towns where they might worship in their own way. After about a hundred years, however, in 1685, the powerful French king, Louis XIV, took that right away and punished the Huguenots cruelly if they came together to worship in their way. Then hundreds of thousands fled from France to Protestant countries, and a good many escaped even to colonies that Protestant countries had by that time founded in America. Paul Revere, who made the famous ride to call the Minute Men to arms at Lexington, was a descendant of one of those Huguenot families that came to Massachusetts.

In England, for a long time, many hundreds of people were put in prison or even burned at the stake, for refusing to accept the state religion — which at one time was Protestant and at another time Catholic. Finally, during the long reign of the great Protestant queen Elizabeth, who ruled forty-five years (1558–1603), most Englishmen became Protestants. **England was then the most powerful of the Protestant countries.** Parliament voted not to look on the Pope as head of the English Church any longer. The " Church of England " changed some of the old ways and

DEATH OF GUSTAVUS ADOLPHUS (page 313). — From a modern painting. Many soldiers still wore armor, as in this picture, although firearms were much in use.

During the long wars in France between Catholics and Huguenots, a Huguenot prince at one time became king of France. This was Henry IV. This picture shows him entering Paris victoriously. To secure the crown, Henry had accepted the Catholic religion, but it was known that he would look after the welfare of his Huguenot subjects. After his death, however, things did not go well with them. See page 314.

became much like our Episcopal Church. Every Englishman was supposed to attend its services and pay taxes for
its support. After about the year 1600, the government
no longer put men and women to death for being Catholics,
but it did still punish them severely in other ways — and
indeed it punished other kinds of Protestants just as it punished people who remained Catholics.

Spain, on the other hand, **was the chief Catholic country.**
The Spanish kings managed to keep out the new ideas — by
putting to death great numbers of freedom-loving Spaniards.
Then Spain took the lead in trying to put down the Protestants in other countries. But there was one little country
under Spain's rule in which there had come to be many
Protestants who insisted on their right to worship as they
chose. That country was *Holland.*

In the Sixteenth Century, Holland Became Independent, And had More Freedom of Religion than any other Country

What we now call Holland was for a long time part of the
Netherlands (or Low Countries) at the mouth of the Rhine.
For centuries the people of the Netherland districts had
been ruled by French or German princes, but soon after
1500 they came under the rule of Spanish kings. They
had always loved freedom, and, long before, they had won
a charter from one of their old rulers giving them a right to
a sort of parliament. But **when King Philip of Spain became
their ruler, he paid no attention to any of their old liberties
and even tried to force them all to become Catholics again.**

The Dutch nobles protested — even many of those who
were Catholics — but Philip sent his most pitiless general,
the cruel *Duke of Alva,* to make them obey. Alva set up a
court that came to be known as the " Council of Blood."
Citizens who were Protestants, or who complained of Spanish rule, were called before this court and condemned to

death without any chance at a fair trial. Thousands of men lost their lives in this way, and thousands more fled across the North Sea to Protestant England.

> This was a good thing for England. The Dutch were the best weavers in Europe, and they now started the manufacture of woolen cloth in England. The industry grew rapidly, and for more than two hundred years England led the world in making cloth.

Instead of giving up to Philip's cruelty, **the Dutch now rose in armed rebellion.** Their heroic leader was *William of Orange*, often called " William the Silent " because he was wise enough to keep his plans to himself. At first, William had been a Catholic ; but the cruel tyranny of Alva, and the sufferings of his country, made him a Protestant and a rebel, and he soon came to believe that a government ought never to force people to worship in ways they did not believe right.

Spain was now a rich and powerful country, and the king sent against Holland his best Spanish generals with mighty armies of trained soldiers. William the Silent was a wise statesman and a man of tireless energy and patient courage, but his army was made up only of untrained citizens. For a long time Alva kept winning battle after battle and capturing and sacking town after town as savagely as ever any barbarians could have done.

Still neither the Dutch people nor their leader would own themselves beaten. As soon as the rebellion was put down in one place, it broke out in another. **Finally the Spanish general decided to capture Leyden.** This was the turning point in the war. If the Dutch lost this town, as they had so many others, it seemed as if they surely must give up the fight. So the Spaniards set their armies all about the city, to starve it into surrender.

William could not possibly gather an army that could drive the Spaniards away. Still he urged the people in the city to hold out as long as possible, for if they gave up, the cause of Holland would be hopeless. The siege lasted nine months. During that time the people suffered horribly from hunger. They ate even the cats and rats, till those also were gone. Finally they sent word to William that they could hold out no longer.

There was just one thing more that William could do. All the land around Leyden was below the level of the ocean. The only thing that kept the fields and villages from being drowned by the sea was the wall of dikes which the Dutch had built with the labor of many years. Now the people of the countryside agreed with William when he said, " Better a drowned land than a lost land ! " **So the Dutch cut the dikes,** letting the waters in over their farm homes and rich fields. The Spanish soldiers had to retreat before the ocean flood, and a fleet of Dutch ships, loaded with food, came sailing across the fields, among trees and farm buildings, up to the walls of Leyden.

The parliament of Holland wanted to reward Leyden for its splendid courage, and so offered to let it go forever after without paying any taxes. But the citizens chose instead to have Holland build a university in their city. That University of Leyden soon became one of the most famous schools in Europe.

This victory gave the Dutch new courage. They now made a Declaration of Independence from Spain, and the little Dutch States united in a Confederation, as the American colonies were to do in the Revolution against England nearly two centuries later. For their first president they chose William the Silent, who is sometimes called " the Dutch Washington."

Soon afterward the Dutch lost this great leader. The Spanish king was cowardly enough to offer an immense reward to any one who would assassinate him, and in 1584

William was murdered in his own house.   But this did not end the war.   The brave Dutch fought on stubbornly for twenty-five years more — until **finally, in 1609, Spain gave up trying to conquer them.**

The Dutch had always been a sea-faring people; and all through the forty years of that famous war for independence they had fought Spain on sea as well as on land.   Even in those times when they seemed to have lost most of their towns to the invading armies, **the Dutch " sea-beggars,"** as the Spaniards called them, **were winning victories at sea and building up a great empire** *outside Europe.*   The Spanish king had conquered Portugal, for a time, and had become master of Portugal's colonies in the East Indies.   But before the war between Spain and Holland came to an end, the Dutch had seized those rich Eastern islands for their own. Some of the Spice Islands have remained possessions of Holland ever since.

Then in the very year that they made Spain stop fighting them, the Dutch hired *Henry Hudson,* an English sea-captain, to explore new lands for them in North America. Hudson was the first white man to sail up the river that we still call by his name.   He hoped that it might be one end of a water road through the continent — and on to the Dutch East Indies.   The Hudson River did not prove to be a short route to the Indies, but the Dutch soon built up a rich fur trade with the Indians along its shores.   Their trading posts grew into towns, and they gave the name *New Netherland* to their colony in America.

In 1588, during the War between Spain and Holland,
Bold English " Sea Dogs " Defeated the Spanish Armada

The one country that had given Holland help against Spain was England.   From the beginning of the war, thousands of young Englishmen had gone to the Netherlands to fight for Dutch independence.

One of these young heroes was the famous *Sir Philip Sidney*. Sidney was one of the finest scholars of his time. When only eleven years old, he wrote letters to his father both in Latin and in French. As he grew a little older he began to be noted as a poet, and he had become a chief favorite of Queen Elizabeth and indeed of all her court.

This young Englishman left all his fine friends and his chances at home, and enlisted in the Dutch army. Once his little company charged a Spanish force many times as large, and Sidney showed great daring. When one horse had been killed under him, he managed to get another, and fought his way

Sir Philip Sidney. — From a portrait.

successfully through the ranks of the Spaniards. He was badly wounded, however, and when at last he got back to his own men, he was fainting from loss of blood. Some one brought him a bottle of water to drink; but Sidney saw one of the common soldiers, near him on the ground, looking at it longingly. The man was dying and was parched with thirst. Sidney waved away the water, pointing to the dying soldier. " Give it to that man," said he, " his need is greater than mine." Soon afterward, Sidney himself died of his wounds.

Englishmen had other reasons for wanting to fight Spain besides their sympathy for brave little Holland. They were bold sailors; and they felt angry indeed that Spain would not let them found any colonies in America or even trade along its coasts. The Spaniards seized English sailors anywhere in the " Spanish Sea " (as they called *all* the waters around America) and hanged or drowned them.

For a long time Queen Elizabeth did not think England strong enough to carry on war with Spain — though she did *secretly* send money and other supplies to help Holland. But while the governments of England and Spain were still at peace with each other, many daring English seamen did sail off to attack Spain in the New World. Sometimes they captured the great fleets that were bringing gold and silver from Mexico and Peru to the Spanish king. Sometimes they raided rich Spanish towns on the coasts of Central and South America.

The chief English hero in this war at sea was *Francis Drake.* In 1577, Drake sailed around South America into the Pacific, where no English ship had ever been and where the Spaniards had always thought themselves perfectly safe from any attack. He swooped down on the unprotected ports along the western coast there and loaded his vessel with rich booty. He captured Spanish trading vessels, too, returning from trips to China, and took from them their cargoes of silk and pearls and precious stones.

Drake wisely determined not to try to go back by the way he had come, because the Spaniards there would surely be on the lookout for him. So, in his little ship, loaded deep with Spanish treasure, he sailed northward instead, up the west coast of North America, " till the icicles hung from his masts," claiming all that western coast for England. Then he left the angry Spaniards behind him, hunting vainly for the bold English " dragon," as they called him, and turned west across the Pacific. In the Spice Islands he filled the remaining space in his ship with pepper and cloves, and, after a voyage of three years, he at last reached England again.

Elizabeth Knighting Drake on Board the Golden Hind.

This voyage of Drake's brought on open war between England and Spain, which was just what many Englishmen had been wanting. The people of England went wild with enthusiasm for their daring champion and hurried to fit out more ships for other voyages like Drake's. King Philip demanded that Queen Elizabeth should surrender Drake to be put to death as a pirate. Instead, Elizabeth visited him upon his ship (*The Golden Hind*) and made him a knight, with much splendid ceremony. Soon, too, she sent an English army to help the Dutch *openly* in the war they were still fighting for independence from Spain.

The angry Philip vowed he would conquer England, and began to get ready a mighty fleet. But when his armada (as the Spaniards called such a fleet) was gathered in the harbor of Cadiz, just about to sail, Sir Francis Drake swooped in with a small fleet of English ships. Drake took the Spaniards completely by surprise. He burned or sank many of their vessels, captured some of the rest, and carried away or destroyed vast quantities of supplies. As the daring knight said, he had "singed the Spanish king's beard." This delayed the expedition for many months.

Still in 1588, the "Invincible Armada" did set sail, to conquer Protestant England. The one hundred and thirty-two great ships were crowded with soldiers — for Philip expected the Armada to brush away easily any English ships that might dare attack it and then to land the trained Spanish army in England. Spain at that time was looked upon everywhere as the strongest power in the world, and almost no one thought that the English could win.

England had only thirty-six ships of war. But in that day it was not hard to turn a merchant vessel into a war ship — just by putting a few cannon and a few more men on its decks. So nearly two hundred little vessels were finally gathered in the English Channel, some of them only small fishing schooners, to meet the mighty and boastful " Invincible Armada."

Many of the Spanish galleons were the largest ships that had ever been seen upon the sea. But they were built to stand high out of the water (so as to have more room for troops), and that made them clumsy to handle in high winds. Besides, the Spanish admiral, though a brave soldier, knew little about fighting at sea. The English sea-captains and sailors and ship-gunners were then the best in the world — unless perhaps the Dutch were as good — and their small ships could be handled and turned about much more quickly than the huge ships of the enemy. Often they would sail up close to a Spanish galleon, fire a deadly broadside into its hull, and dash away before the Spanish cannon could be brought to bear upon them. And the Spanish guns were so high up anyway that most of their shots passed above the low decks of the English without doing much harm except to masts and sails.

After getting much the worst of it for some hours, the surprised Spanish fleet tried to sail away and continue its voyage to the harbor of Calais (on the French side of the Channel), where it was to take on board more Spanish troops from the army in Holland. But it could not shake off the English sea-dogs. It had to move up the Channel slowly, so as to keep in one solid body ; and the little English ships hung close on its rear, dashing in every little while to cut out an injured Spanish vessel, or one slower than the others, and so wearing down the mighty fleet.

Most of the Armada did get into the harbor ; but before it could take on the Spanish army, the English (helped now by Dutch vessels that had joined them) drove it out again in wild disorder. At midnight they silently rowed eight ships, all smeared with tar and pitch and filled with fuel, in among the crowded Spanish vessels. Suddenly those eight fire-ships burst into flame ; and the surprised and terrified

Spaniards had to cut loose from their anchors and hurry out to sea — where the English and Dutch at once attacked them again.

The battle went on for two days more before the Armada gave up and decided to try to get back to Spain. But it had waited too long. As it ran north through the North Sea, to pass around Scotland and Ireland, a frightful storm came upon the battling navies, and dozens of the heavily loaded and clumsy Spanish ships were wrecked on the coasts of the British Isles. Not half the Armada ever got back to Spanish harbors.

This defeat of the Spanish Armada is a turning point in *our* history. It is one of the main reasons why people who live in the United States to-day speak English instead of Spanish. The power of Spain from that time began to go down. She was still able, for a long time, to hold the colonies she had already started; but it was soon plain to all the world that she was no longer " mistress of the seas." She never had held much land north of Mexico. So the way was now open for other countries to plant colonies in North America.

SUMMARY

After 1500, little groups of people began to teach different ideas about religion, and many different Protestant churches grew up. In each country the ruler tried to make all the people believe as he himself did. This led to wars between Catholics and Protestants. Protestant Holland became independent of Catholic Spain; and in 1588 Spain's claim to all the New World was broken when England defeated the Spanish Armada. Other countries then started colonies in North America.

NEW WORDS

Protestant	freedom of religion	Church of England	armada
Catholic	state church	dike	galleon
Lutheran	Huguenots	colony	broadside

THOUGHT QUESTIONS AND THINGS TO DO

1. Put on the time line the important dates in this chapter. Which came first, — the defeat of the Armada or the founding of New Netherland?

2. On an outline map put the important places mentioned in this chapter. At the bottom of the map put a list of those places and explain what important thing happened in each.

3. Imagine yourself a Dutch child in Leyden during the siege by the Spaniards and write the story of that siege.

4. Imagine yourself a sailor with Drake and write the story of one of his voyages.

5. On an outline map trace the routes of Magellan and Drake. Drake's voyage was about fifty years later than Magellan's. Compare the two in importance.

6. Give reasons why " the Dutch Washington " is a good name for William the Silent.

7. Good accounts of events in this chapter are given in Tappan's *European Hero Stories*, O'Neill's *The World's Story*, Banks' *Boy's Motley* (about Holland), and Church's *Stories from English History*. Read in one or two of these books about the man you are most interested in, and then write an account of him, telling why he interests you.

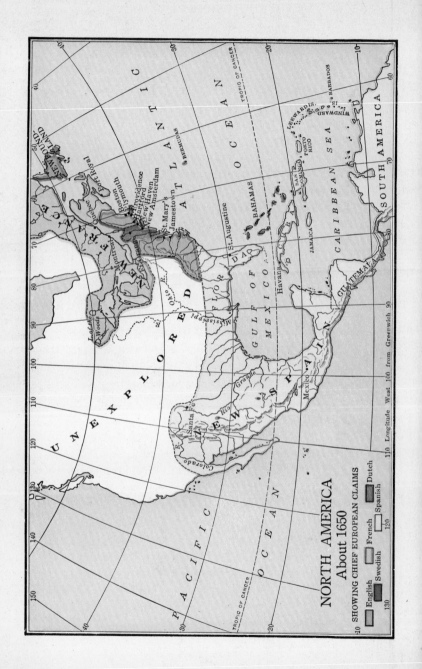

NORTH AMERICA
About 1650
SHOWING CHIEF EUROPEAN CLAIMS

English · French · Dutch
Swedish · Spanish

An Early Colonial Swedish Church, still standing, at Wilmington, Delaware.

CHAPTER XXIX

SPAIN'S RIVALS IN AMERICA

The Dutch and the Swedes

Now that the way to North America was open, Spain's rivals lost no time in starting colonies there. We have already told about New Netherland, **the Dutch settlement on the Hudson.** That colony belonged to Holland only about fifty years. Then it was seized by the English, who at that time were fighting the Dutch in Europe about trade. This change of rulers, however, did not hurt the Dutch settlers in America. England gave them more freedom than they had had before, and they grew into the great colony of New York. Theodore Roosevelt, one of the greatest of our Presidents, was descended from one of the old Dutch families there.

In much the same way, **Sweden founded and lost a colony.** Soon after the death of Gustavus Adolphus (page 313) the government of Sweden built a fort in America at the mouth of the Delaware River, and sent over several shiploads of colonists. But after only about twenty years this settlement was swallowed up by Dutch New Netherland — only a few years before that colony was herself gobbled up by the English. By that time both Sweden and Holland had become too weak to protect colonies in the New World, and **the chief rivals of Spain for North America had come to be England and France.**

ENGLAND

Even *before* the Armada, two English gentlemen of Queen Elizabeth's court had *tried* to start settlements in America. These were *Sir Humphrey Gilbert* and his half-brother, *Sir Walter Raleigh.* They believed that English colonies there would help keep Spain from growing too powerful and dangerous and would make England stronger and richer. The Queen gave them permission to found colonies at any place

Ewing Galloway Photo.

This photo of a "historical painting" shows one of New York's most famous streets (Broadway) in 1681 when cattle were watered at the town pump there.

in America that was not already occupied by Europeans. First, Gilbert tried Newfoundland, but found it cold and stormy, and, on the way home, he himself was drowned. Then Raleigh sent out explorers to find a better spot. (He was so great a favorite of the Queen's that she refused to let him risk his own life by going along with his expedition.)

The explorers brought back tales of a beautiful land, — "the most plentiful, sweet, fruitful, and wholesome of all the world." The Indians there had been friendly and had sent many gifts to Raleigh and the Queen. This land was *Roanoke Island,* off the coast of what is now North Carolina.

(At that time the English called all the land they claimed by the name *Virginia* in honor of Elizabeth, their " Virgin Queen.")

But starting a colony in even so delightful a place proved harder than any one had expected. Raleigh sent out many

BOYHOOD OF WALTER RALEIGH, who grew up near the coast of England and listened often to stories of adventure at sea. Raleigh is the nearer of the boys to the sailor. — From a modern painting.

settlers; but the leaders foolishly quarreled with the Indians, and the colonists spent their time in hunting for gold and pearls instead of cutting down trees to get ground ready to raise corn.

Then came the war with Spain, — and for a long time Raleigh could not send any supplies to the colony because England needed at home every ship and man, to guard against the attack that was coming (no one knew just when) from the Spanish Armada. When at last Raleigh did send another fleet of ships to Roanoke, the settlers there had all disappeared. No one has ever been able to learn what happened to them, and they are always spoken of as " the Lost Colony."

Raleigh could not start another settlement, for he had already spent all his own fortune and all that he had been able to borrow from his friends. Then, when Queen Elizabeth died, he himself was thrown into prison by the new king, James I. There he spent the rest of his life; but even in prison, he was not idle. He wrote a famous " History of the World," and he managed also to do some experiments in chemistry, in which he was much interested. Above all, he continued to urge his fellow-countrymen to start colonies, as the surest way to make their country greater. Gilbert and Raleigh had not failed. They had made all England feel that building colonies was a glorious and patriotic adventure. When near death Raleigh said of Virginia, — " I shall yet see it an English nation."

One lesson the English had learned from Raleigh's attempts — namely, that **it took large sums of money to set up a successful colony.** In 1606 some London merchants started a big *stock company.* That is, they all bought " stock " (or shares in the business), and raised enough money in that way to found a colony — just as rich men now sometimes form a stock company to build a railroad. They expected to get their money back, and more, from the trade of the New World — for England needed the lumber and furs and fish that could be found there.

This London Company got permission from King James to start a colony in Virginia; and **in 1607 the first permanent English colony in America was begun at *Jamestown*.** For many years the settlers suffered terrible hardships; but the

London Company each season sent over new supplies, and finally the colony grew strong enough to stand alone. This was the beginning of the splendid State that we still call Virginia.

The first Englishmen to come to America in order to worship God in their own way were the *Pilgrims*, who settled at

By permission of the Yale University Press.

EARLY DAYS AT JAMESTOWN. From the "Chronicles of America" photoplay, *Jamestown*. The picture gives a good idea of the sort of stockade that had to be built around many early English settlements for protection against Indians. The flag is, of course, the English flag, "The Cross of St. George."

Plymouth in 1620. They were Protestants, but they were persecuted by the government in England because they had separated from the Church of England. Probably you know their story, and remember how they escaped first to Holland and then finally to America in *the Mayflower*. (Perhaps the last chapter has helped you to understand why they went first to Holland, instead of to some other country in Europe.)

Plymouth was in New England. **Other colonies, too, were soon founded in New England by English Protestants who disliked some of the ways of the Church of England** and who therefore came into the wilderness, leaving their old homes and friends and comforts, in order to worship in their own way. But in nearly every one of these colonies, most of the people still thought (much as Europeans thought) that the kind of church *they* had set up was the only *true* church

Pilgrims at Plymouth going to church — or, as they said, going to "Meeting." — From a modern painting.

and that everyone who came to their colony ought to be made to attend its worship.

There were a few men in the world, however, far-sighted and broad-minded enough to believe (as we all do now) **that governments** should keep order and protect their citizens but **should let each one choose his religion for himself.** Three such Englishmen took the lead in starting colonies: *Lord Baltimore*, an English Catholic, *founded Maryland* (1632); *Roger Williams*, a Baptist, *started Rhode Island* (1636); and *William Penn*, a Quaker, *founded Pennsylvania* (1681). In these three colonies, Christians of all kinds were allowed to have their different churches side by side, with no more favor for one than for another.

For a time the leaders in the other colonies criticized this plan severely and said it must lead to disorder and bad government. Roger Williams made a good answer to this. Said he, — " On a ship it is necessary that all sailors and passengers obey the captain in matters that concern sailing the ship, but it is *not* necessary that they all attend the ship prayers." And before long a still stronger answer was given by the good order and happiness of the people in the three colonies. Their success *proved* that a government could keep order without making all its people worship in one way.

OLD HUGUENOT CHURCH IN CHARLESTON (South Carolina) as it looks to-day.

Then at last the other English colonies began to let people of different religions settle in them. True, in nearly every colony the majority of the citizens still showed special favor to their own church, but they "tolerated" other kinds of religion also. The whole country did not get complete " religious freedom " until after the colonies became an independent nation — the United States of America. But long before that time the colonies that were later to grow into that nation did have *more* religious freedom than any European land except perhaps little, overcrowded Holland.

And so those colonies became a refuge for people from many countries. This was one of the chief reasons in those early days why people came here who were not English. We have already spoken about the French Huguenots (page 314). Toward the year 1700 there began also a much larger immigration of German Protestants. After the religious wars in Germany stopped (page 312), the Catholic princes there ordered all their people to become Catholics or leave their homes. So hundreds of thousands of such fugitives finally found their way to America. Many of them settled in Pennsylvania and became the ancestors of our " Pennsylvania Dutch." Others settled a row of counties in South Carolina. (Do you know of any people who have come to the United States in later times so that they might worship in their own way?)

By 1750 there were thirteen English-speaking colonies on the Atlantic coast of North America, with settlers from many parts of Europe. Those colonies filled a solid band of territory from Maine to Georgia, and reached back from the ocean into the valleys of the Appalachian Mountains. True, this was a small territory compared with the vast Spanish America or French America at that same time; *but it had many times more people (and more prosperous people) than either of those larger districts had.* (See map facing page 335.)

One reason for this splendid growth was that **England let her colonists have more liberty than other European countries gave *their* colonies.** Every one of the English colonies had its own Assembly, or little parliament, and made most of its own laws. Usually the English government appointed the governor of a colony, but a governor could do very little without the consent of the colonists. Every colonist had certain important rights, such as jury trial, not found in France or Spain in those times but which Englishmen had boasted about with good reason ever since the days of Magna Carta. England did interfere with the colonists' freedom to trade as they wished — a very silly interference and sometimes a very selfish interference — but even in that matter

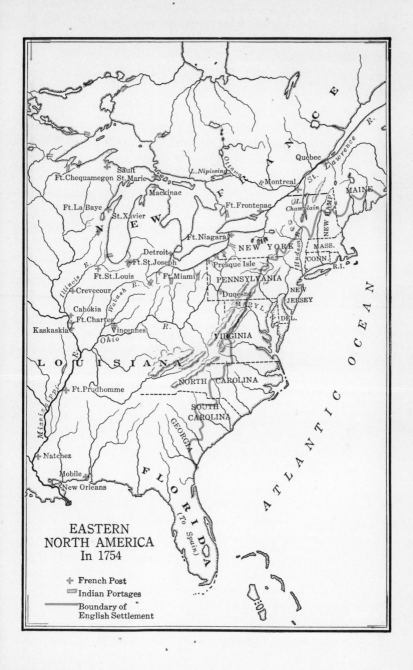

EASTERN
NORTH AMERICA
In 1754

+ French Post
⊟ Indian Portages
⎯⎯ Boundary of
    English Settlement

she left her colonists much more freedom than France or Spain left theirs.

FRANCE

The French, too, had *tried* to settle in America *before* the Armada, but without success. One of their explorers, *Cartier*, did discover the mouth of the St. Lawrence and even sailed up that mighty stream as far as where the city of Montreal now stands. There he was stopped by wild rapids — which afterward were named *Lachine*, because it was believed that China must be only a little way beyond them. Another French leader started a colony on the Carolina coast, but it was destroyed by the Spaniards from Florida and all the settlers were killed.

Then, finally, in 1608 (the year after Jamestown was founded) *Samuel de Champlain* began the first permanent French settlement at Quebec, on the St. Lawrence. Champlain is called the Father of *New France*. For thirty-five years he endured all the hardships of life in the wilderness, fighting the Indians and exploring new lands for France. Up the St. Lawrence he made his way, past the rapids that had blocked Cartier's path, even into the Great Lakes. With his Huron Indian guides, too, he paddled his canoe up the little streams that flowed into the St. Lawrence from both north and south.

When Champlain found the lake south of the St. Lawrence that bears his name, a very important thing happened — very unfortunate for the French. His friends, the Huron Indians, were at war with the Iroquois tribes, who lived near that lake. Champlain helped his Indian friends attack these enemies. Now the Iroquois were a very powerful Indian people, — far the best warriors among all the Indians of North America, and for more than a hundred years after that, they were bitterly hostile to the French. If it had not been for this, New York and New England might have been French instead of Dutch and English.

The French heard much from their Indian friends about a very great river farther west of the Great Lakes, flowing to the southward. Here at last, they thought, must be the short water way through North America to Asia, and they set their hearts on finding that river and following it to the

This is a picture that Champlain himself drew of his battle with the Iroquois, when he and the Hurons attacked an Iroquois fort. The Iroquois had never seen firearms, and Champlain's death-dealing musket terrified them and won a victory this time, as Champlain's Huron admirers had expected. Soon, however, the Iroquois ceased to be terrified by this new weapon.

sea. In 1673, after many attempts, the trader *Joliet* and the brave missionary *Marquette* found their way from Lake Michigan over to the Illinois River, and on down that stream to the Mississippi. They even explored the Mississippi as far south as the mouth of the Arkansas, but then turned back, because of hostile Indians and Spaniards.

The task was then taken up by perhaps the greatest of all French explorers — *La Salle*. For many years this hero, too, had to struggle against all sorts of trials and hardships.

CHAMPLAIN DISCOVERING LAKE CHAMPLAIN in 1609. From a painting by
F. W. Kelley.

LA SALLE TAKING POSSESSION OF THE MISSISSIPPI VALLEY FOR FRANCE at the mouth
of the river, in 1682.

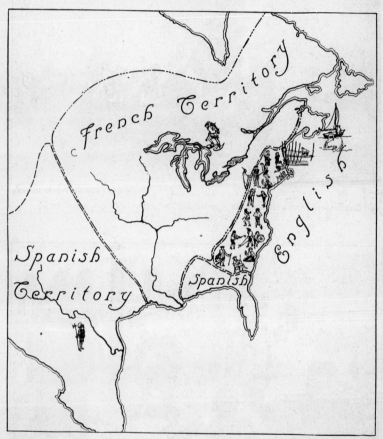

SETTLED PARTS OF NORTH AMERICA IN 1750. — This " graph " indicates (truly) that English America had twenty times as many people as the larger French America — and also that it had more kinds of work. (See pages 332 and 335–336.)

The governor of New France was jealous of him and tried to have the king call him back to Europe, and for many months La Salle had to give all his attention just to getting permission to keep on serving his country.

To do his work more successfully, he built a ship on Lake Erie, above Niagara Falls. It was made out of green timber cut from the forest near by; and all its ropes, sails, and guns had to be brought from Europe. Then *The Griffin*, as La Salle called the vessel, was soon wrecked in a storm, so that all the precious supplies he had been gathering were lost — arms, ammunition, medicines, and trinkets with which to trade with the Indians. La Salle's men, too, grew weary of tramping through snow and ice and of danger from Indians and of living on scanty food, and they deserted him just when he most needed them. Many times he nearly lost his life.

But at last, in 1682, La Salle did reach the mouth of the great river. There he set up the French flag, claiming the whole vast valley of the Mississippi for King Louis of France — for whom he named it *Louisiana*. The river had not proved a path to India; but La Salle was sure it would be a very valuable possession for his country. He had visions of fleets of ships setting sail for France each year from the river's mouth, loaded with precious furs of beaver and fox and buffalo, which traders and trappers would collect from all the vast valley. He did not live to carry out his plans. While he was exploring the shores of the Gulf he was killed treacherously by one of his own men. But not long afterward, the important French colony of New Orleans was begun.

France then owned more then half of what is now the United States, besides almost as much more land north and northwest of the St. Lawrence. **But it proved hard for her to get settlers enough of the right kind.** She had many splendid leaders and explorers, as we have seen. She had also large numbers of daring traders who pushed on into the wilderness, west and north, even to the Rocky Mountains, seeking larger supplies of the furs that sold for high prices to fashionable ladies and gentlemen in Europe. With the traders, or close behind them, came bands of French soldiers, to build forts at important places, so as to hold the new lands

BIRD'S-EYE VIEW OF THE BUSINESS PART OF NEW ORLEANS TO-DAY. If La Salle could see that city, would he feel, do you suppose, that his dreams had come true?

for France. Even ahead of the traders, devoted missionaries forced their way through all dangers and hardships, sometimes at the cost of life itself, to bring the Christian religion to the Indians. **But the French colonies had very few busy little towns, with many kinds of work,** such as were found in the English colonies, **and they did not have many farm homes either.** The men indeed did not often bring their families with them from France. So, as we have said, the vast French possessions had few inhabitants.

You may be wondering why the Huguenots went to the English colonies (page 314) when there was so much French territory unoccupied in America. The answer is that the French government would not let them go to French colonies. The kings of France were Catholics, and they were determined that only good Catholics should live in their colonies. This undoubtedly was one reason why the French colonies did not get settlers enough to make them able to stand against the English.

Summary

Soon after 1600, Spain's rivals (especially France and England) started colonies in North America. Some of the English colonies were founded for trade and riches, but several were started to escape religious persecution. Rhode Island, Maryland, and Pennsylvania welcomed all kinds of Christians equally, and soon the other English colonies adopted the plan of religious toleration. Then many people from European countries came to them so as to worship as they chose.

French explorers, traders, and missionaries claimed vast territory for France. But the French kings would not let the Huguenots settle in the French colonies, and other Frenchmen did not want to come in large numbers or bring their families.

New Words

stock company   *permanent*   *fur trader*   *religious toleration*

Thought Questions and Things to Do

1. Write an advertisement, or make a poster, urging settlers to join an expedition to some colony that we have been talking about. Give good reasons for going to the one that you choose.

2. Suppose you had been sent out in the seventeenth century to find a place for a colony, — what are the things you would have looked for? Write a report about the spot you choose. (Why were rivers important?)

3. Imagine yourself one of " the Lost Colony," and write the story of what happened to it.   Imagine yourself a Huguenot after 1685, and tell what plan you decided on to avoid persecution.

4. French is still the speech of many of the people in some parts of the United States.   Can you find out where?   Make a list of French place-names in the United States, and see whether you can explain how some of them came to be used.

5. Show on a map the parts of the United States first settled by Dutch, Swedes, Spanish, French, and English.

6. Read stories of some of the explorers in McMurry's *Pioneers on Land and Sea* and *Pioneers of the Mississippi Valley*, Tappan's *European Hero Stories*, or Evans' *America First*, and then write or tell what you can remember about one of them.

About the year 1500, King Henry VII in England gave a sum of money to the abbot and monks of Westminster Abbey in London, in return for which they were "for ever" to lodge and feed thirteen poor men — who were to repay the king by praying daily for him ("King's Bedesmen"). This picture is part of the initial letter in the deed from the king.   It represents the abbot and three monks and some of the bedesmen behind them — each with the king's emblem (rose and crown) on the shoulder.

There were three or four hundred such small "foundations," established by rich men, in England in the Middle Ages.   Some of them still exist. Along with the usual monastery care of the helpless, they took the place of modern "poor houses."

CHAPTER XXX

LIFE IN EUROPE WHEN AMERICA WAS NEW

In England Many People had More Comforts Than in the Middle Ages

By the beginning of the sixteenth century **English traders were bringing in new luxuries from all parts of the world** that Europeans then knew about, and skilled artisans at home were learning to manufacture many new things. Richard Hakluyt, an English clergyman of that time, wrote an interesting book about the voyages and adventures of English seamen. In it he told how ships from London and Bristol traded as far as Sicily, Tripoli (in Africa), and even Syria. He named six different kinds of linen and cotton cloth they carried to those distant countries. (That list shows only some of the things that English artisans were making for merchants to sell in foreign lands.) The ships brought back from those voyages, adds Hakluyt, silks, several kinds of wine, sweet oils, " raw " cotton (not yet made up into cloth), Turkish carpets, pepper, cinnamon, and other spices.

Princes and great lords lived no longer in gloomy and damp castles, but in fine country houses with wide windows from which broad marble stairs led down to lovely gardens where fountains played among the trees. The rooms were filled with richly carved furniture and with curiosities from many lands; the floors were carpeted with costly Oriental rugs; and the walls were hung with finely woven silks and

A GENTLEMAN RIDING WITH HIS WIFE "a-PILLION." — From an English manuscript of the 16th century. This was a favorite way for ladies of this class to travel.

embroidered tapestries. Through the spacious halls moved stately groups of ladies and gentlemen, clad in silks and velvets, wearing wide starched ruffs of lace and linen, and gleaming with precious jewels. A story about Sir Walter Raleigh describes him as wearing a costly jewel hanging from the tip of a feather on his hat, and with gems on his shoes worth "six thousand six hundred pieces of gold."

Next to the nobles stood the country gentlemen (page 252). They lived in manor houses which now were almost as handsome as the homes of the nobles. They were very proud of their well-kept estates. Most of them lived always in the country, and were rarely seen at the royal court. Still, Queen Elizabeth selected her wisest advisers from this class. Sir Philip Sidney (page 319), whom she called the brightest jewel in her crown and whom William the Silent thought one of the greatest statesmen of all Europe, was a country gentleman.

A country gentleman at his death did not *divide* his lands among his sons. Instead, all the land, or nearly all, went to the oldest son — so that the family might not lose importance by having its great estates broken up into small ones. The younger sons usually became lawyers or clergymen or

BALL ROOM OF HADDON HALL — a sixteenth-century English country house where Queen Elizabeth spent much of her girlhood.

LOCELY HOUSE, an English country house of the seventeenth century.

PALACE OF A GREAT FRENCH LORD, built in the seventeenth century.
The tower at the left (except for the top) is part of an older feudal castle.

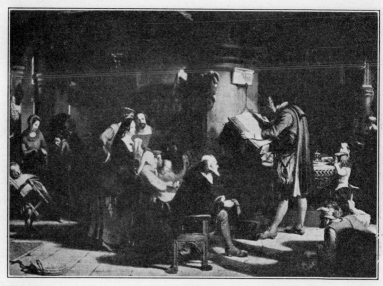

This old English painting represents a reading from an early English Bible (chained
to a reading desk) in St. Paul's, London.   See page 353.

perhaps merchants, or (very often) they sought fortune as adventurers in new lands, or as soldiers in many parts of the world. Among such younger sons of country families were Gilbert and Raleigh, of whom we have been reading.

In the towns **the most important people were the merchants** — the men, that is, who traded with foreign countries. A merchant's wealth was not in land but in ships and warehouses. Many a merchant was richer than the average country gentleman, and indeed than many nobles, and his town house was as comfortable as a manor house, even if not quite so grand.

ENGLISH WOMAN WEAVING in the 16th century. Compare with the picture on page 12. It was to be two hundred years more before the loom was much improved.

Nobles, country gentry, and merchants made up what is called the *upper classes* of that time. All together they were only a small part of the people. "Below" them were much larger *lower classes*. Here, too, there were three different groups.

1. **The best off were the yeomen,** or small farmers (page 243). They tilled their own farms with only the help of their families, or perhaps with that of one or two farm laborers. A yeoman's house had become more comfortable than in earlier times. Often it had two rooms, with perhaps also a loft (a sort of low attic) where the children slept when old enough to climb the ladder that led up to it. Usually, too, the house had a chimney and a wide fireplace about which the family could gather. The light was rather dim, even on the brightest day, for houses were taxed according

to the number and size of their windows; but the few small windows were filled with panes of glass.

Some of these houses had floors of stone or wood, though many still used only the packed clay covered with straw or reeds. Pewter dishes were taking the places of older wooden bowls and spoons; and the important members of the family slept on feather beds, instead of on heaps of loose straw, and rested their heads on feather pillows instead of on wooden blocks.

Sometimes a very rich yeoman might marry a merchant's daughter and so get money enough to buy more land. Such a man might come to be a country gentleman. From such a rising yeoman family came Francis Drake.

2. **A much larger class of men,** and a very much poorer class, **tilled the lands of nobles and gentry** but owned no land of their own. These "*farm laborers,*" or "cottagers," lived in miserable huts, or cottages, in villages on their landlord's land. Usually each family was allowed to use a small patch of ground to raise its food, and it had also the right to pasture its cow or goat or geese or pig (if lucky enough to have any of these) on the village common. In the woods belonging to the village, too, the family could gather brush and broken limbs from the trees for fuel. The farm laborer got very little wages, and it was almost impossible for him to save any money. But if he stopped working for the landlord, the family had to leave its wretched home and wander away — with small chance of finding another even as good.

3. **The third group of these lower classes was made up of the artisans and small shop-keepers in the towns.** These men were growing more important and better off. They made and sold the goods of many kinds that the merchants gathered together and sent to foreign lands, and so they were almost as much interested in seeing trade grow as the merchants themselves were. They lived plainly, but with

far more comfort than the farm laborers. As yet, however, there were not a great many of them in England.

Of course, **if *we* could go back** to the houses of even the very richest nobles or merchants of that time, **we should miss many of the things we think necessary to-day.** Fireplaces were the only way of warming a house or of cooking meals. Baking was done in outdoor brick ovens. When an oven had been heated by a fire *inside* it, the coals were scraped out and the loaves of bread were put in. The only lights were candles or rushlights (made by dipping long reeds in melted tallow or wax). The family washing was done two or three times a year in the nearest stream, as women in many parts of Europe do their washing to-day. There

From Ewing Galloway, N.Y.

This modern photo shows the women from the village in the distance at their regular washing in the river. The medieval castle, by which the stream flows, is one of the few castles in northwestern France which have lasted on to this day.

was no way to keep things cool in summer except in a hole in the ground, and no way to preserve food except by salting or drying or smoking. Europeans did not yet use corn, potatoes, lettuce, tomatoes, or indeed most of the vegetables that we have now, and we should soon have tired of their food. At dinner, too, we should have looked in vain for a fork, unless we were in a very wealthy home.   Queen Elizabeth herself was particularly proud of her forks — though she had only *two*, while she had two thousand gorgeous dresses.   And more than anything else we should have missed fresh air and baths — two things that most people of those days, rich or poor, thought quite unnecessary and indeed rather dangerous.

The saddest thing, however, about that day in England was that *so many people were without any homes at all.*   This

was before England began to make woolen cloth, of course (page 316) ; but the Netherland clothmakers were paying high prices for English wool, and so **the landowners were fast turning their farms into sheep pastures.**   It took only one or two shepherds, with their dogs, to herd sheep over wide stretches of land where it had needed many laborers to plow and sow and reap.   Most of the old laborers, therefore, lost their jobs.

Besides, the big landlords, to get still more sheep land, began to fence in the *public* land, the

FRYING FRITTERS for a " party " — An English picture of the 16th century.   These young folks are of the gentry (gentleman) class.

village commons, along with their own.   Then the poor cottager could no longer keep a cow or goat to furnish milk, because he had no pasture.   This fencing in of public lands is called " enclosures."   (Do you remember how bad it was for Roman Italy when something of that sort once happened there?) Even the English yeomen had depended a good deal on the common lands for pasture and wood; and many of that class, too, were soon in great distress. Then some neighboring landlord was always ready to buy them out; and indeed if a yeoman refused to sell, the landlord's men often made it uncomfortable for him in other ways until he did.

The poor people who no longer had jobs, and who had no land of their own, had to leave their old homes. Between the years 1500 and 1560, half the villages in England lost a large part of their inhabitants, and many disappeared altogether. Some of the old villagers learned trades and found work in the towns that were growing up — but towns in that day couldn't furnish work for many new people at a time. A few found work on farms. Many built themselves wretched mud huts on waste land along some roadside, and kept alive as best they could, by working when they found a chance, but, most of the time, by begging or stealing. Great numbers had not even such poor homes as these, but became tramps, or "sturdy beggars," as they were called.

Parliament, which was then made up of landlords and merchants, made stern laws against such tramps. They were forbidden to move from one district to another; those who begged were put in prison or flogged; and those who stole the smallest thing were to be hanged. Seventy thousand *were* hanged during the reign of Elizabeth, and the jails were always full. (Parliament did pass laws, also, to try to stop enclosures, but the government did not enforce *those* laws until the landlords were *ready* to stop.)

Another thing added to these troubles of the poor. Prices kept rising very fast during that century, so that a grown man found things costing two or three times as much as when he was a boy. The merchants, who brought in goods from foreign countries, and the artisans, who made things to sell, got along well. But *wages* for common labor and for farm help stayed down, because there were so many people without jobs.

It is no wonder, then, that **many an English yeoman and many a laborer were ready to take the risk of going to America** as soon as England started colonies there. He might meet many dangers and might even die from famine or disease on the way, or while getting started in the New World. But things couldn't be much worse for him than they were already; and there might be a *chance* for him, or for his children, to make a fortune. At least there was plenty of wild land, and no fear of " enclosures."

There seemed a fine opening, too, for the younger sons of the gentry families. Their families could usually spare them a little money to get a start with, and they were likely to become leaders in the colonies. Even the *heads* of some gentry families were finding it hard to get along in England in the style of living they had been used to, because the prices of the farm products they had to sell did not rise as fast as the prices of all things they had to buy. So some such men, also, came to America. John Winthrop, the famous leader of the Massachusetts colony, gave as one of the reasons why he and his followers ought to leave England, — " England grows weary of her inhabitants; so that man, who is the most precious of God's creatures, is here more vile and base than the earth we tread upon, and of less prize among us than a horse or an ox."

The hope of making a better living, then, was one of the chief causes that sent men to the New World, — " the land of opportunity " in those days as now. The Englishmen who came here for that reason were largely sturdy yeomen, and many of their leaders were from the country gentry; but a large part, too, were common laborers.

Not many working men were able to get *money* enough to pay their own way to America. It cost several hundred dollars in our money for one person to take that long, hard voyage. But if the man was able-bodied and industrious, there were several ways by which he might get his way paid for him. The London Company, for instance, was always ready to carry good workmen (and also their families) to its colony, and to furnish food and shelter and clothing, if they would bind themselves to work there for the Company for a few years under its overseers — cutting down trees, fishing, getting furs by trapping or by trading with the Indians, or raising tobacco or sugar or corn. The well-to-do colonists, too, who had paid their own way and who had large farms, found it hard to get laborers enough and often were glad to pay a man's passage money in order to have his labor for four or perhaps six years.

People who had bound themselves to work for a master in return for their passage were called *indentured servants*. In the seventeenth and eighteenth centuries a great many English and German settlers came in these ways to the English colonies, and many of them, after their terms of service were out, became fine citizens. Charles Thompson, the secretary of the Continental Congress when it adopted our Declaration of Independence on July 4, 1776, had been one of these indentured servants.

In Most Countries Things were Worse Than in England

In France, Spain, Italy, and Germany, most of the men who tilled the soil were still serfs. In the towns the merchants and artisans lived much as the same classes did in England, but the towns held only a small part of the people. At least nine-tenths of all the people were terribly poor.

France had no class of men like the English country gentlemen, but it had far more nobles than England had.   French nobles, however, seldom lived in their castles or country houses, as the English nobles and gentry did. Instead, all of them who were at all rich spent nearly their whole lives at the king's court, living extravagantly and foolishly on the profits that their stewards sent them from the toil of their serfs.

One reason why the poor were poorer in France than in England was the different way in which taxes were raised there. In England all taxes were raised, and spent, by vote of Parliament; and the richer a man was, the more taxes he paid. But in France the king and his advisors taxed just as they liked. So the rich nobles got off by paying very small taxes, or even none at all; and the poor town workmen and village peasants had to pay almost all of them.

When it came to spending the money, the king did that, too, just as he liked — on his wars, on his many gorgeous palaces, in giving splendid pageants and shows, and in paying pensions to his relatives and favorite courtiers. Louis XIV, who ruled in the seventeenth century, could not ride out, or do business, or eat, or even go to bed or get up, unless he was surrounded by a whole swarm of the greatest nobles to wait on him. One particularly favored noble would hand him his shirt; another proudly claimed the right to hold a bowl of water (with rose leaves floating in it) for him to wash his hands in; still another laced his boots, and so on. It was to keep up a foolish show like this that the poor peasants slaved and toiled and starved.

Every king in Europe envied Louis his luxury and his fashionable court, and French became the court language over nearly all Europe. But of course the more money the king spent in keeping up wasteful luxury, the poorer his people grew, until the time came when no more taxes could be squeezed out of them. What happened then we shall see a little further on.

So far in this chapter we have been talking about how the different kinds of people in Europe got their living and whether they were rich or poor. Here are some other things about life in England.

"MERRIE ENGLAND"

The village people in the England of Elizabeth's day were fond of play and of all sorts of games, when they could find time for them. On almost every Sunday and on other Holy Days, after the church service, they met on the village green

From an English manuscript of the 14th century. In those times this game was called "Hodman (Hoodman) Blind." Why?

to enjoy themselves. Some of the things they liked most to see — like cock-fighting and bear-baiting — were rather cruel; but most of their sports were much like ours, except that grown men and women played games that only children play now.

Their *morris dances* were something like the dance games you may have played in school or kindergarten, except that usually a merry dancer was hung about with little bells ("Rings on her fingers, bells on her toes") that jingled a gay tune. *Prisoners' Base* was a common game. So was *Blind Man's Buff*. (The word "buff" in that name came from the fact that the players "buffed," or buffeted, the "blind man" with their coats or scarfs or hoods, to draw him away from some player he was about to catch.)

AN ENGLISH LADY OF THE 16TH CENTURY, painting her own picture.

If you had been present, you would easily have recognized the early ancestors of our *baseball* and *football* games, though some of the rules used then would have seemed very strange to you. In the spring, every one played *marbles*. Indeed a famous American writer has said recently that every school game in America today came from the England of that time. *Wrestling* and *archery matches* were favorite contests, and often traveling actors gave a *play* on a rude out-of-door stage. **Always the gayest day of all the year was May-day,** as for hundreds of years before (page 199). All the night of that day, in every village, the young people danced about the village May Pole, to tunes played by the village fiddler, after they had chosen a "Queen of the May."

The nobles and gentry and the people of the court had entertainments of their own, — tennis, croquet (which they called "pall mall"), fencing, bowling, and the game from which golf has descended, as well as hunting, hawking, and fishing. Cards and dice, too, were much used. Ladies played upon many kinds of musical instruments.

"BANDY-BALL." — From an English 14th-century manuscript. Here the game is played by peasants.

There were rich feasts and gorgeous shows and pageants which cost huge sums of money and sometimes took hundreds of actors.

The Theater: William Shakespeare

In the towns the first English theaters were being built. Plays were always given in the day-time, and all classes of people delighted in them. The cheapest part of the theater, where the poor went, was not the gallery, as now, but on the floor just in front of the stage. That place was called the "pit." The crowd there might get wet from a sudden shower, because, far above them, the roof was left open, so as to get light for the stage. They had to stand, also, for there were no seats in the pit. Most of the spectators sat in the balconies, and very important people were given chairs on the stage itself — where they often interfered with the actors by talking and criticizing what was going on.

The most famous name of all the sixteenth century — greater than Drake's or Raleigh's or even Elizabeth's — **is that of *William Shakespeare*.** When hardly more than a boy, Shakespeare ran away from his home in the small town of Stratford-on-Avon, to escape being punished for killing a deer. He went to London; but he was so poor there at first that he had to earn his living by holding gentlemen's horses in front of the theaters while the performances were taking place. Then he got a job as an actor, and soon he began to write plays himself. When he had grown rich, he went back to Stratford to live.

Not much is known about Shakespeare's life in London or afterward, but we know very well indeed the people he put into his dramas. Men and women, and boys and girls, have laughed and cried ever since over the adventures of his characters. He was the greatest play-writer the world has ever seen, and his plays are still acted in almost every country of the world. They contain much of the most beautiful poetry and of the highest wisdom ever put into words. Every great actor hopes sometime in his life to act in one of Shakespeare's plays.

Every year hundreds of Americans go on a sort of pilgrimage to visit Stratford. The house where Shakespeare was born, and the grammar school he went to, are still standing. A beautiful and splendid theater, planned by an American woman-architect, has been built there recently by Americans, so that now, three hundred years after his death, Shakespeare's plays can be acted in his own town. Because English is our language also, we Americans claim him as one of *our* poets — as indeed we do other great English writers.

SCHOOLS AND BOOKS

By Shakespeare's time, nearly every English town of any importance had a grammar school like the one at Stratford. A *grammar school* was an upper school where students studied Latin grammar and learned to read some Latin writers, as students may do now in our high schools. A hundred years earlier there had been hardly any such schools in England; but in the sixteenth century the brother and father and grandfather of Queen Elizabeth had all started a great many, putting up buildings for them and giving large amounts of money to keep them up year after year. Many a rich man, too, used his money to set up such a school in his own town. But these schools were not kept up by taxes, as our schools are, and the money given for them had to be helped out by fees. That is, each student had to pay something for his schooling — unless he was known to be very bright. Then indeed his way might be paid for him by some " scholarship fund " started by some patron of the school who wished to educate bright poor boys.

Girls did not go to school. If they belonged to a noble family or to a very rich family, they might have tutors in the home, as the sons also of such a family usually did. Elizabeth, for instance, had become a great scholar, speaking and reading seven languages, before she became Queen. But that was a rare exception. A girl was considered well educated if she had been taught the catechism, good manners, embroidery, and perhaps her letters.

But as the printing press made more and more books, it became more and more common for even poor people in small villages to learn to read. Children learned their letters from a horn book — a printed sheet of paper covered with transparent horn and hung around the neck or from the belt. Sometimes they used the horn book at home, but usually they were sent for a few weeks to some " dame school," kept by an old woman of the neighborhood. They had no primers and first readers, like those in our schools now, and their first real reading was usually done in a book rather hard for beginners — the Bible itself.

THE ENGLISH BIBLE AND THE PURITANS

Elizabeth's father, King Henry VIII, had ordered the Bible translated into English, so that everyone could understand it better. A copy was placed in every church (chained to a reading desk so that it could not be carried off) ; and after a while a copy was found in nearly every English home, even though no other book might be there.

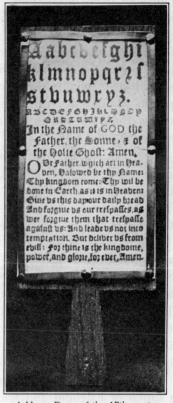

A HORN BOOK of the 17th century A photo by the Keystone View Company from one kept in the New York Public Library.

Then in 1611, eight years after Elizabeth's death, a new translation was published in strong and simple and very beautiful English. This translation is known as " **the King James Bible.**" From the first it was used in homes and churches even more than the older translations had been, and soon its words and phrases became a part of the everyday speech of Englishmen, so that to-day we often quote it without knowing we are doing so. The English colonists brought this translation to America, and it is the one still most commonly used by all English-speaking Protestant people, though in quite recent years more exact and careful translations have been made.

In Elizabeth's reign, especially toward the close, there grew up in England large groups of people who wished to live more exactly as they thought the Bible commanded. They wished also, as they said, to " purify " the English Church of many of its customs, and so they were called *Puritans*. They were very strict in their ideas, and thought that much of the gayety of " Merrie England " was wrong. So **the England of the seventeenth century became much more serious** than the England of Elizabeth had been. People dressed more plainly; and at times when the Puritans had the most influence, laws were passed against playing games on the Sabbath. Even the ringing of the church chimes was forbidden, or the playing on the church organ.

Some groups of Puritans separated entirely from the Church of England and tried to worship in their own little congregations. They were called *Separatists*, and were punished severely by the government. One of these Separatist congregations became the Pilgrims who settled at Plymouth in New England (page 329).

Most Puritans in England, however, stayed in the Church of England, but tried to make it over according to their own ideas. When they failed in doing that, after a long struggle, many thousands of them, too, came to New England, bringing their ideas to America.

We may think that the Puritans were too strict about little things and certainly we do not agree with them that it is wrong to enjoy music and pictures and other beautiful things. But we must always remember **two great debts we owe them.** (1) They were very brave men, ready to suffer anything for what they believed right, and, as we shall see, they had a large part in saving English liberties in the seventeenth century both in England and in the English colonies. And (2) they believed that every one ought to be educated enough so that he could read and understand the Bible for himself. But the Puritans who made colonies in New England did not have men among them rich enough to found grammar schools out of their private fortunes, as rich nobles did in England (page 352); and so the Puritan colonies set up such schools in every town of any size by taxing *all* the citizens. This was the beginning of our great **American public school system.**

Summary

Write a summary of the first two divisions of this chapter, using not more than 100 words. List the topics that are written about in the rest of the chapter.

New Words

Puritan	*pewter*	*merchant*	" *enclosures* "
Separatist	*ruff*	*artisan*	*indentured servant*

Thought Questions and Things to Do

1. Imagine yourself a visitor to a friend in London in Elizabeth's time, and write home a letter about what you saw and did.

2. Can you now add to the list of reasons for going to America that you made at the end of the last chapter?

3. Try to find a horn book in the picture on page 266.

4. Read Mark Twain's *Prince and Pauper*, if you can find a copy of the book. It tells a good story of how a prince and beggar happened to change places. Perhaps your class can make a play out of the story. Other good books on the life of that time are: Quennell's *History of Every-day Things in England*, Tappan's *European Hero Stories*, Greenwood's *Merrie England*, Bennett's *Master Skylark* (a story about the young Shakespeare), Barnes' *Drake and His Yeomen*, Major's *The Little King* (Louis XIV), Martin's *A Warwickshire Lad* (another Shakespeare story), Dix's *Blithe McBride*, Hall's *Boys of Scrooby*, Meigs' *Master Simon's Garden*, Pyle's *Jack Ballister's Fortunes*. (Some of the last of these are stories of life in both England and America.)

SIGNING THE DECLARATION OF INDEPENDENCE

From the painting, by Trumbull, which hangs in the Capitol, Washington, D. C.

CHAPTER XXXI

REVOLUTIONS IN THE OLD WORLD AND THE NEW

When a wheel turns all the way around, we say it has made a revolution. So when a nation suddenly changes completely its way of living, or of doing some important thing in its life, we say it has gone through a revolution. Sometimes the change comes about through war between those who want it and those who do not. Such a sudden and violent change always causes much suffering for many people, even though it may in the end bring good to the world. But many a revolution comes peacefully, though of course more slowly, so that most people do not really know what is happening until it is over.

In the seventeenth and eighteenth centuries, there took place **four great revolutions** which affected both Europe and America.

I. The English Civil War and the Glorious Revolution of 1688

You remember that ever since the time of Edward I (page 259) the English people had been electing representatives to Parliament and so had had a large part in governing themselves. (Look on your time line to see how long that had been going on before 1600, and compare that with the length of time since 1600.)

But when Queen Elizabeth died, in 1603, **a family came to the throne who meant to take away this liberty of the English people.** The new *Stuart* kings were Scotch cousins of Elizabeth. They did not believe in the English idea that a king's power was limited by the consent of the people. Instead they believed in what they called " the divine right

of kings," — the idea that kings were next to God in power
and that they received their right to rule directly from Him,
so that it was a sin for anyone to criticize the doings of a king
or to interfere with him in any way.   The first Stuart kings
(*James I* and his son, *Charles I*) tried to make the Puritans
give up their forms of worship — just by a mere command —
and they tried also to tax the people without first getting
the consent of Parliament.

If you remember what happened in the reigns of King
John and his son (chapter xxiv), you will understand that
the English people were very angry at these acts.   Bitter
quarrels broke out between them and their king.   Many
gentlemen, who refused to yield to the king's wishes, were
imprisoned — sometimes without any trial — and thousands
of Puritans crossed the Atlantic, to build up free governments in America.

**Finally a civil war began between the supporters of
Charles I and Parliament,** which stood for the rights of the
people.   Most of the people's party were Puritans, and they
were called " Roundheads," because many of them dressed
very plainly and clipped their hair short, instead of wearing
it in long curls as had been the custom for gentlemen.   The
followers of the king were called " Cavaliers."   They were
largely gentlemen and nobles, and they made splendid soldiers.   At first it looked as if they would win and put an end
to the old English liberty.

But **soon the Roundheads found a great leader,** a Puritan
gentleman named *Oliver Cromwell*.   His army was made up
mostly of yeomen and shopkeepers, who were not much used
to fighting; but Cromwell trained and drilled them until he
was able to defeat the king's gallant forces in battle after
battle.   Charles himself was finally taken prisoner and was
tried and put to death for " treason to England."

**Then for twelve years (1648–1660) England was ruled by
the Puritan Parliament and Cromwell.**   The country built

CHARLES I OF ENGLAND WITH HIS FAMILY — a photo of the portrait by Van Dyck. This bad king was a good husband and father.

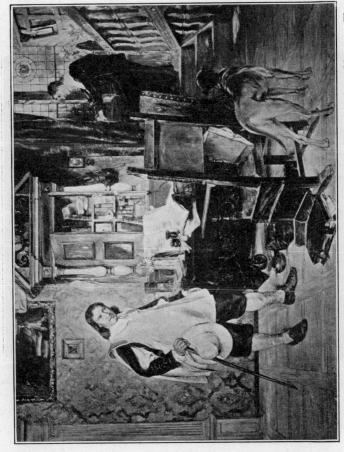

OLIVER CROMWELL (page 358) was a friend and neighbor of the poet JOHN MILTON. This painting represents Cromwell visiting Milton, whom he finds playing upon the organ. The picture has to do with a time some years before the civil war in England.

up a prosperous trade during that time and became more powerful than ever before. But still most Englishmen were not satisfied. They had been glad to support the Puritan leaders against the despotic idea of the " divine right of kings," but they did not like to have the stern Puritan government take away their sports and pleasures (page 354). Besides, when Cromwell died, the Puritans had no one fit to take his place ; so, **in 1660, Parliament and people welcomed back the son of the dead king.**

The new king, *Charles II*, had no wish, he said, " to go on his travels again," and so he interfered very little with Parliament. But after his death, **the next Stuart king, *James II*, began to act worse even than the first Stuarts had done.** He gave orders contrary to laws that Parliament had passed, and he dismissed from office any judges who would not obey his unlawful commands. At last, Parliament declared England would no longer be ruled by such a tyrant, and it invited his oldest daughter *Mary* and her husband, *William of Orange* (grandson of William the Silent), to take the throne.

James found very few supporters, so he fled to France. But before William and Mary were crowned, they had to promise solemnly never to disobey the laws made by Parliament or to try to rule without Parliament. They were obliged also to pledge themselves to protect Englishmen in all their old liberties. All these promises were then put into a long *Bill of Rights*, which every king of England since then has had to sign. And more important than any promise was the plain fact that Parliament now could make and unmake kings. **This was the " Glorious Revolution of 1688."** Ever since, the Parliament has been the real government of England, rather than the king.

The English colonists gained almost as much from the English Revolution as England itself did. During the long

quarrels between Parliament and kings, the government had
been so busy at home in England that it had left the colonists
pretty much to themselves.   But when James II came to
the throne, he planned to do away with colonial Assemblies.
He sent a despotic governor, *Sir Edmund Andros*, with a
force of soldiers, to rule the New England colonies and New
York according to the king's will.

The colonies were not yet large enough or rich enough to
fight successfully against the king of England, though they
were getting ready to try anyway.   But the English Revolution made things better for them.   As soon as they heard of
that, they rose against Andros and drove him out.   Then
they restored their legislatures and all their old ways of governing themselves.   The English Parliament and the new
king and queen respected their rights ; and it was more than
seventy years before any king interfered seriously with them
again.

The rights claimed by Englishmen in the Bill of Rights
belonged also to English colonists in America.   When the
Americans declared themselves independent of England,
in 1776, it was because they felt that the English government was trying again to take those rights away from them.
And when they drew up constitutions for their new States
and for the whole United States, they put into those constitutions many parts of the English Bill of Rights in the
very words of that great document.   **The Bill of Rights,
even more than Magna Carta, is part of the foundation of
our liberty.**

New Words

revolution   civil war   " divine right "   legislature   constitution

Thought Questions and Things to Do

1. Put on your time line the important dates in this chapter.
Do you see one reason now why England did not take part in the

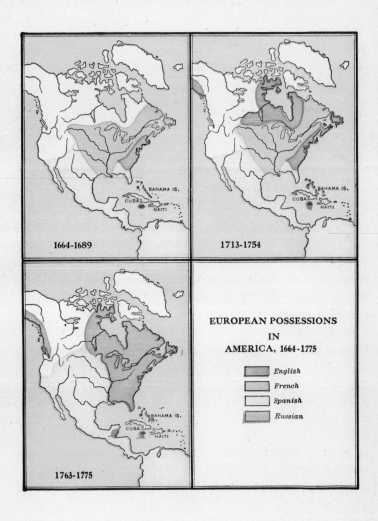

1664-1689

1713-1754

1763-1775

EUROPEAN POSSESSIONS
IN
AMERICA, 1664-1775

English
French
Spanish
Russian

Thirty Years' War, when almost every other important country did?

2. Make a poster calling on the people to defend their liberties against the Stuart tyranny.

3. Why were so many Englishmen willing to go to prison rather than pay a small tax at the king's command? Do you see how the saying " No taxation without representation " arose? Who decides about *our* taxes?

4. Good accounts of England's Civil War and Glorious Revolution are given in O'Neill's *The World's Story* and in Tappan's *England's Story*.

5. Can you add now to the list of reasons why Englishmen came to America?

II. EUROPEAN WARS AND THE AMERICAN REVOLUTION

Spain lost her place as the most powerful nation of Europe after the wars with Holland and England, as we have seen. In the next century, Englishmen were busy saving their liberties from Stuart tyrants, and Germans were busy fighting one another about religion. So French rulers seized the chance to make their country the leading nation.

It was in the long reign of Louis XIV (1643–1715) **that France reached the height of her power,** but it was at that time, too, that she *began* to go down. Louis was ambitious and selfish. He wanted to make himself the most powerful ruler in the world. To be sure, he wanted his people also to prosper, and for a time he did many things for their welfare — building roads and canals and helping their trade to grow. But he cared more for the pomp and splendor of his own court (page 348), and still more for robbing weak neighboring countries of lands and trade.

In his early wars he added much German and Belgian territory to France. **But soon nearly all Europe became afraid of his schemes and formed alliances against him.** Then slowly, in his later wars, he lost much of what he had gained. Besides, he had made such bitter foes for France that the wars against her went on long after his death. He had weakened France, too, by driving out the Huguenots (page 314). And one of the worst results of his reign was the crushing taxation which kept the people poor.

The **wars of Louis XIV had important results for America.** Some of those results will be mentioned further on, but *one* ought to be told here. While Louis was conquering some parts of Germany, in his early wars, his generals cruelly drove all the people from their homes, so that French settlers might come in. The poor homeless Germans sought refuge in other lands, and great numbers of them found their way to the English colonies in America. This added a new German immigration to the one we spoke of on page 332. This was one thing that made the English colonies strong enough so that France could not conquer them.

In 1690, soon after the English Revolution, **England became the leader in the European alliances against France,** and those two countries were at war with each other most of the time for the next seventy years. King William of England (page 359) had been fighting France for some time before, while he was a Dutch prince, and had saved Holland from Louis XIV by cutting the dikes and letting in the ocean, as his grandfather had saved it from the Spaniards a hundred years before. Besides, France and England had already become rivals for North America. They were also rivals in India, because each wanted to get complete control of the rich trade there in tea, silks, spices, and jewels. Some of the wars of this next seventy years were caused by matters in Europe, like the greedy ambition of Louis XIV, and most of the fighting was in Europe; but back of everything else was the rivalry of France and England for land and trade in the New Worlds.

Soldiers of Louis XIV Ravaging a German Town (*Heidelberg*). — From
a modern painting.

The ruler of Prussia ("the Great Elector") welcoming fugitive Huguenots to his country, after Louis XIV drove them from France. These Huguenots had much to do with founding the prosperity of Prussia.

The last of these wars is sometimes called *the French and Indian War*. When it closed, **in 1763, France had lost her mighty empire in North America.** All east of the Mississippi and all north of the St. Lawrence was taken from her by England. Spain had been helping France, and so victorious England had taken Florida away from *her*. To repay Spain for loss, France then gave her the west half of the Mississippi valley (which kept the name "Louisiana"). So North America was left to rising England and decaying Spain, with the Mississippi for the dividing line between them — though Spain did have also the little island of New Orleans just at the mouth of the river.

England came out of the long wars the most powerful country in the world. But wars are costly, and **the English people had to pay dearly for their victories in heavy taxes.** Besides, they had to keep up large armies to protect the empire they had won. It seemed to them that the colonies in America ought to help pay for an English army to defend them against the Indians and to guard against any attempt that France might make to win back North America.

So in 1765 Parliament began to tax the colonists. This led to ten years of bitter quarrels between England and the thirteen English-speaking colonies (page 332), and at last these quarrels broke into war that lasted eight years (1775–1783). This was the *American Revolution.*

In the English colonies from almost the very beginning, the settlers had managed nearly all their affairs in their own way, and **the common people had enjoyed more freedom than was then known in any other part of the world.** England, however, had interfered somewhat with their trade (page 332). But the colonies were now grown strong enough so that they felt quite able to take care of themselves and they saw no reason for putting up with any interference at all.

So **the attempt of Parliament to tax America was like a
spark to a fuse.** The colonists declared firmly that Parliament had no right to tax them because they had no representatives in it. This was the old English principle of " no taxation without representation." Many great Englishmen saw
at once that the colonists were demanding just such rights
as Englishmen had fought for against the Stuarts a hundred
years before. But the king, George III, and the advisors he
had chosen were stubborn and rather stupid, and insisted
that the colonists must be shown that England had power
to tax them if she saw fit. When the colonists refused to use
taxed goods and mobbed the tax collectors, the English government sent an army to force them to obey. War began
April 19, 1775, with the battles of *Lexington* and *Concord;*
and a year later (**July 4, 1776**) **the united colonies declared
themselves independent, as** *the United States of America.*

The full story of our Revolutionary War you will read in
another book at another time. You all know that our
United States was successful in gaining its independence.
Some other things, however, we must notice here.

**The American Revolution soon became part of a great
world-wide war.** England had now become the country
whom her neighbors in Europe feared, and so they seized
this chance to try to weaken her. She had to fight, therefore, not only the United States but also France, Spain, and
Holland. Except in America, she was everywhere victorious; but the part that those other countries took in the war
was a great help to the United States. Without that help,
indeed, we might perhaps still be English colonists — like
our neighbors in Canada.

**The victory of the United States was a good thing for the
world, as well as for ourselves.** It set up the first independent nation in the New World, and before long most of
the colonies of Spain were to follow our example. More-

over, our new nation had a new *kind* of government.   The
Constitution of the United States arranged, not for a king
as ruler, but for a President and Congress to be elected by
the citizens.   The Constitution said also that there should
never be any nobles or lords in this country.   This made
our citizens more nearly equal than the citizens of any other

BENJAMIN FRANKLIN AT THE FRENCH COURT. — Franklin was sent to France to get
that country to help us in the Revolution against England.   A French artist painted
this picture to show how popular Franklin was with the ladies of the gay French
court.   Franklin (the central figure in the picture) is walking forward to pay his
respects to the King and Queen (the only seated figures).   Since he was a Quaker
in habits, he wore no wig, nor did he have any embroidery on his clothing, such as
all courtiers were expected to wear.

great nation were at that time.   That is, *the United States
was a democratic republic.*   Before long, other countries, both
in America and Europe, began to follow this example.

England, too, learned from the American Revolution to
give her remaining colonies more freedom.   Moreover, in
many ways the revolution in America led up to the revolution in France, of which we are to read next.

New Words

Review the meanings of *democracy* and *republic*.

Thought Questions and Things to Do

1. Study the maps of North America facing pages 332 and 361. Make a map of North America for 1783. (After the American Revolution, England gave Florida back to Spain.)

2. List all the ways you can think of in which the French and Indian Wars helped to bring on the Revolution.

3. Write several news articles for an imaginary colonial newspaper in 1688, in 1763, and in 1775, showing each time how events in Europe affected Americans.

4. A longer account of the aid given us by the French may be found in West and West's *Story of Our Country*. The story of the struggle for North America is told in Hart's *Camps and Firesides of the Revolution*, Southworth's *Builders of Our Country*, and Tappan's *American Hero Stories*.

III. The French Revolution

When the king of France sent men and money to help the American Revolution (page 364), he did it only because he wanted to get part of England's empire away from her. He had no liking for the American ideas of liberty. But many of the brave French gentlemen (like Lafayette) who came over here to fight on the American side did like such ideas and wanted to see at least some of them adopted in their own country.

Ever since the time of Louis XIV, things in France had been going from bad to worse. Wars and extravagance had been putting the government deeper and deeper in debt. The great nobles still refused to give up any of their luxuries or to help pay taxes; and the peasants had nothing left in their wretched huts to pay with. Neither would the bankers *lend* the king any more money. The money he had spent in helping America was the last straw.

So in May, 1789 (just a few weeks after George Washington became the first President of the United States), **the king called together the States General,** the old French parliament (page 260) which had not been allowed to meet for more than a hundred and fifty years. This body was made up of clergy, nobles, and representatives of the towns, sitting usually in three separate rooms.

WASHINGTON AT HIS HOME AT MOUNT VERNON ENTERTAINING LAFAYETTE AS A GUEST — JUST AFTER THE AMERICAN REVOLUTION.

The king (Louis XVI) hoped that this meeting would find some way to get him more taxes. But the representatives of the towns (the " Third Estate," as they were called) refused even to talk about money until the king should consent to changing many of the old unfair ways of doing things. In particular, they wanted a constitution that should set up a government more like that in England — where Parliament, you remember, was more important than the king.

For some weeks no business could be done. Then a good many of the wiser nobles and clergy joined the Third Estate. That body then declared itself *The National Assembly*, claiming that it stood for almost the whole nation.

Louis saw that this meant some sort of revolution and that his power was in danger. So he **tried to break up the meeting. But the Assembly** sent back his messenger with the bold words, — " Tell your master that we are here by the power of the people and that nothing but the power of bayonets shall drive us away." Then the members solemnly declared that any officer who should interfere with them would be a traitor to France, even if he acted at the command of the king!

Louis, however, had begun to gather troops in Paris, and the people saw that he meant to dismiss or imprison the Assembly. **So on July 14, the citizens of Paris** rose in a vast mob to protect it. To show their hatred for the old tyranny, the crowds of citizens, almost unarmed, **attacked and destroyed the Bastille,** — a great castle where kings of France for hundreds of years, often without even a trial, had imprisoned people who offended them. This overthrow of the Bastille is still celebrated in France each Fourteenth of July much as we celebrate our Declaration of Independence on the Fourth.

The king's troops had not interfered with the rising. Some of the regiments in Paris had been among the French armies that had fought in the American Revolution side by side with free American farmers; and now when their officers ordered them to fire on the citizens, they merely rang their musket butts sullenly on the pavement and growled " We are the army of the nation! " So the king saw that he must yield, for a time anyway, and he told the National Assembly that it might go on making a constitution. Large numbers of the most hated nobles then fled from France to other lands.

DESTRUCTION OF THE BASTILLE, July 14, 1789.

To the common people of Paris, and indeed of all France, this old prison-fortress stood for injustice and tyranny. It was in a poor and crowded part of Paris. Its walls were so thick that it had seemed unnecessary to keep more than a small troop of guards in it. It had been used, in part, for a storehouse of guns and ammunition; and so, when the mob rose, it rushed there to get arms. The commander of the fortress refused to let the mob enter, and the unarmed but frantic crowds of men and women began a mad attack. They were joined quickly, as the picture shows, by a few companies of the king's guards — some of whom had been fighting for liberty in America shortly before — and the garrison finally surrendered. The mob set free the prisoners in the dungeons and completely destroyed the mighty building. To-day not a stone of its walls remains — but in the great public square where its battlements once frowned stands a tall column crowned by a statue to Liberty.

One of the risings of French peasants after the fall of the Bastille.

Meantime, terrible disorders were breaking out over large parts of France. The peasants, who had been oppressed so cruelly for more than a thousand years, were rising against their lords, burning the feudal castles and murdering many of the noble families. The National Assembly helped put down these riots; but it saw now, even more clearly than before, that there must be an end to the old feudal customs.

At last the constitution was ready, and Louis signed it — though it turned most of his power over to the representatives of the people. The nobles and the high clergy, too, lost all their old privileges and had now to pay taxes in proportion to what they possessed. All men were declared equal *in rights;* and the words *Liberty, Equality, Fraternity* (or " Brotherhood ") were made the motto of France. Those three words are carved to-day on every government building in that country.

In some parts of France the peasants had remained serfs until the Revolution. Now they were set free; and all the old feudal dues from *free* peasants were done away with. They no longer had to pay tolls for passing through a landlord's gate or for crossing a bridge. In each village they could have their own mill and their own bakehouse. They no longer had to leave their harvest, at some steward's call, to work on the roads or on a lord's buildings. No one any longer had the right to trample down their fields of grain by hunting rabbits or deer through them, as the nobles had been in the custom of doing.

In the old days a peasant had been afraid to keep a goat or a pig, even if he were able to have one. Indeed he had not felt it safe to clean up about his house. If he did, the tax-collector or the landlord's steward would think him able to pay more, and would demand more grain from him. But now the Assembly had made it possible for each peasant to own his little farm outright, and so he felt anxious to improve

it in every possible way. **France became a country of free
and prosperous small-farmers,** whose sons often became
educated men and sometimes rose to the highest offices.

But the Revolution was not over. Before many months
it was discovered that Louis was secretly getting ready to
overthrow the constitution. He was collecting *hired* German and Swiss soldiers, who could be depended upon to do
his will as long as he paid them, and he was writing to the
kings of Europe, begging them to invade France and put
down the Revolution.

**Then came the violence and bloodshed known as the
*Reign of Terror.*** The Assembly ordered that Louis and his
Queen should be tried for treason, and they were put to
death along with hundreds of their friends. France was
made a republic; and many who had been leaders of the
Revolution in its earlier days were executed because they
opposed this kind of government or the stern measures it
used.

To-day every one is sorry there was so much injustice and
cruel suffering. But the people of France were in a panic
lest they lose all they had gained from the Revolution; and
fear like that often makes men cruel. But at all events
the good work of the Revolution was saved. The foreign
invaders were driven back on all sides. The royalist risings
in France were put down. And then the Republican armies
in their turn began to invade Spain, Italy, and Germany,
spreading their motto of " equality," freeing the serfs, and
putting an end to feudal customs.

We ought to remember, too, that the new Republic
gave every man in France the right to vote. This
seems natural to us now, but it was a new thing then
for any large country. In England no one could vote
for members of Parliament unless he owned a good deal
of property; and even in the United States there was

only a very small part of the country that had " manhood suffrage " until some years later. (Of course, no one thought yet about woman suffrage.)

To be sure, things did not go forward *steadily*. Sometimes there was a swing backward. About ten years after the Revolution began, a great French general, *Napoleon*, overthrew the republican government and made himself master of France with the title of Emperor. Free government was lost for a while; but even during that time the other gains of the Revolution went on growing and spreading.

And the *idea* of free government lived on. France had to have more revolutions before that idea won a complete victory, but for the last sixty years she has been a strong and free republic. For about that same length of time, too, in all the other countries of Western Europe the people have had at least a large share in the government.

During the fifteen years of his rule, Napoleon waged many wars, and at one time he was master of almost all Europe. England was the only large country he did not conquer: he could not reach her, because she was mistress of the seas.

Early in his rule, he planned to build again a French empire in America, and he forced the king of Spain to give him " Louisiana " (page 363), which France had given to Spain in 1763. This made the United States uneasy. We were not a very powerful nation yet, and our people did not like to have the ambitious Napoleon for a neighbor — especially since he would now be able to interfere with our trade down the Mississippi which had become by then very important to us.

So our government sent agents to France to try to buy at least New Orleans. It is not likely they could have succeeded except for one thing. Napoleon had just decided to attack England; and he knew that if he were at war with that country her fleets (for a time anyway) would surely seize any possessions he might have across the ocean. So, **in 1803,** for a small sum, **he sold us the whole Western half of the Mississippi valley** — which was then called Louisiana. Before that purchase the United States had reached only from the Atlantic to the Mississippi. Now it had doubled its size, and reached to the Rocky Mountains.

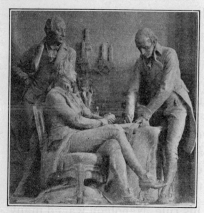

SIGNING THE LOUISIANA TREATY. — A relief on the base of a memorial monument. One of the American negotiators, Robert R. Livingston (standing at the left, in this sculpture), wrote : "This is the noblest work of our lives. The treaty we have just signed will change vast solitudes into a flourishing country. It will cause no tears to flow. It will prepare centuries of happiness for innumerable generations."

Napoleon and England remained at war for twelve years, until Napoleon was finally overthrown at the battle of Waterloo in 1815. During all that time both parties interfered with our trade. Each wanted to prevent us from trading with its enemy, and each seized sailors from our ships for its own navy; but since England was much more powerful at sea, she was able to trouble us most. **So in 1812 we began our second war with England** — usually called the War of 1812. This went on until the European wars ended. Then England and America also made peace, since they no longer had anything to fight about.

There was one more important connection between the wars of Napoleon and the United States. In 1807 Napoleon seized Spain for one of his brothers and put the Spanish king in prison. He tried also to have Spain's colonies in America recognize and obey this new government; but they all refused to do so, and he could not reach them because of England's fleet. So for several years they were really independent nations.

After Napoleon's overthrow, the old king of Spain was restored to his throne, **but the Spanish-American nations refused still to become colonies again.** They liked too well the taste they had had of freedom and the right to trade where they chose, and, soon after 1815, they declared themselves independent nations. The rulers of some European countries, like Austria and Russia (which had now become great powers in Europe), planned to help Spain put down these "rebellions." But in 1823 our **President Monroe announced that the United States would not permit European powers to interfere with free American states** or to make any more colonies in the New World. England, too, declared that she would oppose any expedition from Europe against the liberty of the Spanish-American States. So all idea of such an expedition was given up; and Russia soon agreed to found no more colonies on the Pacific coast south of her own colony of Alaska (see map opposite page 361). Ever since that time this "Monroe Doctrine" has played an important part in our history.

NEW WORDS

Third Estate   *fraternity*   *royalist*   *manhood suffrage*

THOUGHT QUESTIONS AND THINGS TO DO

1. List in order of time the different countries that have claimed the territory which Napoleon sold us. Which ones of our States have been made out of that great territory?

2. List things accomplished by the French Revolution that show how well-chosen its motto was.

3. Good accounts of the French Revolution are given in MacGregor's *Story of France* and O'Neill's *World's Story*.

IV. The Industrial Revolution

While the American Revolution and the French Revolution were giving more freedom to the peoples of America and Europe, there was also going on a *peaceful* revolution that was to affect the everyday life of people in all parts of the world. We call this **The Industrial Revolution** because it **was a complete change in the ways of doing work,** — that is, in *industry*.

For thousands of years before that time there had been very little change in ways of work. Until after 1750, all over the civilized world, farmers in the fields, artisans in the shops, women in the homes, were using almost exactly the same tools that had been used in Egypt in 5000 B.C. Then suddenly **inventions began to crowd one upon another,** until they changed not only all ways of working but also most ways of living.

We have told how men had learned in the Middle Ages to use water power to run grist mills (page 153) and saw-mills (page 284), as well as to use windmills for pumping water. And we have mentioned a few other inventions that belonged to the period of Rebirth in Europe. But that sort of change had been so slow that it seems like standing still, when we compare it with what was now to come.

One of the men who did most to bring about the Industrial Revolution was *James Watt*, who invented *the steam engine* in 1765. This engine furnished a much greater and more convenient power than water to turn the wheels of many new machines that were just then being invented for spinning and weaving. Soon, thousands of threads could be spun at a time, instead of only one, and whole bolts of cloth could be woven with less labor than had been necessary before for weaving a few yards. Then machines to be driven by steam power were invented also for working in wood and iron and for every sort of trade, so that all sorts of goods could be produced in vast quantities.

Artisans then could no longer do their work in their own homes or in small shops, as in the days of the gild and of the domestic system (pages 231–234). It took great factory buildings, also, to house the mighty engines and the many machines that each of them could run; and a workman could not afford to own the new huge machines. So the domestic system came to an end, and **the factory system of manufactures began.**

Many a single factory could give work to hundreds of people. Crowded cities, therefore, grew up around the factories and about the mines that turned out the iron ore and the coal for making and running the machines. In those cities the workmen had to live, packed together, near the factory buildings. They no longer had room around their houses for the little gardens which in earlier times had given them food and some out-door work. At first this was very hard on them, — especially as they had to work from " dawn to dark," twelve or fourteen hours a day. But after many years, they learned to combine in " unions." Then they could make better bargains with their employers, and get better wages and shorter work-days.

There are still many bitter disputes between the factory workers and the men who own the factories; but the two parties are learning better and better how to settle their disputes so that both sides may have fair treatment. Quite possibly the men who do the hard work do not yet get their fair share of the new wealth that comes from machinery. But certainly they are better off than workmen ever were before in the world. Machinery has at last put an end to slavery. No human slave could do so much work so cheaply as these slaves of wood and iron.

As cities grew larger and larger, it became hard to bring food enough to them on pack-horses and in carts and wagons. But **early in the nineteenth century, clever inventors** (like Robert Fulton in America and George Stephenson in England) **learned how to use steam-engines for moving ships and railroad trains.**

The railroad could haul in food for the largest city. It also brought to each manufacturing city " raw material "

This recent photo shows a steamship unloading its cargo directly into freight cars at a New Orleans dock. Compare with the vessel shown on page 265. It would take several hundred of those 15th-century ships to carry as much freight as this steamship.

for its factories to use — cotton or wool or iron, as was wanted — and then carried away to other cities or to other parts of the world the things the factories made. Better than ever before, **each city could " specialize " now** in the kind of goods that it could make most easily and cheaply. Some made silks; some made steel; some made watches; some made cotton or woolen cloth; still others made shoes or gloves. Except for the railroad there could not have been so much of this specializing.

The Industrial Revolution began in England. Soon after 1800 it reached the United States, but the long wars of Napoleon kept it from passing from England to any of the other countries of Europe for many years more.

It was in America that the Industrial Revolution first reached the farm. The factory towns needed more and more workmen, but they couldn't get them except by drawing people away from the farms. Then the people *left* on farms would have found it hard indeed to feed those growing cities if farm machinery had not been invented, to make their work easier.

In 1831 *Cyrus McCormick* of Virginia invented a *reaper*, to be drawn by horses. This machine cut grain much faster than a man could do it with the old sickle. Before long there was joined to the reaper a *binder*, which tied the grain in bundles as it was cut; and by 1900 there had been twelve thousand different improvements to that reaper and binder — to say nothing of all the many kinds of machinery that we have now for doing other kinds of farm work. One man, with our modern machinery, can do more farm work than twenty could do a hundred years ago.

It was natural enough for America to lead in inventing farm machinery. No other country at that time had such vast prairies to turn into fruitful fields. If it had not been for the new machinery, our people could never have spread out over the wide Mississippi valley so rapidly as we did, especially over the vast " Louisiana " district that we had bought from Napoleon. Nor, without it, could we feed our 120 millions of people to-day, besides millions more in other parts of the world.

The Industrial Revolution is still going on — and faster than ever. Steam power has been followed by electric power and by the use of gasoline engines that make possible automobiles and airplanes to carry goods. For more than a hundred years the United States has been *one* of the leaders in this mighty movement, but we must not think that the advance is the work of any one or two nations. **The scientists of every land are working together constantly to find new and better ways of adding to man's comfort and happiness, to his knowledge of the world in which he lives, and to his understanding of his fellow men in every part of it.**

New Words

industry   *factory*   *raw material*   *specialize*

Thought Questions and Things to Do

1. In the sixteenth century, English writers complained that their island was· overcrowded. It then had about four million people. To-day it has about forty million. Why does it seem no more crowded now than it did then?

2. List some of the raw materials that have become more valuable since the Industrial Revolution began. Where are they to be found?

3. Historians say that the Industrial Revolution has made the world more democratic. Can you see any reasons why that is true?

4. Imagine yourself a hand-worker at the time when machinery for your trade was first invented and tell how your life was affected.

5. List the things you have used to-day that you would not have had if the world still did its work by hand-power.

The New World and the Old To-day

Our story of Old World *foundations* for the United States comes to an end with the eighteenth century, when our country began its life as an independent nation. But Europe did not stop *influencing* us when we came to have a government of our own. Our life continued to be bound up in many ways with that of the rest of the world.

Great changes took place in Europe in the nineteenth century. Groups of little states united into new and strong

nations like Germany and Italy. Peoples like the Irish,
Greeks, Belgians, Poles, and Bohemians, who had long been
ruled by foreign powers, became independent states, or at
least secured more freedom than before. (Map after page
378.) Everywhere the people threw off the power of despotic kings and took a hand in their own government.
Some of these changes were not completed until after the
World War of 1914–1918. All of them came about only
after long struggles; and during those struggles hundreds of
thousands of people, who despaired of getting liberty in their
old homes, found it by coming to the United States.

In fact, from the beginning, **the Old World has given us
our citizens.** Colonies of England, Spain, France, Holland,
and Sweden grew together into our United States. And
ever since, people from all the lands of Europe have flocked
to our shores for much the same reasons that brought the
colonists here — for more freedom in government or in religion, or for adventure, or to make a better living. From
each European land we have gained something new, to make
life in America richer, finer, more interesting, and more
beautiful. Together we have been able to clear our forests,
cultivate our vast prairies, develop our mines, build our network of railroads and our mighty cities. All of us together
make up the American nation and carry on our government.

**Then also we are all the time trading with the other coun-
tries of the world.** For a long time we sent Europe our raw
materials, for the most part, in exchange for European
manufactures. But now we have become a great manufacturing country ourselves. We send to all the countries
of the world our specialties — steel, machinery of all sorts,
wheat and flour, and canned foods that we can raise in
greater quantities than they; and they send to us *their*
specialties. Without that trade, our business would fall off
and our factories would be out of work. We need other
countries and they need us.

And modern inventions have brought the different parts of the world closer together. Steamships cross the Atlantic in less time than it took George Washington to go from his home in Virginia to New York; and the flights of Lindbergh and other airmen have shown that soon any of us may cross from the New World to the Old in a few hours. Besides,

FIRST TRIAL EXHIBITION OF THE TELEPHONE (March 18, 1877). — Alexander Bell, a school teacher, had invented a telephone a few years before, but very few people knew of it or believed it would really work. This picture shows the inventor talking from a lecture-room platform in Salem, Massachusetts, to scientific men in another hall in Boston, several miles away. Some of the chief men of Salem sat on the platform with Mr. Bell, to take turns at the phone and to testify to the amazed audience that friends in Boston really heard and answered.

men at their own desks in New York City or Boston can do business by wireless telephone with men in London or Paris or Berlin, and (by television) even see the faces of the far-off friends with whom they talk.

The story of almost any important invention shows how **scientists of different countries help one another.** In 1846 the American *Morse* invented the electric telegraph. Just a few years later, daring Englishmen made use of that invention to lay the first under-water cable on the ocean floor — from England to France.   Then an American, *Cyrus W. Field* took up *their* idea, and extended it, until, after a life time of heroic effort, he had a cable working across the wide

FIRST PUBLIC TELEPHONE (*Wireless*) TALK ACROSS THE ATLANTIC (January 7, 1927) — just fifty years after one town in America first talked with another (see opposite cut). The President of the American Telephone and Telegraph Company picked up his phone in his New York office at 8 : 30 A.M., and asked to speak with the Head of the English Postoffice. In less than a minute, word came back from London that that gentleman was at his phone, and the talk began. The guests in the New York office, you notice, listened in through phones placed at each chair. That same day there were thirty-one wireless talks between banks, newspapers, and business men in New York and London.

Atlantic from the United States to England.   That was accomplished more than sixty years ago ; and to-day many oceanic cables cross the Atlantic and Pacific and Indian oceans, binding all the continents together, so that important news flashes around the world more quickly than it used to travel from one village to another, ten miles away.

Without the American inventions of telegraph and telephone, it is hard to see how the Italian *Marconi* could have invented *wireless*, as he did about thirty years ago; and except for Marconi, our very recent American and English inventors could hardly have given us the *radio* and *television*, and the other wonders that belong with those inventions. To-day physicians from all over the world come to see the marvelous work of American doctors in the little Minnesota town of Rochester; but those famous *Mayo brothers* could not even have begun their work if a French chemist, *Pasteur*, had not first discovered that many diseases are caused by germs, and if a German professor, *Röntgen*, had not discovered the *X ray*, and if a French woman-scientist, *Marie Curie*, had not discovered *radium* — to say nothing of many much earlier men, like the English *Harvey* who, three hundred years ago, first found out just how the heart sends the blood through our bodies.

In the last century and a half, we have learned that the wars and troubles of our neighbors hurt us also. Wars in Europe have checked our trade, and, more than once, in the end we ourselves have been drawn into the struggle. Diseases in distant countries have been carried to our shores. Business panics in other parts of the world have caused business panics in America. If sheep-herders in Australia lose their flocks by disease, many of our woolen factories have to shut down and all of us have to pay more for clothing.

But we have learned also that most of these evils can be kept from spreading, and perhaps from even starting, **if the different nations will only arrange to work together.** And more and more that is being done. Each year now sees *international congresses* to which come delegates from all

WILLIAM HARVEY, who discovered how the blood circulates in our bodies.

LOUIS PASTEUR, who invented (among other things) the way to kill disease germs in milk by "pasteurization."

MARIE CURIE, discoverer of radium.

WILHELM RÖNTGEN, discoverer of X rays.

SAMUEL F. B. MORSE, inventor of
the magnetic telegraph.

CYRUS W. FIELD, creator of the first
Atlantic cable.

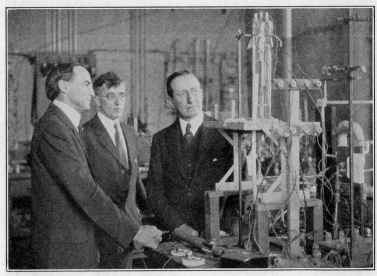

MARCONI (at the right), the inventor of the wireless telegraph. With other famous
scientists, he is watching an experiment in the Research Laboratory of the (American)
General Electric Company.

parts of the world.   Business men gather to study problems
of world business; doctors and nurses to plan how to check
and prevent disease; social workers to study the needs of the
poor and helpless in every land ; scientists to discuss the new-
est inventions and to give one another the benefit of their
latest discoveries; educators to compare the methods used

THE WORLD COURT HOUSE AT THE HAGUE. — This building is one of Andrew
Carnegie's gifts to the cause of world peace.   The Permanent Court of International
Justice holds its sessions here.

in the schools of different lands and to take home new ideas
for the betterment of their own schools.   Radio congresses
decide on a uniform wave length.   Workers' congresses
consider the best ways of helping fellow workers in other
lands.

**The most important of all these world meetings are those
that gather year after year, to find better ways of settling
the world's quarrels.**   During all the nineteenth century

the United States was a leader among the nations in working to prevent wars. But since the great World War, which lasted from 1914 to 1918, Europeans are perhaps even more eager than Americans to find peaceful ways for settling disputes in future. The fighting of that war took place in the Old World, and people there learned, by a terrible experience, how wasteful and horrible war must be, now that men have invented such frightful machines of destruction. Their long struggle to restore their homes and farms and factories, and to build up again their business and trade, has made it plain that war does not " pay," whether a country wins or loses.

Before that World War ended, many great Americans (like Woodrow Wilson, William Howard Taft, Elihu Root, and Charles Evans Hughes) had suggested plans for a world-wide League of Nations to deal with matters that concern more than one country. They planned also for a World Court, to *settle* disputes between countries just as our law courts settle disputes between persons. **Soon after the war, nearly all the nations of the World did join in a League of Nations and a World Court.** Woodrow Wilson, who was President of the United States during that war, did more than any other one man to set up the League of Nations; and Mr. Hughes is one of the justices of the World Court.

The United States has not joined the League, but we do work with it in various ways. We have also made many treaties with other countries in which we promise to find peaceful ways of settling any troubles that may arise. **And finally in 1929 the United States joined with all the other great nations of the World in the famous Pact of Paris.** The important parts of that treaty are printed just below, and you can certainly understand it, though some of the words may look a little hard. We have good right to be proud that Americans had a chief part in drawing up this treaty. Indeed, it is often called *the Kellogg Pact*, because Mr. Frank Kellogg, our Secretary of State, proposed it to the other nations. We may hope that it is a sign of a time to come in which all men, wherever they live, may work together for the good of all.

CHIEF PARTS OF THE PARIS PACT

Article 1. The High Contracting Powers solemnly declare, in the name of their respective peoples, that they condemn recourse to war for the solution of international controversies and renounce it as an instrument of national policy in their relations with one another.

Article 2. The High Contracting Powers agree that the settlement or solution of all disputes or conflicts, of whatever nature or of whatever origin they may be, which may arise among them, shall never be sought except by pacific means.

NEW WORDS

international congress   *World Court*   *League of Nations*

THOUGHT QUESTIONS AND THINGS TO DO

1. List all the ways you can think of in which each of the revolutions mentioned in this chapter has helped the world. In some ways the Pact of Paris marks still another revolution. Explain what you think it is.

2. Plan a pageant in which each country we have studied brings its gift to America.

3. Make a list of places in other parts of the world which you would like to visit, and write briefly why. What places in America do you suppose a European would like to visit?

INDEX AND PRONUNCIATION OF WORDS

Many words are given here that would not be put into this index, except that it makes a convenient place to show their pronunciation if students need the information. Sometimes a word is merely divided into syllables. The marks of pronunciation are those used in Webster's dictionaries. Where an Anglicized pronunciation is permitted for a foreign name, it is used in this book. (In a few cases the teacher may wish to consult the pages toward the close of the "Unabridged" for the pronunciation of certain letters from German and French.)

The index also indicates on which map each place name may be found. Usually the map so referred to is the earliest one in the book on which the name occurs, but sometimes several successive map references are given.

1